Living for Jesus and Japan

Living for Jesus and Japan

THE SOCIAL AND THEOLOGICAL THOUGHT OF
UCHIMURA KANZŌ

Edited by

Shibuya Hiroshi and Chiba Shin

WILLIAM B. EERDMANS PUBLISHING COMPANY
GRAND RAPIDS, MICHIGAN / CAMBRIDGE, U.K.

Published 2013 by
Wm. B. Eerdmans Publishing Co.
2140 Oak Industrial Drive N.E., Grand Rapids, Michigan 49505 /
P.O. Box 163, Cambridge CB3 9PU U.K.

Printed in the United States of America

19 18 17 16 15 14   7 6 5 4 3 2

Library of Congress Cataloging-in-Publication Data

Living for Jesus and Japan: the social and theological thought of Uchimura Kanzo /
edited by Shibuya Hiroshi and Chiba Shin.
pages   cm
Includes bibliographical references and index.
ISBN 978-0-8028-6957-9 (pbk.: alk. paper)
1. Uchimura, Kanzo, 1861-1930.
I. Shibuya, Hiroshi, 1932- editor of compilation.

BR1317.U22L58   2013
275.2′082092 — dc23
2013020939

www.eerdmans.com

Contents

Editors' Preface   vii

Acknowledgments   xiii

Introduction: A Biographical Sketch of Uchimura Kanzō   1
  Shibuya Hiroshi

Part I. Historical Context and Social Thought

Japan for the World   21
  Andrew E. Barshay

Uchimura Kanzō and American Christian Values   36
  Ohyama Tsunao

Uchimura Kanzō and His Pacifism   55
  Takahashi Yasuhiro

Prophetic Nationalism: Uchimura between God and Japan   69
  Yagyu Kunichika

The Legacy of Uchimura Kanzō's Patriotism:
Tsukamoto Toraji and Yanaihara Tadao   93
  Shogimen Takashi

Part II. Biblical Studies and Theological Thought

The Biblical Research Method of Uchimura Kanzō   115

    Miura Hiroshi

Uchimura and His *Mukyōkai-Shugi*   127

    Shibuya Hiroshi

Uchimura's View of the Atonement in *Kyūanroku*
(*The Search for Peace*)   143

    Lee Kyoungae

Uchimura Kanzō on Justification by Faith in His *Study of Romans:*
A Semantic Analysis of Romans 3:19-31   162

    Chiba Kei

Uchimura Kanzō and His Atonement Eschatology:
On "Crucifixianity"   198

    Chiba Shin

Contributors   221

Editors' Preface

Uchimura Kanzō (1861-1930) was a representative Christian leader and thinker in the Meiji and Taishō periods of Japan. He is well known in Japan as a prolific biblical commentator, a pacifist Christian thinker, an advocate of the nonchurch (*mukyōkai*) type of Christianity, as well as an astute social critic, especially early in his career. Our general purpose in publishing this anthology in English is to make Uchimura Kanzō's Christian thought better known to the world at large. The authors believe that it has strong relevance to the needs and aspirations of the present world, as we suffer from the loss of meaning of life, ecological crisis, conflicts and wars in many parts of the world, and so forth. Uchimura is worthy of continued study and remains inspiring and refreshing not merely as a Christian thinker but also as a social thinker.

Uchimura Kanzō was one of the representative men of modern Japan. He wrote an English book, *Representative Men of Japan,* published in 1894. If someone were to expand this book today, it is highly likely that a critical biography of Uchimura would be included. What makes him one of the representative men of modern Japan?

Uchimura tried earnestly to link Japanese cultural traits with an influential universal religion, that is, Christianity. In so doing he wanted to make the Japanese spiritual heritage and cultural legacy comprehensible and intelligible in international society. We hope that our volume can introduce Uchimura Kanzō to the reading public in the English-speaking world in a manner similar to the way he himself introduced a few representative Japanese people whose lives and thoughts he described in *Representative Men of Japan* more than a century ago.

The study of a thinker such as Uchimura must be made from various angles. Therefore, the contributors to this volume represent different specialties and nationalities. And their disciplines spread across such diverse fields as theology, philosophy, American studies, intellectual history, and history of social and political thought. In publishing this kind of collection of essays, one might correctly say that we are in a sense following Uchimura's footsteps. For two years he was an owner-editor-writer of an English monthly magazine, the *Japan Christian Intelligencer* (*JCI;* 1926-28); he wished to let the world, especially the United States, know about his and his comrades' beliefs, which they considered to be among Japan's "best" spiritual heritage. Unfortunately, he was too old at that time to be the owner-editor-writer of two magazines (since 1900 he had edited *Seisho no Kenkyū [The Biblical Study]*). *JCI* started almost immediately after 1924, one of the most critical years in the prehistory of the Pacific war between Japan and the United States, when the so-called Anti-Japanese Immigration Act was put into effect and the Japanese were not allowed to immigrate to the United States. Uchimura understood that this was the United States' one-sided repeal of the Japan-America Treaty of Amity and Commerce, which had been concluded in 1854. Uchimura and his comrades were so disappointed with this move by the U.S. government that they organized the Christian Council of the Problem toward the United States. They wanted to form and mobilize public opinion in Japan against the American government by means of mass communication to change the U.S. policy. Soon after, however, Uchimura began to think over their protest movement, and found fault also with Japan herself. The country was always silent and hid her true intentions as well as her own treasures behind an enigmatic smile. And by so doing, Japan "hid" her views of God, of humanity, of life and the world, like the servant described in Matthew 25 who kept "in the ground" the one talent entrusted to him by his master.

During Uchimura's lifetime, the Japanese did not keep good company with people of the neighboring countries of East Asia nor with those of the West, including the Americans. The Americans were generally open and frank and naturally expected foreigners to be frank with them in return. Uchimura thought the Japanese should have satisfied, at least to a certain extent, their reasonable expectation. That is to say, the Japanese should have shared their traditional thoughts and cultural traits more openly with the foreigners. This would have been a kind of good "return" that the Japanese could make to their international neighbors. For Japan continued to receive so much rather one-sidedly, Uchimura thought, since the two countries had established the diplomatic relations. Most conspicuously, Japan received a universal religion, that is, Christianity, and a number of worldly, scientific, and technical inventions. The reverse seldom happened. This kind of basic unevenness provoked American antipathy against Japan. Therefore, the task of the *JCI*, as Uchimura understood it, consisted in reducing that unevenness to some extent.

As Uchimura suggested in the first issue of *JCI*, one of the purposes for publishing this English journal was to make known to the world what could be considered "the best" in Japan, and by so doing to make a little contribution to world-thought and world-progress. "What nation is there which is without some good in it? . . . there is no best, that is, all-perfect nation in the world, and Japan certainly is no such nation. But there is good that is specially hers; and it is her duty to recognize it, and to give it to the world, and receive back in return the best in other nations. . . . We believe in the perfectibility of the world by the contribution of the best in every people" (29:422E; see p. xii for explanation of citation method).

Here Uchimura embodies, on the one hand, what political sociologist A. D. Smith called "polycentric nationalism." Smith wrote as follows: "'*Polycentric*' nationalism, by contrast [to 'ethnocentric' nationalism], resembles the dialogue of many actors on a common stage. As the term implies, this kind of nationalism starts from the premise that there are many centres of *real* power; other groups do have valuable and genuinely noble ideas and institutions which we would do well to borrow, adapt. . . . ['Polycentric' nationalism] seeks to join the 'family of nations,' the international drama of status equals, to find its appropriate identity and part."[1]

Smith also wrote about the unevenness we described above. And we suppose that Uchimura was at least one of the most original and stimulating Japanese thinkers at the end of the nineteenth and beginning of the twentieth century. Therefore, by publishing this anthology, we are trying to introduce one of Japan's "best" during that era in the hope of contributing to the "perfectibility of the world." So the title of this book can be explained at least in part in terms of our effort to do justice to Uchimura's lifelong commitment to contribute to the world what can be regarded as each people's "best."

*   *   *

1. Anthony D. Smith, *Theories of Nationalism* (London: Duckworth, 1983²), 158-59.

The title, *Living for Jesus and Japan,* is also related to Uchimura's famous essay "Two J's" (1926). In this essay, he proclaimed as follows:

> I love two J's and no third; one is Jesus, and the other is Japan.
>
> I do not know which I love more, Jesus or Japan.
>
> I am hated by my countrymen for Jesus' sake as *yaso* [Christian], and I am disliked by foreign missionaries for Japan's sake as national and narrow.
>
> Even if I lose all my friends, I cannot lose Jesus and Japan. . . .
>
> Jesus and Japan; my faith is not a circle with one center; it is an ellipse with two centers. My heart and mind revolve around the two dear names. And I know that one strengthens the other; Jesus strengthens and purifies my love for Japan; and Japan clarifies and objectifies my love for Jesus. Were it not for the two, I would become a mere dreamer, a fanatic, an amorphous universal man.
>
> Jesus makes me a world-man, a friend of humanity; Japan makes me a lover of my country, and through it binds me firmly to the terrestrial globe. (30:53-54E)

This "Two J's" essay can be misunderstood easily, especially when Uchimura's commitment to Japan is too narrowly interpreted as an expression of egocentric nationalism, which often characterized his age. His devotion to Japan should be regarded rather as an expression of the Christian idea of neighborly love. Thus, despite Uchimura's rhetorical and paradoxical embellishment of the "Two J's" language, its real meaning should be understood as either christocentric or theocentric but not nationalistic in intention. This short piece should be read together with his youngish aspiration that he wrote down on the reverse side of the cover of his cherished Bible while he was living as a sojourner in America and studying at Amherst College (1885-87):

> To Be Inscribed upon my Tomb.
> I for Japan; Japan for the World; the World for Christ; and All for God.

∗   ∗   ∗

As is clear from the title, the subtitle, and the table of contents, the book is divided into two parts. Especially important is the subtitle: *The Social and*

Theological Thought of Uchimura Kanzō. The first part of the volume deals with Uchimura's social thought: his ideas on Japan for the world, his youthful encounter with America, his pacifism, and his nationalism and the legacies of his patriotism. The second part is related to his biblical studies and theological thought: his biblical research method, his nonchurchism *(mukyōkai-shugi)*, his views on atonement and justification by faith, and his atonement eschatology.

For Uchimura Kanzō, the rich social meanings that his religious and theological thought embodies are very significant. Unlike many religious thinkers of the nineteenth and twentieth centuries, Uchimura did not remain within the individualistic and private, inner and existential forms of belief. On the contrary, his theological thought is inseparably connected with his dedication to the public world (neighbors, society, the country, the region, and the world). And his commitment to the public world is based on the principle of love. It takes a reformist approach of concentric and centrifugal extension from the soul (the inmost depth) of each and every individual to the outer world: the self, family, neighbors, society, country, region, and entire world.[2]

To be sure, the series of religious experiences and encounters that Uchimura had undergone and assimilated took place in the vertical level of his inner soul "alone with God." But they were nonetheless open and acted out to the public world in the horizontal level. Thus, this book is the expression of a collective effort to elucidate the "interaction between the social and theological thought" that characterizes this highly original and interesting pioneer Christian leader and thinker of modern Japan. We will seek to shed light on the inner logic, meanings, and modes of this stimulating interaction between the social and theological thought observable in Uchimura Kanzō.

Thus, Uchimura's theological commitment to inner values of Christian faith goes hand in hand with his social commitment to the public world. His religious commitment is grounded in his experiences and understandings of the gospel of Christ based on his redemptive theology of the cross, the resurrection, and the second coming. These theological values are organically linked with his admonition for living and practicing such evangelical and social values as prophetic existence, neighborly love, reconciliation

2. E.g., 8:455-56; 10:276-77. Cf. Shibuya Hiroshi, *Kindai shisōshi niokeru Uchimura Kanzō (Uchimura Kanzō in the History of Modern Thought)* (Tokyo: Shinchi Shobō Publishers, 1988), 119-38.

and peace, social justice, patriotism, and internationalism. We are hoping that the book will elucidate as much as possible this meaningful interaction between the social and theological thought in Uchimura.

*   *   *

Finally, a few editorial notes.

1. In this volume, Japanese names are printed with surnames first, given names last, according to the Japanese custom. So Uchimura is the surname; Kanzō is the given name. This practice is applied not only to historical figures like Uchimura Kanzō but also to contemporary Japanese authors and thinkers.
2. The readers will often find citations in the text. The first number in the citation corresponds to the volume number of *Zenshū* or *Works: the Complete Works of Uchimura Kanzō,* 40 vols. (Tokyo: Iwanami Shoten, 1980-84); the number following the colon is the page number; "E" means that the quoted or referred sentence is written in English by Uchimura. So, 8:455-56, for instance, means volume 8 of the *Complete Works,* pages 455-56. The absence of "E" means that the quoted or referred sentence is written in Japanese.
3. Quotations from Uchimura are, as a general rule, used in the original expression. But they are sometimes slightly changed to suit the present-day English writing style.
4. Unless otherwise indicated, Scripture is quoted from the Authorized Version (King James Version), which Uchimura himself generally used and relied on.

Acknowledgments

The editors of this volume are greatly indebted to many individuals and organizations for their support and encouragement. The volume is the outcome of a four-year collaboration among scholars who have been doing research on Uchimura Kanzō and his thought in one way or another. We fondly recollect our stimulating first seminar that we held in November 2008 for initiating the preparatory collaboration for our volume at Keiō University, Tokyo. The editors of the volume are deeply grateful to the authors of the chapters for their willing cooperation and commitment to our book project.

We would like to express our deep gratitude to Kyōyūkai (Christian Association of Friends) at Imai Hall for their funding support. Four years ago, the Committee of the One Hundred and Fiftieth Anniversary of Uchimura Kanzō's Birth Memorial Events was established. And our book project was fortunately accepted as one of these memorial events. We are deeply grateful to Kyōyūkai's chief director Dr. Arai Akira and its general secretary Mr. Fukushima Atsushi for their generosity, patience, and moral support.

In addition, we would like to express our sincere thanks to Professor Andrew E. Barshay of University of California–Berkeley for participating in our book project despite his extremely busy schedule. As a renowned expert in modern Japanese intellectual history, Professor Barshay contributed a stimulating and thoughtful essay to the volume. We also want to give our deeply felt thanks to Professor Trent E. Maxey of Amherst College, Massachusetts. Professor Maxey initially sought and began to prepare an essay for the publication of this volume. But, due to his multiple works and duties at the college, he could not contribute one to it. Yet Professor Maxey's editorial and managing support and advice throughout the past four years were of immense help for completing the volume.

Moreover, we would like to extend our heartfelt thanks to Alice Davenport, Ernst Schwintzer, Derrick McClure, and Elizabeth Dorsch. They assisted improving and editing the language and expressions of the chapters written by nonnative English authors with their marvelous expertise in English. And finally, the editors would like to thank Eerdmans Publishing Company and President William B. Eerdmans Jr. for their willingness to publish this volume. We are greatly indebted to President Eerdmans and to his generosity that made this publication possible. Finally the editors would like to express sincere thanks to Tom Raabe, Eerdmans' editor, for his superb, concientious, and laborious work. Without these precious helping hands and the good will of these individuals and organizations, this book would never have been published.

A Biographical Sketch of Uchimura Kanzō

SHIBUYA HIROSHI

Uchimura's Birth and Origin

Uchimura Kanzō was born on March 23, 1861, in Edo (the old name of Tokyo) as the eldest son of a *bushi* (colloquially, samurai). His father, Nobuyuki, was a lower-class *bushi* of Takasaki *han*.[1]

The Meiji Restoration started in 1868. This sociopolitical disturbance brought much Western civilization to Japan. However, I remember listening on two occasions to speeches by Emil Brunner in Tokyo while I was a college student. In both speeches he stressed that Japan had imported almost all of Western civilization except Christianity, and that because Christianity is the basis of Western civilization, Japan has never had a realistic expectation of *civilizing* herself in the true sense of the word. Of

---

1. From 1192 to 1868, the leader of the nationwide samurai class, after winning victories in a series of civil wars, was designated "Great General for Suppression of Savage Enemies" and acknowledged as the political ruler of the entire country. The emperor was the supreme priest of the Shintō religion, but only nominally the ruler of the nation. The general's headquarters was called the *Bakufu*; it is often referred to as the shogunate.

The *Bakufu* or shogunate distributed the power of local government to councils called *han*, of which the captain was called *hanshu* or *daimyō*. The *Han* (the fence to defend the lord of *Han*) was considered to be the *daimyō*'s enlarged household; his family and his followers, the samurai, were its members. *Daimyōs* generally enjoyed extensive powers of self-government, but they were always carefully observed by the *Bakufu*, and sternly punished on even a suspicion of treason. In the final years of the *Bakuhan (Bakufu-han)* system, the number of *han* was fewer than 300.

Each *han* was identified by the *hanshu*'s family name, that of the town where he resided, or that of the county he ruled.

1

course, Brunner used this hyperbole to warn the Japanese against over-looking the extent to which Western culture was influenced by its religious foundation. Nevertheless, the Restoration still gave no small shock to the course of young Uchimura's life. Those who suffered most from the Meiji government's destruction of the Tokugawa *Bakuhan* system were the lower-class *bushi*, especially those of the pro-Tokugawa *han (fudai han)*. Almost all of them lost their employment and were given a small severance pay. Uchimura Kanzō, the eldest son in his family, was studying at Tokyo School of Foreign Languages, a preparatory college for the prestigious To-kyo Imperial University; but since Takasaki *han* was one of many small *fudai han*, Uchimura's father could not afford to let him graduate. Owing to lack of funds, he was obliged to transfer to Sapporo Agricultural College (SAC), which was free from fees and organized the lives of students like a military academy.

An Encounter with Christianity at Sapporo Agricultural College

It was at this college, however, that Uchimura was unexpectedly intro-duced to Christianity. The first president of the college, Dr. W. S. Clark, was a devout layman evangelist who had led all the first year's intake of students to Christianity. (This was a brand-new college in the new state system, and Uchimura entered in its second year.) Dr. Clark's stay in Japan was only eight months long. When Uchimura arrived at the college, he had already left Japan for the USA to resume the presidency of Massachusetts Agricultural College. At Sapporo, Clark had drawn up the Covenant of Be-lievers in Jesus, which all the students of the first year's intake had signed. When they moved up to the second year, they put pressure on the fresh-men to sign the covenant. Uchimura withstood their efforts for a while, but at last he yielded and signed it. "I often ask myself," he said, "whether I ought to have refrained from submitting myself to such a coercion. I was but a mere lad of sixteen then, and the boys who thus forced me 'to come in' were all much bigger than I" (3:15E). He admitted that his "first conver-sion" was rather immature and somewhat lacking in depth. However, that did not mean that his signing the covenant was a mere formality with no spiritual significance. After signing, he embarked with his classmates on a keen study of Christian doctrine, reading, among other things, the com-mentaries of Albert Barnes; the publications of the American Tract Soci-ety, the London Tract Society, the Society for the Promoting of Christian

Knowledge, and the Unitarian Association of Boston; and issues of the *Illustrated Christian Weekly*. His discussions with his fellow students sometimes even descended to quarrels. Uchimura and his classmates were baptized by an American Methodist missionary, but this missionary did not visit Sapporo frequently enough to provide his baptized students sufficient pastoral care. They therefore had to study by themselves; as a result their understanding of Christianity became focused excessively on its ethical aspects. The *bushi* class had been deeply permeated with Confucian ethics, and most of the students came from that class. Moreover, the Covenant of Believers in Jesus was almost puritanical in its strong ethical stance. All in all, it might not be an exaggeration to describe the college Christianity as a kind of ethical monotheism. As Uchimura had been a very sensitive boy whose religious feelings prompted him to recognize the moral contradictions in nonethical polytheism, this form of Christianity came to him as a joyous emancipation.

When we observe the young Uchimura's spiritual growth, we cannot overlook the state of Japanese thought at the time. At the period in Japanese history in which he grew up, the early Meiji era, nationalism[2] was the zeitgeist. "When we escaped the old *han* government to return to that of the Emperor, our aspiration spread out from Takasaki Han of eighty-two-thousand-koku[3] to the whole of Japan" (36:218), wrote Uchimura to his father. As he was writing, the Meiji Restoration was clearing away the feudal *Bakuhan* system and founding in its place a government with centralized power, combining modernization and absolutism. For the first time in their

---

2. To readers in Western countries, "patriotism" might be a more appropriate word for Uchimura than "nationalism." However, the Latin word *patria* means "fatherland, native place, dwelling place, home, etc.," none of which exactly corresponds to "nation" as a concept of historical or political sociology. For Uchimura, it was a historically or eschatologically based nationalism (it was his belief that the nations would reach their ideal states at the eschaton) that fostered his patriotic zeal.

3. *Koku* is a unit of volume of grain, wood, etc., or a measure of the quantity a vessel can hold. One *koku* of rice is about 180 pounds. A samurai's salary was paid in rice, and a *daimyō's* status was determined by the amount of rice, measured in *koku*, which his domain produced. Takasaki (a town about 100 kilometers northwest of Tokyo) *han* was evaluated as producing 82,000 *koku*, which meant that the *han* was a lower medium-sized one. The Uchimura family had received 50 *koku* as annual salary. The lord of the family had to be ranked as a lower samurai. In several *han* during the closing years of the *Bakuhan* system, however, samurai from low-ranking families were appointed to high positions on personal merit in order to reform the *han*. Uchimura's father was one of these samurai whose individual excellence brought them promotion.

history, the Japanese had united under a strong central government. This was the founding of the Japanese *nation*. The last feudal revolt, and no insignificant one, occurred and was suppressed on Kyūshū Island in 1877, the year in which Uchimura entered SAC. His formative years thus coincided with the period when Japanese nationalism was developing. Uchimura was not a politically oriented youth. But no one possessing normal sensitivity, of whatever orientation, can fail to absorb the spiritual atmosphere that permeates his or her society. Of course, it is quite another question whether the atmosphere an individual absorbs in youth will remain the same when maturity is reached. Uchimura imbibed deeply the air of nationalism, in a highly characterized Christianized form. We will be returning to this subject later.

Uchimura graduated from the college, receiving the degree of bachelor of agriculture. At the college he had made a special study of fishery science, and he went on to take up a post in the Sapporo Prefectural Office as a fishery engineer. His most remarkable work as a prefectural officeholder was perhaps in the field of ocean biology: the discovery of the egg cell of abalone. When he found this under his microscope, he went up a hill at the back of the laboratory and, shedding tears, offered a prayer of thanksgiving to God as the Creator of everything. As a biologist, he could not fail to confront a new biological theory: Darwinism. After all, he was committed to the doctrine of theistic evolutionism: that God alone decides and leads the course of evolution.

Because of ill health, he resigned from Sapporo Prefecture in June 1883; in August he went to Annaka, a town adjacent to Takasaki, to give a speech to the Annaka Congregational Church. It was there that he got acquainted with Asada Také. Though the same age as he was, she was one of thirty people who were baptized by Niijima Jō at Annaka, their hometown, on March 30, 1878, the day of the dedication of Annaka church. Niijima was a leading minister, indeed the best known in Japan at the time; and Annaka church soon became famous as the local headquarters of a campaign to abolish licensed prostitution.

Také had studied at two schools founded by missionaries, Doshisha School for Girls (Kyoto) and Union School for Girls (Yokohama); she had received the highest level of education available to women in Japan at that time.

In March 1884 Kanzō married Také.[4] The couple at first lived with *his*

4. Také was Uchimura's first wife, and gave birth to Nobu, his first daughter, after the breakup of their marriage. When Nobu grew up, she learned the Christian faith from her fa-

parents, according to an age-old custom. Before long, however, there occurred a sharp confrontation between Také and her mother-in-law, who
was a nervous, old-fashioned woman. In the increasingly bitter conflict,
Uchimura at last felt obliged to side firmly with his mother, and Také left
his house in October of the same year. Soon after that, he wrote to a close
friend (an alumnus of college) at Sapporo:

> I shall not write thee the minutiae of the affair, for they are too long; but
> this much I tell thee that after deliberate considerations, asking my con-
> science and the Bible for the true solution of the problem, *I determined
> to give her up.* She is now in Annaka.
>
> Brother, sympathize with me under such a blow. My parents are ex-
> ceedingly sorrowful, and I have no words to console them. I feel much
> ashamed for my thoughtlessness in the selection of my wife; but I wish
> thee to pity me in this respect, for I did it because I *thought* it to be God's
> will. Trust me, friend, though others may laugh at me. Pray for me that I
> may not be cast down.
>
> The storm is not wholly past, and its after-influences threaten my
> family with continued disturbances. The way to avoid the shock was
> consulted, and the unanimous advice of parents and friends was to leave
> the country for a moment, and to find relief either in America or En-
> gland. (36:115E)

Uchimura's Visit to America for Study:
How He Became a Christian

He decided to follow their advice, and made his way to America. This interesting letter shows that the situation into which Uchimura had fallen was
indeed deeply tragic; but he seemed to understand that it was a domestic af-

---

ther and led a Christian life. His second wife was Yokohama Kazuko, whom he married in
July 1889. Her character was said to be different in every respect from Také's. In January 1891,
at the time of "the affair of *lèse majesté*," Uchimura contracted influenza, which developed
into pneumonia; though he soon recovered, Kazuko caught pneumonia from him and died
on April 19. This chain of afflictions made him write *Kirisutoshinto no Nagusame (Consolations of a Christian)*. In December 1992 he married Okada Shizuko, who was his companion
until his death. With her he had a daughter, Rutsuko (Ruth), who died at the age of eighteen,
and a son, Yūji, who became a doctor of psychiatry and a master of the Medical School of
Tokyo University.

fair and tried to deal with it as such. For example, a major part of the blow was his parents' sorrow, which was too deep for his attempts at consolation. Another problem may have been his fear that other people would "laugh" at him, or at his "thoughtlessness in the selection of [his] wife." The "unanimous advice of parents and friends" to travel abroad may have been specifically to avoid this mockery. Here we find that Uchimura was very sensitive about his honor, and extremely afraid of bringing shame on himself and his family. Uchimura in his early days in America lived in what the anthropologist Ruth Benedict has identified as a "shame" culture; his spiritual pilgrimage in those days, therefore, had to take him from this world to that of righteousness and sin (and not to Benedict's "guilt" culture).

The world of shame culture as the starting point of his pilgrimage has been theorized by the Confucian ethical system, of which the cornerstone is filial duty. In this respect, the young Uchimura's understanding of Confucianism was noticeable:

> Looking back upon my past, I have received special education in spite of tight family finances, from eleven years of age on. However, at the precise point when I graduated from college and was just about to devote myself to the country, I committed a *grave* blunder; I committed a work of the devil instead of acting like a believer. When I think of it, I often lose my vigor and cannot recover it again. Nevertheless, when I considered the cause of the blunder, I found that it never sprang from ill will; I fell into that failure because I had been too seriously worried about how to serve my country and people. My basic failure, I believe, resulted from a misunderstanding of the Bible. If such words as *"a man shall leave his father and his mother, and shall cleave unto his wife"* were taken literally, human nature itself would be gravely threatened and the world would likewise be confused. (36:151)

However, he went on to write of finding, to his wonder as well as delight, that a contemporary scholar of the first rank had interpreted those words in a totally different way. Unfortunately, Uchimura neither mentioned the scholar's name nor described his new interpretation. Perhaps we have to satisfy ourselves that Uchimura was making an all-out effort to put his parents at ease.

Moreover, we can find under the surface meaning of the sentences quoted above that the ethic of filial duty could not quench the flames of pride or self-love. Self-love, doesn't it deceive the self-lover himself? The young Uchimura in Elwyn, Pennsylvania, however, had not yet become aware of it.

From January to June 1885, he worked as an attendant at Pennsylvania Training School for Feeble-Minded Children at Elwyn. He had taken an early chance, perhaps even before leaving Japan, of obtaining a scholarship offered by the Medical School of the University of Pennsylvania, through his close friend Dr. Willis Whitney, an oculist practitioner in Tokyo. At Baltimore on May 8, however, Uchimura met Niijima Jō, a leading minister of the Congregational Church of Japan, who was on an inspection tour of European and American universities as advance preparation to raise Doshisha English School to the status of a university. Niijima earnestly suggested that Uchimura enter Amherst College. Two alternatives were thus before him: University of Pennsylvania or Amherst College? This had important implications for his future career: Would he become a medical missionary with a large income or a missionary wholly focused on God's Word with a small income? Which way was he to take? To contemplate this question and pray for guidance, he left Elwyn and went to Gloucester, Massachusetts. During his seventeen-day stay there, he wrote to Niijima, "I intend to go to Amherst, availing your kind concern, and to fulfill my long intention to be a minister of the Gospel" (36:191E). The letter suggests that he was not entirely happy with this decision; but another one written twelve days later informed Niijima of his delight: "The greatest burden of my soul was cast into the bay of Gloucester never to be even looked at." Nevertheless, Uchimura himself wrote between the lines of the same letter: "Maybe I exaggerated a little," and in his autobiography, *How I Became a Christian* (1895), he looked back on his "Gloucester experience" and said, "For two weeks I wrestled in prayer upon a rocky promontory of Eastern Massachusetts. . . . I returned to Boston somewhat becalmed" (3:110E). It is unlikely that he appreciated the experience as highly as some contemporary scholars of his life and work believe. However, it may well have been the tug-of-war between Pennsylvania and Amherst that made him realize that the mortal enemy was self-love.

Since he had become a believer, he had never received pastoral care. At Amherst, he received it for the first and last time in his life from Dr. Julius H. Seelye, the president of the college. Seelye taught him that selfishness is really hatred of self, for anyone who really loves himself should first hate himself and give himself for others (3:114E).[5] Uchimura wrote, "I con-

---

5. Selfishness, or self-love, is based on a kind of misunderstanding. Your self was cre-

7

fess Satan's power over me began to slacken ever since I came in contact with that man. Gradually I was exorcised of my sins original and sins derived" (3:114E). By "sins original" he of course meant self-love, and by "sins derived," feelings of shame plausibly flavored with Confucianism. When one learns to understand the difference between these two kinds of sin, it is a sign that one has already converted to the Lord. *How I Became a Christian* does not point out exactly when Uchimura converted.[6] It may have been one day in the first half of 1886; or it may have taken place over those months, a "conversion term" rather than one particular day.

Two Events: The Hokuetsu Gakkan Event and the *Lèse Majesté* Incident

Uchimura came home on May 6, 1888. In July he wrote to Alfred Struthers, a former classmate at Amherst, to let him know how he was getting along: "In that city [Niigata] is a small wooden structure within which 170 eager students are trying to master [English]. They call this building a college! . . . They have invited me to become its superintendent, — they like to call me Kyōtō, president. Prexie Uchimura, — does it sound good? . . . I am now scheming my plan for the autumn . . . the inauguration address (do not envy me, Alf.) is to be prepared. . . . I am a president of a College! Hello! boys, how are you!" (36:298f.E).

In fact, during his stay in the USA, Uchimura had already received a few offers of positions. (Studying abroad was *indeed* advantageous for job hunting.) Among them was the presidency of Hokuetsu Gakkan in Niigata. (Gakkan may be translated as "academy." This school was the equivalent of a private high school in the modern school system.) Uchimura liked

---

ated by God; so *it is God's property.* Your self is not original with you. You have borrowed it from God. Then if you want to use it for ungodly private purpose, it should be returned to him. This chain of behavior is called "to hate on the basis of misunderstanding." And if we may use the words "the proper hate," it must be the hate against misunderstanding, that is, the hate against our belief in self-property. Arriving at this understanding, you will be able to appreciate the words of the Lord: "Greater love hath no man than this, that a man lay down his life for his friends" (John 15:13).

6. Some scholars suggest March 8, 1886, for his conversion day, perhaps because of the entry in his diary: "Very important day in my life . . ." (3:117E). This may well be correct, but he wrote nothing conclusive about his conversion, and at no time specifically associated it with a particular day.

Hokuetsu because it was "national, and Christian too," or "the first Independent Christian College in Japan." "National and independent" identified the college's financial position; it received money neither from foreign missions nor from the Japanese government, but from local non-Christian magnates. All things considered, Uchimura was in high spirits indeed! Unfortunately, whenever he dashed forward in high spirits toward a goal, some hindrances would invariably appear in his way. This was the first occasion, and he would meet with this kind of experience several times in later life. This time, the hindrances were the American Board missionaries stationed in Niigata and a Japanese clergyman collaborating with them. The idea with which Uchimura had inadvertently provoked the missionaries was stated in *How I Became a Christian:*

> Dec. 5. (1886) — Much impressed by the thought that God's providence must be in my nation. If all good gifts are from Him, then some of the laudable characters of my countrymen must be also from on high. We must try to serve our God and the world with gifts and boons peculiar to ourselves. God does not want our national characters attained by the discipline of twenty centuries to be wholly supplanted by American and European ideas. The beauty of Christianity is that it can sanctify all the peculiar traits which God gave to each nation. A blessed and encouraging thought that J——— *too is God's nation.* (3:124E)

This is the first theoretical expression of Uchimura's lifelong belief, Christian patriotism. The missionaries did not object to this theory directly. The problem was that he put theory into practice too simply and too arbitrarily. He tried abolishing the missionaries' practice of giving free English lessons, which they valued because it gave them a chance to influence the school curriculum and to make its Christian basis real instead of merely nominal. He also invited Buddhist priests to lecture on their doctrine, which caused indignation among the missionaries as it lessened their opportunities to proceed with their work. This practice was based on the theory stated in the diary entry quoted above, namely, "We must try to serve our God and the world with gifts and boons peculiar to ourselves." Uchimura then made a serious mistake by announcing to the college students on October 24 that if the committee of local promoters would not consent to his idea, he would resign and found a separate school with the students who supported him: a threat that was seen as amounting to a betrayal of the college of which he had been president. The only possible excuse for his conduct was his youthful vitality; it had the regrettable result of his losing the friendship of several Congregational missionaries, even an Amherst boy who was among their number. He resigned from Hokuetsu Gakkan on December 18, and left Niigata.

After having taught at two schools in Tokyo, Uchimura obtained the post of lecturer and dormitory superintendent at Tokyo School of Foreign Languages, the governmental preparatory school for Tokyo Imperial University where he had once studied, which had been renamed the First Higher Middle School.[7] The First High, as it was called, brought together the brightest young students in the entire country. Uchimura wrote to an American friend: "My work at present is among the young men who are preparing themselves for Tokyo University. The school I am engaged in has 1200 students. The *flower* of the future Japan is there. The work is quite bracing. Religion, politics, philosophy, science, are to be discussed. . . . The little house I and my wife now live in is opened to the students of this school and of the University. . . . My nationalistic conception of Christianity has met thus far no objection from them" (36:327E).

This letter too was written to Alfred Struthers, his former Amherst classmate, but the high-spirited tone of "Hello! boys . . . I am a president of a College!" was no longer evident. Nonetheless, even in this letter we can detect his quiet confidence in the new occupation. Unfortunately, however, the First High was a governmental school, and the government was now beginning to infiltrate the new morality into the nation. The content of the morality had nothing especially new in it; it was based on traditional Confucian teachings. It was the form in which it was now presented that was new. The government made the teaching of moral standards an integral part of the Imperial Rescript on Education (issued on October 23, 1890); that is, the teachings of Confucian sages were transformed into those of the emperor. The government authorities had set up both Westernization and nationalism as its two main policies from the beginning of the Meiji era. During Uchimura's stay in the USA, however, they began to focus principally on the latter policy, and on February 11, 1889, promulgated the

---

7. During Uchimura's school days (till 1886), the Japanese educational system was in disarray owing to its rapid modernization. The formation process of Tokyo Imperial University showed this: Tokyo Imperial University, the first university of Japan, was set up in 1877, but its curriculum included preparatory courses among the regular programs for students. In 1886, these were separated from the university and integrated into the First Higher Middle School, leaving the specialized courses to form the curriculum of Tokyo Imperial University. This system remained in place until 1949.

Meiji constitution, by which power was centered on the emperor. The Imperial Rescript on Education was a result of their determination to give the emperor the status of moral as well as political leader of the nation.

The First High received a copy of the rescript with the emperor's authentic signature, and held the ceremony of reading it on January 9, 1891. The deputy principal, after reciting it, ordered all the teachers and students of the school to bow deeply to the imperial signature by turns. Uchimura made a light bow, because a deep one seemed to him to have a religious implication and be tantamount to idol worship. Immediately after the ceremony, some teachers and students began to clamor against Uchimura, saying that by failing to bow deeply enough he had defiled the holy ceremonial hall. Even at this stage, the worst outcome could have been avoided if the teaching staff had united to support Uchimura in his difficulty. However, among the staff were a few influential people firmly united in their determination to expel Uchimura, owing to the offense he had given by his Christian faith. Their plan succeeded. He resigned from the First High on February 3.

Uchimura's failure to bow deeply before the rescript has been referred to as his "*lèse majesté* incident."

A Freelance Writer and Journalist

"After that, I wandered around a few schools. But my zeal for education had been chilled at the auditorium of ethics of The First Higher School" (9:476). He therefore left the world of education and resolved to support himself and his family as a freelance writer in Kyoto, the hometown of his new wife's parents (he had since remarried). His Kyoto period (1893-96) was productive for writing, and the principal works of his middle period were published during those years. In the following six years too (1897-1903) he continued to write, now as the editorial columnist for the *Yorozu Chōhō*, a popular national newspaper based in Tokyo.

As an example of his basic social thought in this period, here are selected quotations from a short essay "God of Liberty." "The Being Perfect in Himself is called God. . . . If the universe should be erased and human beings should perish, God is still God without fail. Therefore liberty, in the correct meaning of the word, belongs to God alone. . . . It clearly follows that perfect liberty is not characteristic of relative existence. . . . We must identify the source of liberty with a Being higher than the State, and higher

11

than the Sovereign: the political theorists of the French Revolution identified this as Nature itself, saying that Liberty was given from Nature and therefore had to be called Liberty-given-by-Nature, or natural right. . . . Liberty, according to Rousseau and Voltaire, originated from unconscious nature, and consequently has brought only mechanical equality to society. . . . [L]iberty is not material but spiritual, therefore its source is not nature but God. . . . If we want perfect liberty, we have to make for God, who alone possesses it, i.e. we only depend on God to have it" (6:76).

These quotations suggest the character of Uchimura's religio-political thought, and they support what he said in his editorials. The remarkable point is that he apparently referred to natural right only once in the entire forty volumes of his work, at volume 6, page 77, and he repudiated that right as merely a product of the mechanistic thought of the French Enlightenment. According to Uchimura, a man who is independent of all other men because of his genuine liberty has been lent this liberty by him who is the Owner of it.

Uchimura resigned from the *Yorozu Chōhō* in May 1898, though retaining the position of guest editorial writer, and started his own magazine of contemporary reviews, *Tokyo Dokuritsu Zasshi (The Tokyo Independent Magazine)*. As editor in chief, Uchimura wrote in tones of sharp liberal criticism seasoned with the spiritual aristocratic irony of Thomas Carlyle,[8] ensuring that the magazine would appeal successfully to intellectuals and students. Nevertheless, in July 1900 the magazine stopped publication on account of internal trouble among the editorial staff. The full-time writers of the *Tokyo Independent* were all so keenly conscious of human rights that between them and Uchimura there occurred a sharp conflict over a nonsensical misunderstanding. Ultimately, the failure of the magazine was due to the difference between Uchimura's concept of liberty as obligation and the other writers' concept of liberty as innate property.

At this period, the most urgent feature of the political scene was the possibility of war between Japan and Russia. Uchimura's view of war had been formed about ten years earlier: he was opposed to it, because he had

---

8. Thomas Carlyle (1795-1881) was a Scottish critic and historian. It was from his work in both those fields that Uchimura learned the meaning of sincerity. The *lèse majesté* affair occurred while Uchimura was engaged in close study of Carlyle's *Oliver Cromwell's Letters and Speeches* (1845). About his critical works, Uchimura commented, "Carlyle was a great man who attacked England. However the English who have allowed and listened to his attacks are greater than he. They have yet a great future. Those who are criticized by this enemy of all men [Uchimura himself], can therefore be said to have a little hope" (3:227).

turned to a kind of pacifist after the Korean war (the Sino-Japanese War, 1894-95). On October 8, 1903, Kuroiwa, president of the newspaper, published in the paper a statement that Japan should declare war on Russia, and Uchimura realized that it was time for him to bid farewell not only to the *Yorozu* but also to the world of journalism in Japan. He left his job as a part-time editorial writer the following day (October 9), and his "farewell memorandum to Mr. Kuroiwa Ruikō"[9] was put on the top of the front page of the *Yorozu's* issue of October 12.

As a journalist, for the *Yorozu* Uchimura preached social reform and vigorously countered public opinion, which was firmly in favor of war with Russia. He was defeated. However, he had already started another project: a magazine called *Seisho no Kenkyū (The Biblical Study)*, designed to spread basic knowledge of the Bible as his characteristic way of evangelism, founded in October 1900; his resolution was that genuine social reform could be achieved through evangelical conversion of individuals. One of his friends, Tanaka Shōzō, the leader of Japan's first anti–industrial pollution movement, asked him to stop studying the Bible and concentrate on social reform. Uchimura, though sympathizing with Tanaka, did not follow his suggestion.

Evangelist: Uchimura's True Vocation

When he left the *Yorozu,* Uchimura had no alternative way of giving meaning to his life except through evangelism. He concluded that God had at last revealed to him his true vocation. That vocation, however, was somewhat strange, because, he wrote, "I am a believer in Christ and the Bible, but am neither a member of any church nor of any sect. Neither pope nor bishop nor clergyman dominates me. Therefore I have not been given permission to preach; and even if I make converts, I have no church building to invite them into. . . . In fact, I have never baptized a single person until today, and no-one is studying under me as my *deshi* [disciple]" (9:480). In

9. Kuroiwa Ruikō (1862-1920: his real name was Shūroku, Ruikō being a pen name), a journalist. In 1892, at the age of thirty, he set up a newspaper, *Yorozu Chōhō*. This, at first, was simply an example of "yellow journalism"; but from about 1897 on, Shūroku endeavored to change it to a quality paper. First, he attempted to enlist excellent editorial writers, and Uchimura, who had been a friend of Shūroku's elder brother in Sapporo, was singled out as the first candidate. Shūroku succeeded in persuading him to accept the post. (Fortunately for them, the public had evidently forgotten the *lèse majesté* affair.)

the first days of his evangelizing, as this quotation suggests, he had not yet arranged a system for taking spiritual care of his converts. In February 1902, however, Uchimura's short-lived magazine, the *Mukyōkai* (*Non-church-*[*ism*]), proclaimed that its editing and accounting, starting with the next issue, would be the responsibility of the Tsunohazu Society for Bible Study. Tsunohazu was the name of the village in the suburbs of Tokyo where Uchimura was then living. "Society for Bible study" was a phrase he and his *deshi* would use frequently from then on, his chosen English equivalent for *Seisho Kenkyū-kai*. This *kai* (society) being set up, his converts could at last find refuge. But at first even Uchimura didn't assume that the *kai* constituted an *ecclesia*. According to him, "A Christian church is a community of lives of those who are newly born in Christ through the Holy Spirit" (12:105).

One further important point should be added to his ecclesiology. "Every church on earth, being different from the ideal church in Heaven, has its historical characteristics" (12:109). Therefore, because of "the historically well-known fact that the church is never a perpetual success if not growing in its native land," the church that will endure forever is the one that has come into being naturally, without foreign interference, through the Japanese believers' heartfelt reception of the Christian truth and deep appreciation of the divine grace of salvation. When such a church is built, he wrote, he will cease to be a *mukyōkai* believer (12:121).

Uchimura's formative years and Japan's period of modernization overlapped. Nationalism was the catalyst Japan required for its modernization. The young Uchimura was profoundly influenced by this spiritual atmosphere, and as a result became a lifelong nationalist. I hope, however, to show that his nationalism was eschatological.

After the autumn of 1904, his routine — producing *Seisho no Kenkyū* once a month and conducting his Bible class every Sunday at his residence in the suburbs of Tokyo — was established. At least, the outer phase of his evangelical activity was stabilized, until January 1918. As the history of Western theology exerted such a decisive influence on Japanese Christian churches since the early years of the Meiji era, Uchimura as a believer lived a life of struggle against natural theology that reached the height of its success in the late nineteenth century. Nevertheless, he retained his belief in the theories of biological and social evolution. This belief in social evolution, or the doctrine of progressivism, had been the view of history on which one of his early works, *Chijin Ron* (*Man and Earth,* 1894), was founded.

World War I and Its Impact on Uchimura

In July 1914, however, the First World War began. This war gave a tremendous shock to Western intellectuals, but caused no major unrest among Japanese intellectuals except for Uchimura; and even for him, the greatest shock came not from the outbreak of war itself but from the entry of the USA into the war. He believed that America would be certain to intervene between the warring states, and compensate them for their losses. In the early spring of 1918, at a lecture meeting, he publicly confessed: "[After this war began,] all that I had to say about the Bible according to the faith I had held until then ceased to be meaningful. Of late I have often wished to stop the publication of *Seisho no Kenkyū*. Especially when confronted with enormous problems concerning the universe and human life, I at last came to a deadlock" (24:130). However, his deeply rooted faith had never left him throughout these troubled times, and at last he found the way out of this situation. The part of his faith that sustained him was his belief in the second coming of Christ. "How foolish I was! I have spent many years trying to improve the world by dedicating this small body and small power. It was not my business; Christ will come and accomplish it. Peace shall at last be realized through His Second Coming" (24:60).

Once this truth was revealed to him, he made up his mind to find a special way to proclaim it. On the afternoon of Sunday, January 6, 1918, he held what he called "a meeting for speeches on the prophetic study of the Bible," at the YMCA hall in the center of Tokyo, with two ministers, one of the Holiness church and the other of the Congregational church. He continued to hold these speech meetings, in various forms, till May of the following year. The press had become interested in this sudden change in the pattern of his activities, and called his new direction "the movement of the second coming." This movement differed from his earlier activities in two respects. Firstly, he had never previously worked in such close cooperation with clergymen of established churches. Secondly, though he had hated central Tokyo, comparing it to Babylon, all his speech meetings were held in the heart of the city; and more frequently than before he would travel to local city centers to make speeches on the second coming. He thought that the precious good tidings suitable to the times had to be proclaimed to as many people as possible, and that for this reason he was bound to cooperate with all believers in the second coming, irrespective of which sect they belonged to or whether they were members of any church at all. For the most part, however, his comrades were from the Baptist church and churches affiliated with it.

One reason the mass media showed interest in the movement was that it gave rise to disputes and skirmishes among Christians. Its most eloquent opponent was Ebina Danjō of the Congregational church. Uchimura himself began to fear that placing too much emphasis on the second coming might alienate believers of a certain spiritual quality, and he gradually shifted the main focus of his remarks to criticism of the Wilsonian humanism in the scheme of the League of Nations.

In the early summer of 1919, Uchimura discontinued his series of speech meetings at the strongly worded request of the board of directors of the Tokyo YMCA, and instead began a Bible class at a large hall in the government office district of central Tokyo. At this hall, he lectured on the Epistle to the Romans from January 1921 to October 1922. The lectures he gave in this period have been considered his best. On September 1, 1923, a violent earthquake, known as the Great Kantō Earthquake, shook the Tokyo area, destroying the hall in which his Bible class was held; but a donation from his *deshi,* Imai Shōtarō, enabled him to build a new hall especially for the class, called Imai Hall.

Uchimura, Tsukamoto, and *Mukyōkai*

Another of Uchimura's *deshis,* Tsukamoto Toraji (1885-1973), was a *mukyōkai* preacher who can be seen as Melanchthon to Uchimura's Luther or Beza to his Calvin. He became Uchimura's *deshi* while a student at Tokyo Imperial University (1909), and soon after the Great Kantō Earthquake, which took his wife's life, he was selected to be Uchimura's assistant. The post of "assistant" was one of the few to be established for convenience' sake in Uchimura's fellowship,[10] and was assigned to a leading *deshi,* one part of whose duties was to preach before the *sensei* (teacher; that is, Uchimura) on Sundays, and to contribute essays to *Seisho no Kenkyū.*

---

10. As Uchimura's principle was *mukyōkai* (nonchurchism), he and his *deshi* had to call their gathering by some other name than *kyōkai* (church). In place of it, he had used the word *shūkai* since about the end of the Meiji era. *Shūkai* has many uses; its basic meaning is, however, a group of people who gather together for a common purpose. But when the word is used to refer to a *mukyōkai* meeting (for example, "*Uchimura Shūkai*"), it should be taken as a translation of the Greek word *koinonia* (cf. 1 John 1:3, 6, 7, etc.), whose English translation is "fellowship." So it seems appropriate to use such an expression as "*mukyōkai* Christian fellowship," and to use the term "Uchimura *Shūkai*" to refer collectively to all the meetings he held within his *shūkai* at Kashiwagi in Tokyo regardless of their size.

Before long, however, Uchimura found that Tsukamoto's outlook differed from his: Tsukamoto's conception of *mukyōkai-shugi* was much stronger. For Uchimura, *mukyōkai* arose from his indifference to *kyōkai;* it is good that a church should exist, he believed, but it can be equally good if it does not. The important question was not whether the church should exist or not. On the other hand, for Tsukamoto, *mukyōkai-shugi* was one and the same thing with fideism, the doctrine of "faith alone," which claims that faith and not work is the true road to salvation. To hold this belief, according to Tsukamoto, is to embrace *mukyōkai.* In December 1929, Uchimura at last allowed Tsukamoto to take an independent course, leaving Uchimura's fellowship and setting up one of his own. Tsukamoto, for his part, tried until the end to avoid a break with his *sensei,* though the degree of difference between their views probably made this impossible. It may be seen as a blessing that Uchimura did not leave a direct successor in his fellowship, because his almost popelike status among his followers could not be maintained after the radical split between his and Tsukamoto's conceptions of *mukyōkai.* Uchimura died on March 28, 1930, of heart disease.

PART I

Historical Context and Social Thought

Japan for the World

ANDREW E. BARSHAY

Preface: Everything Is Connected

This essay is a historical meditation on one phrase in Uchimura Kanzō's famous epitaph, written when he was still in his twenties, during his fateful stay the United States. "I for Japan," it begins; "Japan for the World; the World for Christ; and All for God."

Let me say straight out that I am not a specialist on Uchimura. Long ago I read and was enthralled by *How I Became a Christian*, and was later fascinated by his chastened change of mind after writing "Justification of the Corean War." I admired Uchimura's notion of the nonchurch, or *mukyōkai*, and saw its resonances with Shinran's declaration that he "had not a single disciple." As I learned more about Uchimura's life, I could only sympathize with his deepening pessimism over the course his country had taken, and his ardent faith that God would intervene directly to save a desperate humanity. I have never ceased to be amazed by the sheer intellectual energy and verve he sustained over a writing career of five decades. And who could not be interested in a thinker attacked as a "Spiritual Bolshevick" (27:146), and described by one who knew him as a "Great X"?[1]

But the most I have written about Uchimura was in the course of pre-

---

1. "Spiritual Bolshevick": Uchimura, foreword to *Alone with God and Me*, in *The Complete Works of Kanzō Uchimura*, ed. Yamamoto Taijirō and Mutō Yōichi, vol. 3 (Tokyo: Kyōbunkan, 1972), 6; "Great X": Masaike Megumu, *Uchimura Kanzō den (A Life of Uchimura Kanzō)* (1953), in *Masaike Megumu chosakushū (The Selected Works of Masaike Megumu)*, vol. 19 (Tokyo: Kirisutokyō Tosho Shuppansha, 1996), iv.

paring a study of Nanbara Shigeru (1889-1974), a *mukyōkai* adherent and, as a professor in the Law Faculty of Tokyo Imperial University, a representative "public man" of the late imperial period. That study contained just a few pages on Uchimura, and even those were based on Nanbara's writings. For me the sight of the forty volumes of Uchimura's complete works is nothing but daunting. So let me work my way into my subject — Uchimura Kanzō's view of Japan, its relation to and role in the world — via something of a detour. As I hope will be clear from the prefatory tale that follows, "everything" in the historical world is connected, and sometimes in ways that are less trivial than they might first appear to be.

For a while now I have been working on the repatriation of Japanese from northeast Asia after World War II, which, as is well known, involved more than a million civilians from Manchuria alone. Along with that "epic tragedy" (as John Dower calls it) came the internment of between 600,000 and 700,000 captured soldiers of the vanquished Kwantung Army in the Soviet gulag (most in Siberia), where they were held from two to four years, and others far longer. This was a completely unexpected consequence of the Soviet invasion of Manchuria just as the war was ending and led, among other things, to the writing of memoirs by at least two thousand survivors. Some of these men went on to become important interpreters of the USSR for the Japanese public, while others became major painters, poets, and novelists. The Siberia experience was transformative for all of them and also provides a window on the making of postwar Japan that I think is virtually unknown in the United States and increasingly forgotten in Japan itself.

The vast majority of returnees from the gulag, of course, did not record their experience, and most of the two thousand or so who wrote about it did so amid a life spent on other work — they may have written at the prompting of others or because they wanted to record their own story before age and death caught up with them. One such memoir — it is little more than a short essay — brings me to the subject at hand. It dates from 1972, and was written by Dōshō (now Masuda) Nobuhiko, at the time an official of the Economic Planning Agency. I happened on it in one of the pamphlets *(geppō)* included with my old set of Nanbara Shigeru's collected works, which I was looking through in preparation for writing this essay.[2]

---

2. See Dōshō Nobuhiko, "Shiberiya yokuryū to *Kokka to shūkyō*" ("Siberian Detention and *State and Religion*"), in *Nanbara Shigeru chosakushū geppō* (The monthly report of *The Selected Works of Nanbara Shigeru*), no. 1 (Nov. 1972): 4-7. I have also consulted Agnieszka

If I were not now working on the Siberian internment, I am sure I would not have noticed it. But again, "everything is connected."

Dōshō Nobuhiko was a student in the Law Faculty at Todai (Tokyo Imperial University). In late 1943 he received his red draft notice and was posted to Harbin. At the time of his capture he was a cadet, a paymaster-in-training in the Kwantung Army — he would eventually have received his officer's commission had the war not ended so suddenly. As happened with many officers, including those of modest rank, his time in the gulag stretched to four years.

In his essay, Dōshō recounts an episode that is of surprising relevance to our present subject. One day in late 1944, his elder brother, whose mainland unit was being transferred to northern Manchuria, passed through Harbin. Starved for reading matter, Dōshō asked his brother if he could let him have one of the books he was carrying. His choice was Nanbara Shigeru's *Kokka to shūkyō (State and Religion)*, which had been published only a few years earlier. Dōshō had attended Nanbara's lectures at the university, and like Nanbara he was a Christian. Whether he was also, like Nanbara, a member of the *mukyōkai,* I do not know. But along with his Bible, it was Nanbara's book that Dōshō carried with him into captivity. At one point, he tells us, guards confiscated both books in a search held while prisoners were away at work. Nanbara's, evidently, was judged not to be harmful to "socialist construction," and was left in a storehouse rather than destroyed. There, by a stroke of great luck, it was discovered by a coworker of Dōshō, who had recalled seeing it at his bunk, and returned to him. To keep it safe from then on, Dōshō divided it into four sections of one chapter each, and shared three of them out among a group of his fellow internees. They agonized over how best to keep the chapters from being discovered — carrying them to work, hiding them in the barracks' ceiling, and so on. In the hothouse atmosphere created by the ideological reeducation that internees went through, Dōshō, as a cadet, was subject to periodic attacks by his fellow prisoners as a "reactionary element," and he had to worry whether his choice of reading material might lead to something more serious than confiscation. As Dōshō writes, surrounded by the

---

Kozyra, *Nihon to seiyō ni okeru Uchimura Kanzō — sono shūkyō shisō no fuhensei (Uchimura Kanzō in Japan and the West: The Universality of His Religious Thought)* (Tokyo: Kyōbunkan, 2001); and Ray A. Moore, ed., *Culture and Religion in Japanese-American Relations: Essays on Uchimura Kanzō, 1861-1930* (Ann Arbor: Center for Japanese Studies, University of Michigan, 1981); and T. James Kodera, "Uchimura Kanzō and His Non-Church Christianity," *Religious Studies* 23 (September 1987): 377-90.

closed, even claustrophobic society of the labor camp, the gatherings to read and talk about Nanbara's book became for him a concrete instance of the "kingdom of God" taking shape when "two or three are gathered together" in his name (Matt. 18:20). This was the true "church." And when he was called in for interrogation over some matter or other, he found that by the next day he was at peace, his face astonishingly free of anxiety.

For Dōshō, then, *Kokka to shūkyō* was no mere academic treatise. It had eased his mind during his captivity and, he goes on to say, remained his moral touchstone as he entered the official world upon his return to Japan. But his experience of the Siberian camp reading circle raises an important question for us. In an odd and paradoxical way, did "Japan," as a non-Christian society, stand in the same relation to the "church" as did the labor camp itself? Or, if Japanese society and culture represented more than an alien and hostile backdrop, what were the positive features of the relationship? And from there, given that relationship, how did Japan figure in the "world" to which Uchimura had consecrated it in his famous epitaph?

I propose to answer this question in two stages. First, I will use a small selection of Uchimura's texts on the theme of "Japan for the World" to illustrate the evolution of his thinking. And then, with that evolution in mind, I will return to Nanbara's *Kokka to shūkyō*, which I regard as a sort of *mukyōkai* summa on this same issue of Japan's relationship to the world. As a legatee of Uchimura's teaching, I will suggest, Nanbara strove to ensure its salience for later generations — generations with no direct experience of Uchimura's personal charisma and searching less for an eschatological vision than for spiritual guidance in a postimperial present.

Uchimura on Japan's Mission

Uchimura Kanzō wrote two essays, both modest in length, that are specifically concerned with what he termed Japan's *tenshoku* — its providential mission and role in world history. Needless to say, he wrote much else that is relevant to the theme of Japan as "a nation bearing a distinct ideal and mission."[3] I have chosen to discuss these particular two, first because they

---

3. Uchimura's full phrase was: "aru meiryō naru risō to tenshoku wo obite sonzai suru neishon (*kokka to yakusu bekarazu*)." Note the parenthetical "[nation] should not be translated as '*state*,'" with Uchimura's emphasis. See *Uchimura Kanzō zenshū (The Complete Works of Uchimura Kanzō)* (Tokyo: Iwanami Shoten, 1980-84), 7:442. See also Kozyra, *Nihon*

bear the term *tenshoku* in their titles, and second because they were composed slightly more than thirty years apart: the first, "Japan: Its Mission," was published in the *Japan Daily Mail* in February 1892; the second, "Nihon no tenshoku," appeared in the November 1924 issue of *Seisho no Kenkyū* (*The Biblical Study;* a translation given by Uchimura). They are both sufficiently alike, and sufficiently different, to be illuminating for us here.

In "Japan: Its Mission," a young and optimistic Uchimura Kanzō asked of his country, "what can she do for the world?" (1:245E).[4] He saw Japan in a line of great developers of "civilization" — he spoke in the singular — each with its distinct contribution: "Egypt and Babylon started civilization, Phoenicia dispersed it, Judea purified it, Greece polished it, Italy preserved it, Germany reformed it, and America executed it." That neither China nor India appears on this list is a clue that we are reading the young Uchimura, who, though he was endlessly offended by Western arrogance and racism, was just as upset at being identified as Chinese and therefore less civilized than he actually was. At this stage in his life, Uchimura had considerable confidence that God, "the All-wise Dramatist," was distantly overseeing the process of human evolution in more or less the same way he oversaw that of the natural world. This meant that the methods of history were essentially the same as those of science.[5] We can see that confidence in Uchimura's mobilization of German cultural geography. "Nations" were the conceptual units of this discipline, and these were essentially formed of two elements: land and people. We may pass over most of Uchimura's general discussion here, but it is worth noticing his delineation of Japan's "geographical configuration": that it was insular, lay "in the periphery of the land-hemisphere," and was dually oriented toward the Pacific and coastal Asia. ("Japan turns her back on Siberia," he remarked, and he remained consistently antagonistic to Russia.) Such a Japan had to be adaptable to commerce and navigation, and because "the land is already much too crowded . . . we must conquer the sea as an arena for our ambition."

---

to seiyō ni okeru Uchimura Kanzō, 35. Uchimura's complete works are hereafter cited in the notes by the volume and page number(s) (e.g., 7:442). When cited directly in the text, the volume and page number(s) are provided in parentheses.

4. All quotations in the following discussion are from Uchimura, "Japan's Future as Conceived by a Japanese (Japan: Its Mission)," 1:243-54E. The Japanese version was published in *Rikugō zasshi* (April 1892) under the title "Nihonkoku no tenshoku" ("Japan's Mission"), 1:284-94E.

5. See Kozyra, *Nihon to seiyō ni okeru Uchimura Kanzō,* 53-55.

Fortunately, its peripheral location made Japan safe from foreign attack, and by the same token, the "directions of her mountain ranges, taken in conjunction with the internal configurations of her surface, make national unity with local independence possible" (1:243, 245, 247-48E).

By far the most important of Japan's geographical virtues — and a hint of its broader cultural role — are captured in Uchimura's observation that Japan, stretching "one arm toward America . . . stretches the other arm towards the responding arms of Korea and China, the whole making of Japan a stepping-stone . . . between the Occidental and the Oriental continents. . . . She stands as an 'arbiter,' a 'middle man' (*nakahodo* [*sic*]) between the Democratic West and the Imperial East, between the Christian America and the Buddhist Asia" (1:248-49E).

Uchimura warmed to this theme as he turned to the "ethnic" or "race" characteristics of the Japanese." "It is a doubtful question," he emphasized, "whether we were made to cope with the sturdy Cossacks or the sinewy Scotch Highlanders upon the field of battle." "Perpetual advancement in the art of butchering humanity" had not overridden the disadvantages of short stature. Instead, Japan's cultural and political unity, "impressionable nature," and readiness to assimilate fitted it to "some other form of conquest than that made at the point of a bayonet": "The Japanese alone of all Oriental peoples can comprehend the Occidental ideas, and they alone of all civilized peoples have a true conception of Oriental ideas. In intellectual spheres, no less than in commercial, Japan is a stepping-stone between the East and the West" (1:249-50E).

"Historic indications," Uchimura then argued, make the broader case for this mission. For "civilization marches westward, in a direction opposite to the diurnal motion." And by this law, the "stream of civilization" that had begun in Babylon and passed through Greece and Rome, and moved thence to Germany and England, had "culminated on the Pacific side of America." Here, we note, Uchimura did recognize another, eastward-tending stream that "travelled through India, Tibet, and China, culminating in the Manchoo Court of Peking"; but again, Japan is not in this line. Instead, it is as if the "All-wise Dramatist" had set Japan aside, having in mind a special mission that could not be performed if it were too heavily under the sway of its larger and nearer neighbors. "The moral world," Uchimura argued, "is also a magnet with its two opposite poles on the opposite banks of the Pacific, the democratic, aggressive, inductive America, and the imperial, conservative, deductive China." Constant attempts "for the union of these magnetic currents" had been made, and all had failed. Until now: now it was "Japan's turn to add a new proof to the grand possibility of the human race." "The young Japan . . . has the best of Europe and the best of Asia at her command. At her touch the circuit is completed, and the healthy fluid shall overflow the earth." All of Japan's history had prepared it for this: "*To reconcile the East with the West; to be the advocate of the East and the harbinger of the West; this we believe to be the mission Japan is called upon to fulfill*" (1:250-51E).

But how? It is on this question, of course, that Uchimura's optimism was to falter, and soon. He grandly proclaimed Japan to "stand in our relation to Asia as did the ancient Greeks in relation to Europe." As the adopter of the best of the West, Japan would "give them in marriage as fit brides to our less flexible brothers. We shall, if must be, lead humble Asia to curb the march of proud Europe; but we desire peace." The destiny of "1,000,000,000 Asiatics" was at stake. At that moment, Japan was "the apple of the Oriental eye." But amid his confidence, Uchimura — whether just for rhetorical purposes or out of real doubt — recognized that Asia's one billion "are to be blessed or cursed, as we behave truly or falsely." He went on to wonder whether, assuming its success, Japan's role as advocate and harbinger might not "re-create" America itself, which had stood as cultural mediator for Japan only decades before (1:252-54E). But that one line of doubt — would Japan "behave truly or falsely"? — would only grow more persistent, boring its way ever deeper into his mind and spirit.

There is no need, surely, to rehearse here the sequence of events in Uchimura's life and in the history he witnessed that fed the doubts just mentioned. They are amply reflected in his second text on Japan's *tenshoku*, which I turn to below. If anything, it is important to emphasize, as Uchimura himself did, his unbroken conviction that nations had missions, and that those missions were important to the degree that they contributed to, or manifested, the global character of God's plans for the "human family."[6] On the other hand, it cannot have escaped notice that the mission Uchimura envisioned for Japan in 1892, its mode of being a "Japan for the world," had no explicitly Christian character. The fact that he ends

---

6. Cf. Uchimura Kanzō, "'JAPAN: ITS MISSION' sairoku ni saishite no fugen" (Additional remark at the republication of the essay), *Japan Christian Intelligencer*, August 5, 1924, in 30:25: "[Japan: Its Mission] was written thirty-four years ago, when I was a stripling of thirty-one. . . . My country was not a world-power then, and the Chinese and Russian empires were standing in full strength. The United States of America was then an unarmed, peaceful country, and an ideal of what nations should be and do. The reader will notice, however, that my essential position has not changed since then."

the essay with a little peroration on the "heaven-appointed mission" of the "country of the Rising Sun" is indicative here. It is "heaven," not the Lord, who appoints. Although in opening the essay Uchimura invokes a man's service to "his country and Creator" as his subject, it is evident that God is, so to speak, involved more as an immanent principle in the spread of civilization, or perhaps its final cause. The drama of sin and salvation, at the individual and collective level, is entirely absent.

Seen in this light, the mission Uchimura identified for Japan in 1924 is striking for its thoroughly religious character.[7] This is clear from the start, with its adornment of three scriptural texts (from Acts, Joshua, and the Psalms) that invoke a people's service to God as its very reason for existing. The "contributionist" theme, to be sure, remains, but is framed more in terms of what God demands: offerings and sacrifices suited to each ("wisdom from Edom, learning [*gakujutsu*] from Egypt, and worship from Israel"). A nation's *tenshoku* is defined by and as the duty it performs to God. That is what makes a nation a nation (28:400-401).

Perhaps the most important difference from the earlier text is its far sharper articulation of *who* stands as the representative figure for the nation in the performance of its mission, and why. "Japan," so to speak, was not Japan in every respect. There was a "true" or ideal Japan, and an unworthy Japan. And as Agnieszka Kozyra points out, each was represented by actual individuals or groups of people.[8] So this was not a matter of merely condemning the Japan of the present. In any case, it had become clear to Uchimura over the decades since the mid-1890s that his country had been "officially" worshiping a false God — or to put it differently, that Japan was being falsely represented in the court of history and providence. Departing from its just quest for national independence and (at least potential) role as "advocate and harbinger," Japan had chosen the path of empire and pursued the status of "first-rank power" in the world. This was a double perversion: a betrayal of its future promise for the sake of present "glory," and of its own past as well.

Japan at the time, Uchimura observed, might be regarded abroad as a nation whose greatest strength lies in arms and its martial tradition, as its military conquests over the previous thirty years seemed to prove. But this

---

7. Unless otherwise noted, quotes in the following discussion are from Uchimura Kanzō, "Nihon no tenshoku" (1924), in 28:400-408.

8. Uchimura Kanzō, "Nishu no Nihon" ("Two Kinds of Japan"), *Yorozu chōhō*, November 26, 1901, in 9:464. See also Kozyra, *Nihon to seiyō ni okeru Uchimura Kanzō*, 34-35, 83.

was the self-serving propaganda of Meiji's parvenu leadership. The ideology of "loyalty and filial piety," the so-called national morality, was far too "narrow" a foundation for the state, and one that would ultimately prove insupportable. The real Japan, Uchimura insisted, was a land not of warriors at all but of peasants, or (as he put it elsewhere) of "industrious and honest common people."[9] The "military men, the politicians, the writers [*bunshi*] and businessmen" — all city people — were a noisy and noisome minority. It was the people's love of peace that led the Tokugawa, following Hideyoshi's vainglorious attempt at continental conquest, to bring "three hundred years of tranquility" to Japan. A true history of "the Japanese people," Uchimura summed up, would be "nine-tenths a history of peace" (28:402).

But if not martial might, what, he asked, of commerce and trade? In his earlier writings, Uchimura had advanced a liberal ideal in the strict sense that he envisioned society as a space of free and fair competition. And he ventured that such might also be true of the relations among nations. But he had been disabused of such hopes. Friendly rivalry in trade did not guarantee peace, only the accumulation of frictions and resentments. But beyond that, Japan lacked the basic requirements for the projection of commercial influence. Geographically it was only a partial analogy to England. It had not, as England had, built its might on the three pillars of an imposing navy, commercial prowess, and great manufacture. Instead Japan had followed Germany, which had beggared its economy in building up its military only to lose everything in war (28:402-3). And now America too, despite all its gifts and resources and promise, had proven false: rather than bringing peace, it had entered the world war, turned its back on the League of Nations, and, worse yet, embraced a venomous policy of refusing entry to Japanese. The notion of a "great power" was an absurd and immoral contradiction in terms.

Rather plaintively, Uchimura moved on to observe that even in the realm of culture, Japan was less of a presence (less of a "Japan for the world") than it might appear. It is not that artistic geniuses had failed to emerge even on its soil: Hokusai was a "world figure," and "had they been born in Europe, Chikamatsu and Bakin could certainly have become a Shakespeare, a Walter Scott." But what Japan lacked was originality, the capacity to generate new thought. Japanese were "improvers," not creators.

---

9. "Narrow" foundation: "Kanka no kan" [editors' title], *Tokyo dokuritsu zasshi,* April 15, 1899, in 7:19; "honest and industrious": "Nishu no Nihon," 9:464. See also Kozyra, *Nihon to seiyō ni okeru Uchimura Kanzō,* 71-72, 82.

They could "depict nature with skill, but could not daringly move on to search out its mysteries" (28:403).

But ultimately, none of this is decisive. "What is special about the Japanese as a people?" Uchimura asked. "I answer: it is that they are a people of religion." Then he added, somewhat wryly, "I do not say this out of self-interest." Only now, as "external events have aided awakening within," have Japanese begun to realize this about themselves. Needless to say, this had nothing to with sectarian pride. Between Buddhism and Christianity there was nothing to choose as far as institutional corruption was concerned. Across all lines of affiliation, Uchimura wrote, consider the spiritual men who have emerged on Japanese soil. Genshin, gaze fixed on Amida's Western paradise, was a model of faith for Japanese Christians, Hōnen and Dōgen no less, and Nichiren a true prophet. Uchimura's special admiration went to Motoori Norinaga and Hirata Atsutane — "the pride of the nation, the honor of our people" — for enunciating Japan's "true mission" and the principle by which it could "lead the nations" *(bankoku shidō)*. He quoted Hiraga Gennai: "The day that breaks on the Land of Morning / Is the Day that brings the Spring to the East" (28:403-5). Japanese of today must not sully and dishonor this highest of all patriotic ideals by imagining that it could be served by military conquest.

Working through history, Uchimura argued, God had placed Japan's religious tradition, including Christians now in its line of inheritance, in the position of the Hebrew prophets; not to serve those in power but to prod, to challenge, to vex, but above all to bring light. At a moment when Luther himself was forgotten in Germany, and American religion no more than a drive for quantitative "results" — when "so-called Western civilization" had become "the world's destroyer" — Japan's Christians as a prophetic minority had a duty not only to their own people, but to the world. And as prophets, they and their followers were sure to be tested, as had now happened with the 1923 earthquake and America's turn against Japanese immigration. "In our current state, there is nothing that is not working against us. . . . Who knows, but that the true rise of the Japanese nation will not come after this distress has reached its height?" (28:405-8).

From Uchimura to Nanbara

As of that moment in 1924, no one, least of all Uchimura himself, could have imagined how great Japan's "distress" would become. Perhaps fortunately for him, he died before the scourge his country had let loose in Asia would come back to destroy it. On the other hand, Uchimura had created in the *mukyōkai* a means for the core of his "Crucifixianity" to outlast that conflagration and play a role in Japan's intellectual and spiritual revival after 1945. I indicated earlier that Nanbara Shigeru — joined, to be sure, by Yanaihara Tadao, among others — was central to that role. In the final section of this essay, therefore, I wish to return to Nanbara's *Kokka to shūkyō (State and Religion)*. Particularly in its final pages, I believe, Nanbara provides a *mukyōkai* summa on the question I have tried to address in this essay: What did Uchimura mean when he spoke of a "Japan for the world"?

Kokka to shūkyō is a long exploration of the state-church relation in European thought. Its arguments need not concern us here, but as will be seen, for Nanbara, that relation turned on the issue of the church, its nature and identity. Indeed, he would say, it was not possible to think about "Japan for the world" without considering the church, or community of faith, as the vehicle that could link Japan to the world and make possible action "for" that world. Nanbara was writing at the height of the Pacific war, and his language is therefore both circumspect and daring. Uchimura's own writing is considerably more straightforward. But the contours of Nanbara's position are nonetheless clear, and I propose to use them as a guide for my concluding discussion. To that end, I have placed emphasis on certain phrases.

Here are Nanbara's concluding paragraphs:

We must not lose the power to *grasp and believe firmly in the invisible as invisible, spirit as spirit, ideal as ideal.* . . .

For the church to have developed in the European world it required a unique tradition and historical environment. What is needed in our country, which possesses nothing like the history and tradition of Europe and America, is not to make or imitate that history and tradition, but to create a *point of departure different from the European world.* What would it be? It is a method at once original [*gensho*] and new. That is, through a union with the divine absolute ideal symbolized in the personhood [*jinkaku*] of Christ Jesus above all else, it is [to create] a new relationship based on interiorly regenerated personhood. Now for this, our country, where we have practiced absolute loyalty and obedience as in the relation of sovereign to subject and father to son, in *no wise lacks the foundation of a unique and elevated morality.* In this way, with the incorporation of each individual among our people into this holy and deep union until the whole of our national community finds its final fulfillment in the exalted divine life, the *formation of the city of God [kami no kuni] will not cease.* At such a time, the interior foundation of the Japanese state will be set on the firmest foundation of an eternal spirit and basis. What is called *"Japanese Christianity" is nothing other than this.* Apart from it, we can truly expect nothing, not from any contemporary religious movement or philosophy, nor, indeed, from the "dialectic of nothingness" or mystical pantheism.

What has been discussed above has often been referred to as *"No-Church"-ism [mukyōkai-shugi].* Among the modern thinkers to have most thoroughly advocated such an idea, in Europe one could probably offer the name of *Kierkegaard.* As with Nietzsche he set himself against the condition of the religious world of contemporary Europe — its descent into sensuality, transformation into a political power, and moral decay. But rather than the ideal of a "superman" in Nietzschean fashion, to the end he argued for the "solitary man" standing humbly before God. In our country, it was none other than the late *Uchimura Kanzō who took on the role of Kierkegaard, but dared to do so with even greater prophetic insight and passion.* Half a century ago, in an age that took the fashion for Western civilization to its greatest height and licked at [contented itself with] the leavings [*sōhaku*] of the Christian world and the British and American churches, he it was who opposed all the authority of the churches' dogma and institutions, and *fought daringly for a pure gospel faith [junsui fukuinshugi].* But he was decidedly *not* an individualist, as many of his countrymen mistakenly thought. As I see him, unlike Kierkegaard who merely preached the "solitary man" in the presence of God, Uchimura taught of the true "Japanese" standing before God, and behind his No-Church faith, his *heart veritably pounded with a burning love of his country [sokokuai].*

Whether Christianity is compatible with the national polity is surely an issue that is beyond discussion. As Mitani Takamasa has put it, "The issue is no longer whether to approve of or reject Christianity, but how to adopt it." The Japanese nation [*minzoku*] had earlier adopted the world-religion of Buddhism, making it into something eminently Japanese. At the beginning of modern times, it was the German nation that made itself independent from Roman or Latin Christianity, and resolutely carried out the *first* Reformation. By this means they preserved for humankind the common mission of a universal Christianity, but at the same time, by excluding heterogeneous [*ishitsuteki*] elements that the ancient Germans had accepted, they were able to bring German Christianity to completion. Who could declare that something similar to this, as *a second Reformation, cannot be achieved in the East by the Japanese nation?* No, we may regard the foundation as having already been laid. It must be by removing the cause that led the first Reformation, which sought to revive a primitive Christianity, to fail in that aim. It is abundantly clear from what has been said above that more than anything else, it *must make the "church" itself the issue.* One major way in which Japan can contribute to the spiritual world in the future, I believe, lies in restoring to an originally Asian [*tōyōteki*] and global Christianity its Asian character, and in Japanizing it. Can I be the only one who hopes that, with the dawn that brings these things to completion, *a new Japanese culture, one belonging to the world in a new sense,* will develop?[10]

I think it is fair to say that, allowing for shifts in emphasis here or there, Nanbara's summary statement captures every key element in Uchimura's own mature conception of how "Japan for the world" could be realized. We note first the essential recognition that the invisible was real *as such,* as was the ideal. Such a view was especially important in thinking about the church, or Christianity, in a society where it occupied a minority position. Not only would this serve as a safeguard against what Uchimura had castigated as "quantitative Christianity," it was in fact the only realistic position to take, as even in the older centers of Christian civilization, the visible church suffered ever deeper corruption. In this sense, Japan was poised at the gate of the Christian future. Yet — and this was also a typical Uchimura theme — Japan's church stood at the vanguard of that future precisely because it had been "grafted" onto the healthy stock of its non-Christian past.[11] Uchimura never seems to have gone through a phase of attempting to reject his native culture.

On the other hand, it is also clear that for Uchimura and for Nanbara, Christ was the ultimate model for all that humanity could be, and once that model was actualized with Christ's incarnation, every other value became "limited" or historical in relation to it, the Old Testament in relation to the New. Relativism itself was relative. Believers in that truth — in other

10. Nanbara Shigeru, *Kokka to shūkyō (State and Religion),* expanded ed. (Tokyo: Iwanami Shoten, 1946), 378-82.

11. For the "grafting" metaphor, see Uchimura Kanzō, "Bushidō and Christianity" (July 1915), *Uchimura Kanzō chosakushū,* vol. 7 (Tokyo: Iwanami Shoten, 1953), 21. See also the extended discussion in Kozyra, *Nihon to seiyō ni okeru Uchimura Kanzō,* 36-52.

words, Christians — were called on to witness to it, and to seek to bring within it those outside the knowledge of Christ. In this sense there can be no church without a mission.

Uchimura understood this perfectly, and in the *mukyōkai* he sought to develop a religious style or mode suited to evangelization in the distinctive cultural setting of Japan. That setting was not, as we have seen, the hostile environment of the Siberian labor camp in which Dōshō Nobuhiko read and prayed. It was one whose religious heritage could be positively valued, valued far more positively indeed than the ostensibly "Christian" civilization brought by Western missionaries to Japan. The distinction between Christ (or Christianity) and Christendom in Uchimura's thought goes back to his earliest years, and never lost its salience. Nanbara inherited this stance, as we see in his elevating Uchimura over the figure of Kierkegaard for having "stood *as a Japanese* before God."

The culminating idea of *Kokka to shūkyō*, of a second Reformation to be completed in Japan, comes of course straight from Uchimura.[12] That Christian belief is a matter of permanent spiritual revolution, of believers' groups in a constant process of forming and reforming, lies at its core.[13]

---

12. See Uchimura Kanzō, "Need of Re-Reformation," *Seisho no kenkyū*, no. 333 (March 4, 1928), in 31:132-33E.

13. On this point, see in particular the essays by Ishida Takeshi and Ohara Shin in Moore, *Culture and Religion in Japanese-American Relations.* An interesting contemporary perspective on the theme of the constant self-re-creation of the church is found in Iwashita Sōichi, *Katorikku no shinkō* (1930-49). Iwashita (1889-1940) was the leading figure in Japan's prewar Catholic intelligentsia, followed by Tanaka Kōtarō and Yoshimitsu Yoshihiko. The latter two were originally adherents of the *mukyōkai* and had studied directly with Uchimura. The relevance of Iwashita's work — in form, a catechism or exposition of Catholic teaching — is that it self-consciously takes issue with what it terms "Non-Churchist" (*mukyōkai-shugi*) perspectives. For Iwashita this was a general trend within modern Protestantism, and not limited to Japan. In brief, for Iwashita, contrary to the *mukyōkai* position that "it does not itself justify . . . but rather is premised on faith [*shinkō arite no ue no koto*] and must be its natural result," nonchurchism is "neither faith nor gospel, but a species of 'reaction.'" It is premised and depends on the existence of the church, "just as Protestantism itself is premised on the existence of the Catholic Church." As such, it is no more than an "epiphenomenon of Protestantism . . . and represents nothing essential." At the same time, Iwashita was addressing a Japanese audience and emphasized certain of its Japanese features (or "contradictions") as especially significant. Indeed for him, it was none other than the *mukyōkai* that upheld orthodox Protestantism in Japan. One problem, for Iwashita, was that while its adherents generally "follow Western free-thinkers in their views on the essence of faith, the origins of the church, and in privileging individual experience [*kojinteki taikenshugi*], and so on, when it comes to the content of faith, they are highly orthodox, and

And at the core of the core: the sharp consciousness, or conviction, that the élan of this revolutionary process would never work in a way that was destructive of Japan's spiritual heritage. Now Japan's moment in the drama of sin and salvation had come. Nationality was a permanent structure of human history and aspiration. Here, I think, was the uncrossable horizon of Uchimura's thought, and of all those who follow him.

We may be leery today of speaking too confidently about the religious meaning of any people's history, of national mission, providential rise and fall. Uchimura's milieu was not so hesitant. True, Agnieszka Kozyra has argued that for Uchimura, love of nation was another term for love of neighbor.[14] That may be. But I think there was more to it. For it seems to me that Uchimura always combined it with the notion of providence and mission: this gave it the dynamism of a historical force, one that could be observed and judged in religious terms. But we are bound to ask: If God appoints nations to their missions, does he also punish them for their failures? In the aftermath of the atomic bombings and the Shoah, attempts at collective theodicy can often seem cruel or obtuse. It is hard enough to recognize good and evil within ourselves, day in and day out. If we are less bold now in our thinking about the religious destiny of peoples, perhaps this is one reason.

---

while rebelling against authority, are scriptural absolutists [*seishoshugi*]." This contradiction, Iwashita says, frequently places *mukyōkai* adherents in the position of having to explain or rationalize changes in their understanding of something — the content of faith — that both Protestants and Catholics agree does not change. But never once, he says, "have I doubted that Mukyōkai adherents are honest in their conviction when they claim to be speaking through the Holy Spirit." And for raising basic questions *(Problemstellung)* of the relation between faith, church, and the individual believer, the *mukyōkai* has his deepest respect. In the end, however, Iwashita regards as dubious the essential Protestant claim to have "returned" to the original church. As no more than the "antithesis" to the church, the significance of the *mukyōkai* can only be "negative." It is perhaps superfluous to point out that Iwashita was writing before the ecumenical movement of the postwar era and the reforms ushered in by the Second Vatican Council (1962-65). See Iwashita Sōichi, *Katorikku no shinkō* (Tokyo: Kōdansha Gakujutsu Bunko, 1994), esp. 651, 654, 663, 671-73.

14. Kozyra, *Nihon to seiyō ni okeru Uchimura Kanzō*, 87-88.

Uchimura Kanzō and American Christian Values

OHYAMA TSUNAO

Uchimura Kanzō was born in 1861, eight years after Matthew C. Perry's arrival at Edo (now Tokyo) in 1853, and seven years before the Meiji Restoration in 1868. His childhood coincided with the last stage of the socio-political turmoil that led to the Meiji Restoration, and his adolescence extended from the beginning of the new Meiji government to the high wave of the so-called *Bunmeikaika* (a movement in support of "civilization and enlightenment"). As an individual who grew up in these historical circumstances, Uchimura stood in a unique position among Japanese intellectuals regarding how to respond to America, a nation with which Japan would build a close relationship in the decades to come. This article aims to clarify the history of how young Uchimura encountered American Christian values and learned from them, and will discuss how he later struggled with the concomitant problems that these values presented.

An Ideal Image of America

The information about the United States of America that the Tokugawa government possessed in the early 1850s was extremely limited. Lack of information about America hindered smooth and successful diplomatic efforts by the Japanese government, and this threw the Japanese nation into a state of unprecedented anxiety during this time. Thus, at the beginning of the official relationship between the United States and Japan, Japan had inferior information about the other party. The biggest shock to Japan was the emergence of the United States of America, which had not existed as a nation when Japan closed its door to the world in the early seventeenth century. Some two and a quarter centuries later, however, America was one of the most powerful Western nations in the world. Japan's serious quest to understand the new nation began in haste, right after the shock of Perry's arrival. Recognizing that at this point America did not have territorial or colonizing intentions in Asia, and viewing this country as a model for modernization and civilization, Japanese leaders turned their eyes to America and shifted their focus from older European nations.

Symbolically, Japan's first foreign mission was sent to America. This was *Man-en Kembei Shisetsu* (the Mission to the United States) of 1860. Fukuzawa Yukichi (1834-1901), who accompanied the mission, later published a number of books and articles on America and Europe that were based on this mission and other trips. Fukuzawa played a significant role in disseminating information about America, and he became a leading advocate of catching up with the West and overcoming the disparity between civilizations.

Uchimura belonged to a generation that could walk the road of life in rather stable social circumstances, compared to Fukuzawa's generation. Uchimura grew up after mainstream foreign-language learning in Japan had completely shifted from Dutch to English, and during a period when positive feeling for America prevailed among Japan's intellectual leaders. The *Bunmeikaika* soon became a national motto of the time. As a child of an education-minded ex-samurai family, Uchimura started learning English at the age of eleven, and achieved a level of English language good enough to study at Sapporo Agricultural College (SAC, now Hokkaido University), where most lectures were conducted in English by American professors. His classmates at SAC had a more or less similar educational background. As Nitobe Inazō (1862-1933) wrote, "We studied every subject in English. Mathematics, geography and history. . . . For me, reading English books was far easier than reading Japanese books in my twenties."[1] But considering the educational opportunities for the overwhelming majority of Uchimura's generation, an English-language education was exceptionally rare, permitted only to a small and select elite, even during the days of the *Bunmeikaika*. In this period, Japan's public education system had not been fully institutionalized, and private education was even less so.

SAC attracted capable applicants who had both high aspirations for

1. Nitobe Inazō, *Eigo oyobi Eibungaku no Kachi*, in *Nitobe Inazō Zenshū*, vol. 6 (Tokyo: Kyobunkan, 1969), 354.

founding a new nation and a high level of English-language competency. The college was established by the Japanese government under a grand colonization plan for Hokkaido that resembled the settlement of the frontier in the American West. Its curriculum was modeled after Massachusetts Agricultural College (MAC, now the University of Massachusetts). SAC's graduates were expected to become high-ranking professional officials, and their education was solidly oriented in this direction. However, in spite of the government's original intentions and in spite of the vocational term "agricultural" in the school name, the college became known much more for its liberal arts and its emphasis on character development.

The school's special educational focus has been attributed to William Smith Clark (1826-86), the first president of SAC, who provided the finishing touch to the curriculum and led activities on and off campus in the initial year. With the privileges of a foreign scholar hired by the Japanese government, Clark was able to pursue his educational ideals at SAC. Previously, he had adhered to these educational ideals in the institutions for which he worked in Amherst, Massachusetts: as a professor at Amherst College (1852-67), and as president of MAC (1867-79). More noteworthy is that Clark was a Protestant from a society where the Congregational Christian ethos was deeply rooted. Both his educational ideals and his Christian personality inspired students' minds. Under Clark's well-considered guidance, students were led to the Christian faith and to signing the Covenant of Believers in Jesus that Clark had written.

Clark left SAC four and a half months before Uchimura entered as a freshman. However, through the propagation of Christianity by senior students, Uchimura came to know how spiritually influential Clark had been while at SAC. Uchimura was pressured to become a Christian by the ardent seniors, and he signed the covenant. Though this document included a statement about the cross and the redemption of humanity by Jesus, Uchimura's decision may be better described as a conversion from old superstitious polytheism to ethical Judeo-Christian monotheism, than as a conversion to Christianity. In *How I Became a Christian: Out of My Diary,* Uchimura wrote, "The Christian monotheism laid its axe at the root of all my superstitions. All the vows I had made, and manifold forms of worship with which I had been attempting to appease my angry gods, could now be dispensed with by owning this *one* God: and my reason and conscience responded 'yea!' . . . I was not sorry that I was forced to sign the covenant of the 'Believers in Jesus'" (3:17-18E). The expression "was forced" evidently does not suggest his lingering regret; rather, it suggests that the event symbolically represented a new beginning of his spiritual life. Uchimura also said, "The new spiritual freedom given by the new faith had a healthy influence upon my mind and body. My studies were pursued with more consideration" (3:18E). In this sense, his conversion at SAC was not a matter of salvation from sin, an issue he was to face under the tutelage of Julius Hawley Seelye (1824-95) at Amherst College years later.

Uchimura spent four years (1877-81) at this New England–style college in Sapporo. Most lectures were delivered by American scholars, and textbooks, reference books, and other academic books were brought from America. The reading room even provided American newspapers (like the *Amherst Record, New York Tribune,* and *Springfield Republican*); scientific magazines (such as *Appleton's Journal, American Naturalist*); and a religious weekly *(Illustrated Christian Weekly).*[2] Though the Meiji government repealed its sanction against Christianity in 1873, the translation of the entire Bible was not completed until 1887. Therefore, Uchimura used an English Bible and read commentaries and other books on Christianity in English. It would be no exaggeration to say that he lived and breathed American culture at every level during his life at SAC. He confessed, "I learnt all that was noble, useful, and uplifting through the vehicle of the English language" (3:79E). Moreover, Uchimura gained the ability to think in English and to express his thoughts in English without much trouble. His valuable college experience, coupled with positive impressions of American culture, formed his idealized image of America, to the point that he saw America as a *"Holy Land"* (3:79E). Uchimura looked up to America as a nation of highly advanced Christian civilization. Uchimura's father, who had already converted to Christianity under his son's influence, handed Uchimura a poem on the young man's departure to America in 1884. This poem suggests that oftentimes Christian America was the topic of discussion between the two. "Where I see not, Jehovah seeth; Where I hear not, Almighty heareth. Go my son, be not 'fraid; He thy help, there, as here" (3:77E).

Seeking an Identity in America

"To be a MAN first, and then a PATRIOT, was my aim in going abroad" (3:77E), said Uchimura. Behind this decision were several grave frustra-

---

2. Book lists in *Annual Report of the Sapporo Agricultural College* 1 (1877); 2 (1878); 3 (1879) (in the possession of Hokkaido University).

tions: his failure to discover his vocational calling after graduation, and the breakup of his marriage, which lasted only seven months. To Uchimura, his classmates appeared to be successful, sailing out into their respective worlds with respected vocations. He was aware that he had yet to become a grown man in comparison with his classmates. Going to America meant a serious search for his own identity.

Uchimura's stay at Amherst College (1885-87), or more precisely, his tutelage by President J. H. Seelye (college president from 1876 to 1890), had a decisive influence in establishing his identity. But before Uchimura attended Amherst, he worked for eight months at an asylum for children with mental health disorders in Elwyn, Pennsylvania. He began this work with an idea of devoting himself to philanthropy; however, the hard work at the asylum drove him into a neurotic state. Hearing rumors about Uchimura's difficulties, the Christian educator Niijima Jō, who happened to be fund-raising in America for Doshisha (now Doshisha University), counseled Uchimura and arranged his way to Amherst.[3]

The name Amherst had long been familiar to Uchimura. As mentioned above, the Massachusetts Agricultural College, a model for SAC, was located in Amherst. Clark was both a graduate of and a professor at Amherst College, as well as president of MAC. In addition, Uchimura knew Seelye's name. Uchimura had read Seelye's critical article on Darwin's evolution theory as well as Seelye's proposal for Japanese educational reform that was submitted to the Japanese government in 1872 (3:73).

Uchimura wrote a letter to Niijima in the summer of 1885, after an agonized deliberation that lasted months: "There now remains no other way to go than to Amherst at present" (36:197E). Judging from his academic ability (as shown in his *summa cum laude* graduation from SAC), Uchimura would have been successful at an institution with advanced training in his vocational discipline such as postgraduate study in fishery science, his field of specialty. Despite his demonstrated excellence in a highly focused discipline, Uchimura dared to choose a liberal arts college. Why? Possibly this choice was a last resort in his search for an adult identity, even though it entailed taking a detour. It is obvious when compared to his close friends from SAC who had continued their education in the same or a related discipline. For instance, Nitobe was studying agricultural

3. See Otis Cary, *Uchimura no Ketsudan no Natu — 1885 nen — Niijima. Uchimura no Ōfukushokan ni arawareta Kindai Nihon no Ichidanmen* — , in *Jinmongaku*, no. 24 (Kyoto: Doshisha, 1956).

economics at Johns Hopkins and Miyabe Kingo was at Harvard as a graduate student of botanical science. Uchimura, however, could not see his own future in this type of stable and established way of life. Moreover, he was preoccupied with the failure in his marriage as well as his professional life. Uchimura needed a second college experience to start afresh. Even though he had graduated at the top of his class and a bright future seemed to await him after SAC, Uchimura had gradually developed ambivalent feelings about his own achievements and academic experiences at SAC. The decision to attend Amherst effectively meant coming to terms with his growing disillusionment that SAC was the school to help him shape his identity. This would explain his later ambiguous attitude toward SAC. In "Yo no Hokkai no Uba — Sapporo Nōgakkō" ("My Nursemaid in Hokkaido — Sapporo Agricultural College"), he said, "Sapporo Agricultural College did not teach me the best things . . . it was not my alma mater, but my nursemaid school" (15:235). There is no doubt that Uchimura cherished his days at SAC. However, when it came to questions of his own spiritual and vocational identity, he became ambivalent about his SAC education.

At that time, Amherst College was under the leadership of J. H. Seelye, whose Christian principles of higher education were trusted by orthodox Protestants in New England. However, during this period two universities (Johns Hopkins and Harvard) were developing a German-university-type educational model that emphasized research and objective methodology, rather than liberal arts. A few other influential American universities also adopted this approach, postulating the system's ability to produce academic excellence.[4] Seelye's task was to preserve Amherst College as a Christian liberal arts college against this trend. The trustees evidently supported Seelye's aims, for at his inauguration as college president in 1877, a representative of the board of trustees gave this address: "Sharp, solid, generous, manly Christian scholarship is now, and long has been our watchword. In the great conflict that is now upon us, the conflict between science and religion, this institution has nothing to fear. We shall send you raw boys, to be sent back to us accomplished Christian scholars and gentlemen."[5] Seelye kept to the firm principle of "Give them the light first,"[6]

---

4. See Richard Hofstadter and Walter P. Metzger, *Development of Academic Freedom in the United States* (New York: Columbia University Press, 1955).

5. *Addresses at the Inauguration of Rev. Julius H. Seelye* (Springfield, Mass.: Clark W. Bryan Co., 1877), 6-8.

6. Thomas Le Duc, *Piety and Intellect at Amherst College, 1865-1912* (New York: Columbia University Press, 1946), 56.

and maintained the traditional belief that spiritual eminence comes before academic excellence. Edward Hitchcock, the third president of Amherst College (1845-54), once wrote, "Another danger is that the desire and effort to make the students eminent in scholarship shall be stronger than to lead them to excel in piety."[7] This school of thought must have looked too traditional and conservative to those adopting the new educational trends. Uchimura was aware of Seelye's principles, and though he could have chosen Harvard had he simply wished to follow his own intellectual pursuits (3:72), he nevertheless chose Amherst and was enrolled in the junior class in early autumn 1885. He was already twenty-four years old. For the next two years, Amherst College provided him with a spiritual and psychological shelter, which may have been to Uchimura what the Erfurt monastery was to Martin Luther before Luther became a reformer.

At Amherst College, Uchimura concentrated on a liberal arts curriculum. According to school records, he attended the following classes: German (six terms), history (three terms), Hebrew (two terms), as well as theism, religion of the world, geology, mineralogy, philosophy, and catechism (class discussions with the college president).[8] These subjects (none of which besides the two natural science courses were offered at SAC) would revive one of his earlier dreams of the ministry. As early as January of 1882, Uchimura wrote to Miyabe, "I know not what will be my future. Whether I be a fisherman of Hokkaido [as a fishery scientist], or a fisherman of Galilee [minister], I cannot tell. The will of God be done" (36:36).

Even more than his college classes, what most impressed Uchimura was President Seelye's piety and Christian personality, as expressed in classroom teachings, chapel sermons, and occasional conversations on campus. Uchimura wrote about Seelye, "A single meeting with him is worth reading more than one hundred volumes of Evidences of Christianity" (3:74), and "None influenced and changed me more than the worthy President himself. It was enough that he stood up in the chapel, gave out a hymn, read from the Scripture, and prayed. I never have 'cut' my chapel-service, i.e. absented myself from it, even for the sole purpose of casting a view upon the venerable man" (3:113E).

---

7. Edward Hitchcock, *Reminiscences of Amherst College, Historical, Scientific, Biographical, and Autobiographical; Also, of Other and Wider Experiences* (Northampton, Mass.: Bridgman and Childs, 1863), 208.

8. School record 408, Special, class of 1887, Uchimura, Jon Kanzou of Sapporo, Japan (in the possession of Amherst College). According to his own writings, he failed in psychological philosophy, and seemed to have audited French and Greek.

Under Seelye's pious tutelage, Uchimura was led to a conversion to Christianity that was clearly based on his acceptance of Jesus' redemption. Most scholars call this Uchimura's second, true conversion compared with his first conversion at SAC, which was a simple decision to turn from polytheism to monotheism. On March 8, 1886, Uchimura wrote in his diary: "Very important day in my life. Never was the atoning power of Christ more clearly revealed to me than it is to-day. In the crucifixion of the Son of God lies the solution of all the difficulties that buffeted my mind thus far. Christ paying all my debts, can bring me back to the purity and innocence of the first man before the Fall. Now I am God's child, and my duty is to believe Jesus. For *His* sake, God will give me all I want. He will use me for His glory, and will save me in Heaven at last" (3:117-18E).

The next day W. S. Clark died in Amherst, after a long illness. The pastor who sat by Clark on his deathbed later relayed Clark's last words to Uchimura: that is, Clark felt his greatest consolation in life had been teaching the Bible to his students in Japan (20:421). Uchimura, as a newly born Christian, praised Clark's Christian work in Japan in an article entitled "The Missionary Work of William S. Clark. Ph.D., LL.D." in the April 1886 issue of *Christian Union* (1:136-41E). Uchimura could not help believing in providential guidance on his path from SAC to Amherst. It was probably around this time that Uchimura finally decided to become a minister, a dream he once embraced earlier in life. In his later years, Uchimura recollected Clark and Seelye and compared their work in an article entitled "Kurisumasu-Yawa: Watashi no Shinkō no Sensei" ("Evening Talk at Christmas: My Mentors of Faith," 1925) (29:341-45). Uchimura explained that he was not a direct disciple of Clark; rather he was led to spiritual salvation by Seelye. A seed of faith was sown by one graduate from Amherst College, and it was fostered and strengthened by another graduate from the same school. Uchimura further explained that his faith in Christianity was significantly influenced by these two individuals, both of whom came from New England, home of Puritanism. Later in life, engaged in Christian activities back in Japan, Uchimura often cited Puritanism as the ideal image of true Christianity or Christian America. At Amherst College Uchimura finally found his spiritual and vocational calling. He sought further religious study, and in the early autumn of 1887, Uchimura left Amherst for Hartford Theological Seminary.

Uchimura started his theological studies in order to become a minister. But some biographers of Uchimura contend that he had no intention of taking up the ministry and quote the following passage from *How I Be-*

came a Christian: "I made up my mind to study Theology, but upon one important condition; and that was that *I should never be licensed*" (3:134E). Considering that this autobiography (written at the age of thirty-five) was based on his past life but was also influenced by his belief about his future, this passage should not be cited without careful historical verification. The first question is whether an applicant who intended never to be licensed could be admitted by the seminary. According to the *Catalogue of Hartford Theological Seminary, 1887-8,* applicants were examined in reference to (1) church membership, (2) college graduation, (3) personal piety, and (4) motives of seeking the ministry. Those who were admitted were able to receive a license to preach at the end of the second year.[9] If Uchimura had made a firm decision not to receive a license to preach, he would not have been admitted in the first place (this would have shown a lack of motivation in seeking the ministry). The second issue is a contradiction between his possible desire not to be licensed and the actual letters he wrote to Miyabe before and after he entered the seminary. In a letter of July 27, 1887, he confessed, "I shall go to Hartford. By the time I go back to Japan I want to be a good intelligent priest" (36:263E). Uchimura wrote again of this same hope in a letter of January 4, 1888, "I am studying Theology. I wish to become a good intelligent clergyman" (36:272E). There is no denying that he intended to be a minister.

But Uchimura's study in Hartford lasted only four months, until late January 1888. Again, some biographers quote passages from *How I Became a Christian* that express his disappointment in theological training (3:135E); these biographers contend that this disappointment led to his leaving the seminary before completing his course of study. But to really understand Uchimura's reason for leaving the seminary, one should pay close attention to other passages in the same book. For example, Uchimura said, "But I was not to continue my study of Theology any further. Severe mental strains of the past three years unsettled my nerves, and chronic insomnia of a most fearful kind took hold of me. Rest, bromides, prayers proved ineffectual, and the only way now open for me was one leading toward my homeland" (3:137E). And Uchimura wrote to Seelye in Amherst in February 8, 1888, "I am compelled to write you that my bodily health had been failing to such an extent I was advised to take a long rest before I resume my study again. . . . I was so reluctant of leaving America just at

9. *Catalogue of Hartford Theological Seminary, 1887-8,* pp. 13, 19 (in the possession of Hartford Seminary).

this time. . . . I see now, however, that I *must* go" (in his letters, 36:276E). Moreover, in the Amherst class of 1887 yearbook (issued the next year), there appeared a short report on Uchimura's departure from America: "On account of illness Uchimura was obliged to temporarily suspend his work at the Seminary and, Feb. 20th, 1888, sailed for Japan for a year's rest."[10] These documents tell us that the main reason Uchimura left Hartford was not his disappointment in theological learning but his fatigue from nervous problems and chronic insomnia, even though he was critical of theological studies and the atmosphere at the seminary.

Uchimura had to return to Japan without completing the institutional requirements for the ministry, though he had finally found his calling. On April 16, 1888, almost his last day in America, he wrote a letter from San Francisco to Alfred Struthers, his classmate at both Amherst and Hartford: "*What* to do there [Japan] I know, but *how* I know not yet. . . . Good bye again before I bid farewell to the dear America, which has nourished me, reared me up, and cared for me, during the most momentous period of my life. Let us be true, noble, and good, and as Christ died for our souls, let us die for the souls of our fellowmen" (36:289-90E). Prior to this letter, Uchimura wrote a farewell letter to Carrie Hardy, sister of Edwin Hardy, his classmate at both Amherst College and Hartford Theological Seminary, telling her, "I shall be satisfied if I can preach the Gospel of Christ to them [the Japanese], by deeds more than by words" (36:284E). Judging from these letters, "*what* to do there" undoubtedly referred to preaching the gospel, though *how* to do so remained unanswered. If Uchimura had hoped to resume life at the seminary or to pursue theological studies at any other institution, this question would have been answered. But such a hope was not in sight then. At best, he could write, "*how* I know not yet." Such soul-searching helped pave the way for Uchimura to found *mukyōkai*, the nonchurch movement in Japan.

Progress of Human Beings and War

The time he spent in America was "the most momentous period" in Uchimura's life. Despite having the obvious setback of not being able to complete his studies at the seminary, this was a fruitful time for him. As his

10. *Class of '87, Its Histories, Class Day Exercises, and Statistics* (Cortland, N.Y., 1888) (in the possession of Amherst College).

letter to Struthers implied, Uchimura had many valuable experiences while in America, the most important of which was his journey to the faith of the redemption under the guidance of Seelye. In addition, his encounter with people living within the Christian ethos became a lifelong spiritual asset for Uchimura. His great appreciation for American values did not waver as long as he remembered these experiences.

But at the same time, the reality of American society shook Uchimura's image of America. He was shocked by the profane language, the crime rate, and the materialism of urban America; these factors were enough to damage his image of America as the Holy Land. Uchimura wrote frankly, "Is this the civilization we were taught by missionaries to accept as an evidence of the superiority of Christian Religion over other religions?" (3:89E). Uchimura's contemporary, Christian leader Uemura Masahisa (1858-1925), had a similar impression of America, and he was also critical of the moral decadence of the country. During a three-month trip to America in 1888, Uemura visited New York, Boston, Philadelphia, Baltimore, and Washington, D.C. This was the "Gilded Age," a time of rapid industrialization and great economic and social change, and some social evils may have been visible in the big cities even to visitors. Writing to his wife from New York, Uemura sternly criticized ordinary people and scholars, as well as Christian churches and ministers.[11] But Uemura neither observed America deeply nor analyzed the relationship between Christianity and America's social realities. This difference between Uchimura and Uemura may be partly attributed to their experience with American life. As mentioned above, Uchimura spent time as a worker in Elwyn and a student in Amherst and Hartford. The towns where he lived were small, educational, academic communities in the countryside. They were, so to speak, the hinterlands of urban society. In contrast, Uemura's visits were brief stopovers in big cities. He did not have a chance to deepen his rather superficial impressions of America by actually living among ordinary people. For this reason, Uemura's criticisms remained those of a sightseer.

Uchimura's stance of rational observation was based on his residence in America and his encounters with respectable people of many social groups and religious denominations. This led him to a new understanding of America. Toward the end of his stay in America, Uchimura made several comments on this topic:

---

11. Uemura Masahisa, *Uemura Masahisa Zenshū*, vol. 8 (Tokyo, 1934), 178.

Then observe this optic phenomenon of *the greatest darkness with the greatest light.* The shadow is the deeper, the brighter the light that casts it. One characteristic of Truth is that it makes the bad worse and the good better. (3:149E)

But if Christendom's bad is so bad, how good is its good! Seek through the length and breadth of Heathendom, and see whether you can find one John Howard to ornament its history of humanity. (3:151E)

And not only are there such good men in Christendom, but their *power* over bad men is immense, considering the comparative scarcity of good men even in Christendom. This is another feature of Christendom, that goodness is more possible and more powerful there than in Heathendom. (3:153E)

Uchimura's great appreciation of American values and his dichotomous understanding of reality sustained him whenever the reality seemed to betray his image of America. Against a "false" America that was prevalent in the evils of society, Uchimura often defended a "true" America by citing "Puritanism" and "New England," or by referring to particular historical figures like Lincoln, or even to good (though anonymous), ordinary people.

However, his position on America was shaken by the issue of war. Uchimura asserted the justness of the Sino-Japanese War (1894-95), while he held fast to pacifism during the Russo-Japanese War (1904-5). To explain this radical change we must examine Uchimura's view of history, and the way American Christian values were woven into this view.

Uchimura's theories and opinions on history were formed under the influence of Professor Anson Daniel Morse at Amherst. Morse's definition of history ("a record of the progress of human beings") caught Uchimura's attention and changed his view of history drastically. Until then, his historical knowledge had been mere accumulation of miscellaneous historical events. Though he had already read Peter Parley's *Universal History,* Uchimura did not seem to understand that Parley's view was based on an idea of progress. But Morse's lecture clearly showed Uchimura a way of organizing historical events in a line of progress, and this led Uchimura to the thought that Providence could be sought by the inductive method, that is, through examining facts objectively (2:385-86).

This view of history as progress and Uchimura's great appreciation of America were two sides of the same coin. Uchimura called America "the hope of civilized nations in the history of two thousand years" (2:439), and considered it the epitome of civilization up to that point in history. In his view, the value of a country must be measured by its level of civilization. Applying this view to the Sino-Japanese war, Uchimura wrote in his "Sekairekishi ni Chōshite Nisshin no Kankei o Ronzu" ("On Sino-Japanese Relations in the Light of World History"), "I proclaim as a historian that the collision between Japan and China was inevitable" (3:35). Uchimura also wrote, "The Korean war is to decide whether progress shall be the law in the East, as it has long been in the West. . . . America who first led us to light and civilization, as Japan is now trying to lead Korea. . . . Japan is the champion of progress in the East" (3:45-47E). This was the kind of view shared by most interested American Christians. Professor William L. Neumann writes, "When the Sino-Japanese war began in 1894, opinion ran strongly in favor of Japan. . . . The official American position was one of neutrality, but a benevolent neutrality."[12] There were many sympathetic and well-meaning Americans with pro-Japan thoughts. For example, David Spencer, a missionary in Japan, sent a report from Nagoya to a missionary magazine shortly after the war began. "She [Japan] asks China to do the right things, and China replies with contempt. She asks China to join her in reforming the government in Korea. . . . China refuses."[13] Howard Martin (an ex-American foreign service officer in Beijing who shared Uchimura's views on national rivalries and the consequences of the war) was severer in his evaluation of China: "The success of Japan in Korea means reform and progress . . . in that unhappy country. . . . The success of the Chinese means the forcing back of the Koreans to Oriental sluggishness, superstition, ignorance, and anti-foreign sentiment. It is a conflict between modern civilization, as represented by Japan; and barbarism, or a hopelessly antiquated civilization, by China."[14]

Japan's victory in 1895 seemed to evidence progress of history in the East, but it did not necessarily satisfy Uchimura. He expressed his deep sympathy for those bereaved by war in a famous poem entitled "Yamome no Joya" ("New Year's Eve for a War Widow," 3:273-74). Some scholars think this poem was Uchimura's turning point from advocacy of righteous

12. William L. Neumann, *America Encounters Japan from Perry to MacArthur* (Baltimore: Johns Hopkins University Press, 1963), 104-5.

13. *The Missionary Review of the World* (New York), November 1894, 852.

14. Quoted by Neumann, *America Encounters Japan*, 105.

war to pacifism. But Uchimura's lamentation in the poem cannot be said to be based on his pacifism; rather, his lamentation was derived from his anger at the tragic losses of war and the postwar coldness of Japan's society and government. At this point Uchimura still adhered to possible justification of war, insofar as war was part of the progress of history.

When the Spanish-American War broke out on April 24, 1898, Uchimura promptly sided with America. In his dichotomous comparison of despotic Catholic Spain and democratic Protestant America, it is obvious which side he supported. The Japanese newspaper *Yorozu Chōhō* ran Uchimura's English article, "The Spanish-American War," in the April 26 issue, in which Uchimura wrote, "The outcome of the contest is apparent to everybody . . . in this case the smaller and weaker takes up the cause of Despotism . . . the stronger has taken up the cause of Freedom. . . . AMERICA has her weakness and wickedness too; but we believe, in this case she has taken the better side. . . . Shall Cuba, the Pearl of the Caribbean, alone be unfree? America says, it *shall be* free, and she is going to *make* it free" (5:397-99E). And in another English article entitled "America's Motives for War" in *Yorozu Chōhō's* May 14-15 issue, Uchimura expressed the same opinion: "America will win, and Spain will lose, and Cuba will be free, and *more* righteousness will come upon the face of the earth, by this war, as by other wars for good noble cause" (5:414E).

In the Japanese media of those days, most initial reports of overseas incidents were based on brief telegraph accounts from international news agencies. Additional story details and thorough analysis of the news could not be carried out until weeks after the physical delivery of foreign newspapers and magazines to Japan. Considering the circumstances, Uchimura's quick response to the Spanish-American War was unique among Japanese journalists. No other journalist held knowledgeable and passionate opinions to the same extent. Uchimura's extensive reading of American newspapers and magazines helped him gain substantial knowledge about America. This reading deepened his own view of history, as well as his appreciation for America. Important among these periodicals was the *Springfield Republican*. Uchimura first came across this newspaper during his days at SAC, and became a regular reader. The *Springfield Republican* had a column titled "Current Opinions," which summarized the editorials or opinions of other papers (ranging from top-quality newspapers to so-called yellow journalism). In this way, Uchimura was informed not only of the opinions of the editors of the *Springfield Republican* but also of the opinions expressed by the American newspapers.[15] As far as America was concerned, Uchimura's analysis was far above that of other Japanese journalists who covered overseas issues.

The war was over on July 16, 1898, and Uchimura dreamed that a new, peaceful world order would develop under Protestant American leadership. However, he gradually became suspicious of the American government's attitude during the peace negotiation, which started in Paris on October 1. American public opinion had been shifting its focus from Cuba's emancipation to the annexation of the Philippines. President McKinley yielded to nationwide pressure and gave the Paris delegation instructions to demand this annexation. Uchimura's trust began to waver both in McKinley as a democratic statesman who listened to the *vox populi* (6:119) and in the *vox populi* itself. This may explain why Uchimura, who had quickly published a pro-American article at the outbreak of the war, kept silent for almost three and a half months during the peace talks. He had to reconsider his views of America, a country he had considered the epitome of civilization and progress. It was beyond his comprehension that Christian America would act like an imperialistic expansionist nation.

Uchimura broke his silence on January 25, 1899, when he made a critical remark about an American public that demanded the acquisition of the Philippines. In a brief English language commentary, "1899.NOTES," he referred to the American public as "the American Jingoes," and added, "it is neither very Puritanic nor Cromwellian" (6:398E). Moreover, in the essay entitled "Tosei Rinri" ("The Present Time Ethics") of February 25, Uchimura sternly criticized America: "America finally annexed the Philippines on the pretext of helping neighbors. It was indeed the act of a robber" (6:432).

Nevertheless, Uchimura still managed to place his hopes on good and trustworthy Americans. In an English article entitled "Mr. Hoar's Great Speech" in *Yorozu Chōhō*'s February 27 issue, Uchimura said:

> Senator George F. Hoar's anti-imperialistic speech delivered in the United States Senate . . . is one of the greatest I have read recently. It shows what is still left among the American statesmen of the spirit of their Puritan fathers. . . . It must be remembered that Mr. Hoar left the Republican Party with which he affiliated himself for the last *fifty* years

---

15. For instance, see the *Springfield Republican,* April 21 and 25 (microfilm, in the possession of Amherst College).

on this one score of the annexation of the Philippine Islands. . . . I confess, I for one received with intense relief to my mind the cable announcement that the American Senate passed a resolution that the American occupation of the Philippine Islands shall not be permanent. If America too shall fall, to what other nation shall Humanity look for peace and freedom? Mr. Hoar has my thanks as well for his brave deed and words, for in this case, he fought and spoke for *me* also, a humble dweller in a far-off isle. (6:434-36E)

Hoar's activities were reported in detail in the *Springfield Republican,* which had been developing a campaign against the annexation of the Philippines.[16] Uchimura now distinguished a high-handed America supported by the majority from a conscientious America backed by the minority and represented by such entities as the *Springfield Republican,* and by statesmen such as Hoar.

Later on, at the time of the Russo-Japanese War, Uchimura referred to the *Springfield Republican* in explaining his pacifism. When the war became imminent, Uchimura publicly expressed his strong opposition and developed an antiwar campaign with his fellow intellectuals. After the war broke out, he published the famous article "Yo ga Hisenronja to Narishi Yurai" ("Why I Became a Pacifist") on September 22, 1904. In this article Uchimura explained that his views were influenced by four sources: (1) the Bible, especially the New Testament; (2) the effect of his own past experience of nonresistance; (3) his considerations of world history in the past decade (including the Sino-Japanese War, the Spanish-American War, and the Boer War); and (4) the opinion of the *Springfield Republican.* In the explanation of the third reason, Uchimura remarked that the consequences of the Spanish-American War were far worse than those of the Sino-Japanese War: "It is difficult to express how I have deplored the depravity of America, my second home country" (12:425). Regarding the fourth reason, he acknowledged that the *Springfield Republican* had been his primary source of information about world affairs. Uchimura added that although the peace-loving character of this newspaper was not pacifism, the paper's introduction of famous pacifist opinions had smashed his belligerent stance to pieces (12:426).

Prior to this famous article, Uchimura wrote short but significant es-

---

16. On the *Springfield Republican's* history, see John J. Scanlon, "The Passing of the Springfield Republican" (thesis, Amherst, 1950), in the possession of Amherst College.

says suggesting that he had departed from his original view of the progress of history, a view that supported the necessity of a just war in the name of the advancement of civilization and progress. In "Tarumunakare" ("Do Not Slacken") of November 15, 1898, he wrote, "Justice once loses and rises, and injustice once wins and falls," citing Socrates and Jesus as examples (6:207). This paradoxical explanation of his view of justice contrasts with his earlier view on the victorious advance of civilization throughout the progression of history.

This new view led Uchimura to a repudiation of physical victory during the Boer War (1899-1902). When it was clear that the Boer belligerents (two independent Boer republics) were clearly losing their war against Britain, Uchimura showed sympathy for their side in a short article entitled "Seigi to Wanryoku" ("Justice and Physical Strength") of March 1900: "I am confident that justice is the final winner . . . but justice never wins by resorting to physical strength. Justice always loses and then wins. . . . Even if justice loses, it is justice. We tend to hope in our hearts that justice wins even if using physical power. But this kind of hope is not the hope for justice. It is better for hope to be once beaten. It is the very way for justice to gain the final victory. . . . This belongs to the secret of Christianity" (8:99-101).

On January 25, 1899, Uchimura wrote a significant essay on Seelye, "Senshi Shiirii Sensei o Omou" ("Thinking of the Late President Seelye"). In it Uchimura thanked Seelye for his pious guidance years before, and wrote, "Facing difficulties nowadays in finding ways to walk, I often seem to be able to see the President's face and feel as if I am being taught by him" (6:389). This suggests that as a Christian journalist, Uchimura was driven to such an impasse that he needed to hear Seelye. Seelye's view of history was quite different from that of A. D. Morse, who held the view that history is progress. After being influenced by Morse, Uchimura formed his own view of history by combining it with a great appreciation of America. That is, history was to advance under the leadership of the most civilized Christian nation, America, on a historical line of progress. Since the same idea had been evolving among American Christian leaders, it may be said that Uchimura simply joined this school of thought. On the other hand, Seelye was very critical of such an understanding of history. In his inaugural address of 1877, Seelye said, "The facts of history certainly show a far more prominent law of deterioration than of progress. Over by far the larger portion of the globe to-day, and with by far the larger portion of mankind, retrogression reigns instead of progress, and this is true as we look back through all ages." Seelye's inaugural address also referred to human nature: "We crudely talk as though human nature by the evolution of its own inherent forces could lift itself from a lower to a higher plane, but in no case was this ever done." In Seelye's view, progress can only be possible through humanity's consciousness of sin: "Wild, uncivilized barbarous, savage people are changing to-day to a state of peace and purity and advancing civilization, not by commerce or conquest of arms, not by letters or science, or the knowledge of the so-called useful arts, but by the simple preaching of the gospel, by the story of God's grace, which makes a man feel that he is a sinner, and gives him his first longing for a better state."[17] Seelye's logic of progress showed another way that history can advance in spite of the belligerent stance of the majority. Recollecting Seelye's thoughts must have helped Uchimura remember "true" Americans, though this group was small in number and appeared to be nonprogressive. Uchimura wrote in "Yo no Jōtai to Gojin no Kibō" ("World Situation and My Hope") of June 20, 1902, "If we place the Gospel on the scale of judgment of progress, it is quite clear that the present has not made any further progress than the past" (10:201-2).

In the period between the Sino-Japanese War and the Russo-Japanese War, Uchimura's pacifism gradually crystallized through his struggle as a Christian thinker who sought the Providence of history. Moreover, his struggle was related to the way he viewed Christian America, which was fostering the religion of civilization (Christianity), sometimes even through the means of war. Around this time, Uchimura seemed to have become able to clearly separate the message of the gospel from the achievements of Christian America. It was in such a context that Uchimura developed his Christian pacifism. In this sense, his pacifism was never a mere political response to the Japanese government's imperialistic intentions on the Asian continent, as some biographers have thought. Rather, Uchimura's pacifism was predominantly a religious decision.

In the Climate of Opinions for Modernization

There were at least three popular mottoes used by the Japanese leaders in the days of Japan's modernization: *Bunmeikaika* (civilization and enlightenment), *Wakon Yōsai* (Japanese spirit and Western knowledge), and *Datsu-a Nyū-ō* (quit Asia and join Europe). Uchimura was an individual

---

17. *Addresses at the Inauguration of Rev. Julius H. Seelye*, 15-17, 23.

shaped by his age, and to some extent he shared the national atmosphere engendered by such mottoes. This would explain his continuing passion for Western knowledge from his early teens. He studied *Yōsai* (Western knowledge, or products of the Western civilization) at a New England–style college established in the midst of the *Bunmeikaika* movement. Uchimura's encounters with new cultural and spiritual values at this school widened his intellectual horizon, and made him embrace a new view of life. Deepening his studies, he understood Christian values as a basis of *Yōsai*. In this sense, he was not as influenced by the idea of *Wakon* (Japanese spirit) as many of his contemporaries, though he cherished Bushidō (the way of the warrior, or Japanese chivalry) as an ethical heritage of Japan. Following his education in Japan, Uchimura's experiences in America brought him not only to a new understanding of Christian America, but also to a new evaluation of Japan. During his stay in America, Uchimura wrote, "Looking at a distance from the land of my exile, my country ceased to be a 'good-for-nothing.' It [Japan] began to appear superbly beautiful, — not the grotesque beauty of my heathen days, but the harmonic beauty of *true proportions,* occupying a definite space in the universe with its own historic individualities" (3:92E). Uchimura spared no effort to learn from Christian America in order to make his beloved Japan spiritually blessed. Thus, *Wakon* evidently did not meet Uchimura's spiritual wishes. After coming back to Japan, he was faced with the nationalistic reaction against the Westernization of the 1890s. This nationalistic trend coincided with a shift of academic emphasis from America to Germany, and intellectuals began to maintain the superiority of German *Kultur* to American civilization. In spite of such a trend, Uchimura did not turn away from America. It is no exaggeration to say that among Japanese intellectuals of his day, only Uchimura was capable of discussing American issues in any depth. Analyzing and explaining America, however, was not a simple task for him. The discrepancy between the ideal image and the reality of Christian America always worried him. To Uchimura, discussing America meant re-examining deeply implanted American values. This difficult task lasted until his later days.

Uchimura Kanzō and His Pacifism

TAKAHASHI YASUHIRO

Uchimura Kanzō is one of the towering figures among Christian evangelists in modern Japan. He is well known for his dedication to religious liberty and pacifism. His pacifistic thought, however, emerged through a difficult spiritual struggle. Since he was born and grew up in the late nineteenth century, the era of imperialism and colonialism, the atmosphere of the time had a great impact on his early thought. Deeply influenced by social Darwinism at Amherst College, he was a passionate supporter of the First Sino-Japanese War (1894-95) as a manifestation of social Darwinist nationalism. For Uchimura the war was an inevitable consequence of Japan's manifest destiny to liberate and enlighten the backward Asian civilization. After the war, however, he saw that his own nation had fallen into ignoble and corrupt behavior, boasting of the triumph. "What sort of benefit has Japan gained from this war? Due to this war the original aim of securing the independence of Korea is not promoted but diminished in turn, isn't it? Has not the war led to the disintegration of China, letting the Japanese bear much more heavy burdens, degrading its morale, and endangering the whole Far East?" (11:296).

This was the turning point in Uchimura's conversion to Christian pacifism. He deeply regretted publishing his justification of the war and was thoroughly determined not to justify any war in the future. Some scholars interpret his decision to embrace pacifism as a "conversion" or "socially oriented conversion."[1]

---

1. Maruyama Masao describes Uchimura's attitude toward the Russo-Japanese War as that of a "convert." Maruyama Masao, "Uchimura Kanzō to 'hisen' no ronri," in *Kaisō no*

In this chapter I will describe some unique features of Uchimura's religious pacifism and compare his thought with that of other pacifists in the modern world. I will show several common features of pacifism among them. As we have seen with the 9/11 terrorist attacks in the United States and the subsequent "war on terror," we are now in the stormy era of international terrorism. If Uchimura lived in this age, could he still so eloquently and passionately present the significance of peace through his uniquely religious perspective? We are called on to listen to his voice carefully and develop our thoughts on peace.

The Features of Uchimura's Pacifism

Nationalistic Pacifism as Japan's Mission

Uchimura had a dream in his youth. As encapsulated in his famous phrase "the two J's," his dream was simply to devote himself to Jesus and to Japan. That conviction shaped his vision of the ideal Japan and, in his own words, "Japan's mission." Before the Sino-Japanese War, young Uchimura thought that Japan's mission was to be a mediator between Western civilization and Eastern civilization, "standing between the republican West and the monarchical East, and mediating the Christian America and the Buddhist Asia." He said, therefore, "I believe the Japanese empire's mission as a mediator between East and West, introducing the mechanical Europe and America to the idealistic Asia in order to open the door of the conservative East by means of the enterprising West" (1:293). He had an optimistic hope in Japan's mission as he conceived of it before the Sino-Japanese War.

However, his dream of Japan's noble mission was completely betrayed by Japan's successful invasion of neighboring East Asian countries. He lamented the moral corruption of the Japanese people. Shortly before the Russo-Japanese War (1904-5), he raised a powerful voice in support of an

---

Uchimura Kanzō, ed. Suzuki Toshirō (Tokyo: Iwanami Shoten, 1972), 105. Miyata Mitsuo interprets Uchimura's conversion to pacifism as a result of "social awareness of his sinful experience awakened by his spiritual depth." Miyata Mitsuo, "Kindai Nihon no kirisutokyō heiwashugi," in *Miyata Mitsuo shū — Seisho no Shinkō*, vol. 5 (Tokyo: Iwanami Shoten, 1996), 272-73. Chiba Shin describes Uchimura's conversion as a "socially-oriented conversion." Chiba Shin, "Uchimura Kanzō — hisen no ronri to sono tokushitsu," in *Seijishisōshi niokeru heiwa no mondai* (Tokyo: Nenpō Seijigaku, 1992, Iwanami Shoten Publishers), 100-101.

antiwar war policy, proposing the "abolishment of war": "Some people insist that a war produces benefits. I once agreed to this foolish theory. However, I now confess that this is the ultimate folly. The benefit of war cannot compensate for its vice. Its benefit is exactly the same as the robber's. It is a profit (if someone calls it so) that leads to an everlasting lack of profit. The robbers lose their morality. As a result, they finally have to compensate for their vice beyond what they have illegally gained" (11:296).

In spite of his disillusionment with Japan, Uchimura could not cease to speak of his vision for his own nation. He could not give up on the spiritual growth of his country. In his late years he imagined a renewed vision of Japan's mission: for the nation to be "the religious people." While he denied Japan's imperial and militaristic role, Uchimura gave his nation a new task to protect the significance of religion and to proclaim a renascent form of religion all over the world. "And the world is waiting for the rise of a genuine faith. Western civilization now reaches its peak of prosperity, revealing that it can destroy our world instead of saving it. . . . As a person who has devoted himself to making money tends to move from a business world to a spiritual sphere in his late years, all the nations are now beginning to pay attention to a genuine faith. Who can provide the faith to them? Isn't that a task for the Japanese?" (28:406-7).

Scientific Pacifism

Uchimura was originally a student of ichthyology and started his career as an excellent scientist. After he determined to proclaim his pacifism, he was apt to use his scientific knowledge to back up his thought. Uchimura insisted that his pacifist view uniquely collaborated with "the law of nature." He advanced the theory that the more humankind pursues the achievement of peace, the more the world would harmonize with "the law of nature," improving utility and productivity. He compared a soldier to a nail or fang of a carnivore, while likening a pacifist to a stomach or an intestine of a herbivore:

> If we compare a state to an animal, we can safely say that a soldier is
> equivalent to a nail or fang of a carnivore, while a pacifist is a stomach or
> intestine, which are organs for nurturing. Although the nail or fang is
> necessary to the carnivore, the peaceful function of digestion by the
> stomach and intestine is absolutely essential to it. Especially for those

useful animals such as a sheep, a horse and a cow, aggressive organs are no use and the digestive function is highly advanced. Anti-war policy is just one aspect of pacifism. Another great virtue of it is nurturing and production. (12:154-55)

He further illustrated his view of nature by explaining the meaning of peace. His intention was to disavow the warlike view of the world offered by social Darwinism, the prevailing ethos since the late nineteenth century. He insisted that the notion of peace did not collide with "the law of nature":

In the world of nature there is both war and cooperation. What our world has become today is not only the product of the act of war. It is a poorly perceived understanding of nature that sees natural selection only as a state of war. It goes without saying that lions eat deer and rabbits. Deer, however, have an advantage over lions in that their nature is to cohabitate in mutual and harmonious assistance. Therefore, although deer are easily beaten by lions in battle, the former can be a winner in terms of reproduction. . . . It is a mistake to assume that the world of nature is a reflection of hell. That is not true. We can safely say that the world of nature is a sort of family where love and peace can be triumphant. (16:21)

Biblical Pacifism

Uchimura's pacifism is also based on biblical centralism. After Uchimura declared his antiwar creed in response to the Russo-Japanese War, he continued to proclaim his biblical pacifism. He emphasized the idea that the God of the Bible should be the center of world peace. For Uchimura genuine peace could not be created by any human effort. No politician or political activist could create a true sense of peace. This realistic approach might have derived from his own experience when his passionate appeal for an antiwar creed was not publicly accepted during the Russo-Japanese War. His vision of peace had been refined through his personal pursuit of the issue.

Peace in a fully deep sense, abundant peace without any this-worldly fulfillment — even the British prime minister or the U.S. president cannot create such a deep sense of peace. It is the way to spiritual and physical redemption. Given such redemption, we begin to be satisfied with our life and to have charity for all. Genuine peace will not come to us until this kind of redemptive grace appears in our world. (24:413)

As Isaiah 2:4 says, world peace will come after God comes to reign over the whole nation. Without God wars never cease in spite of every human effort. Therefore, peace will come where the son of God, Jesus Christ, abides with us. First, the true peace will come to our hearts, then each home, community, nation, and the whole world. It is not superficial and temporal peace. It is the profound and perpetual peace beyond imagination. That is why we engage in the work of evangelism as the most reliable method of the pacifist movement. (26:542-43)

Since Uchimura realized the ignoble sins of humankind, he knew that wars would not disappear from the earth so easily. Even so, he would not give up the hope for perpetual peace on earth, never falling into pessimism. He finally realized the necessity of evangelism in order to achieve the hope.

Peace in Action

What, then, is the practical manifestation of Uchimura's pacifism? We now consider the aspects of its social application. In Uchimura's thought, the following elements work together in an organic unity.

Prophetic Spirit

Uchimura severely criticized the vice of war and the corruption of states with the might of his pen. Here we can see the same prophetic spirit that animated the ancient Hebrew prophets. One of the historical lessons he learned from the Russo-Japanese War was that even many Christian churches surrender to the aggressive war policies of nation-states. A human organization, be it a church or a state, is very willing to trample on God's peaceful message: "The more I see the majority of Christians are supporters of wars, the more I am convinced that I would not belong to any Christian churches. The contemporary Christians who call themselves 'worshipers of the peaceful Lord' do not aspire to peace. These days genuine supporters of peace do not live in Christian churches but outside of them" (13:405).

Indeed, he would rather sympathize with Herbert Spencer's pacifism even though he was an atheist philosopher: "Thus, the Russo-Japanese War introduced a lot of new friends to me. I have a new friendship with many strangers in the name of peace. The God of peace has bound me with many people through pacifism. Now, there are two types of people in the world. One is the lover of war, the other is the hater of war. Even if the former are Christians or philanthropists, they are not my friends. On the other hand, even if the latter are agonists or atheists, they are my friends whom I respect" (13:405).

Since Uchimura witnessed the ignoble reality that any human organization, including the Christian church, could abandon an ideal vision for peace and justice, and fall into moral corruption, he decided to be independent from church affiliation.

Awakening of Religious Conscience

To awaken the religious conscience of people is an imperative task of a prophet. War causes devastating effects on human moral character. This was, for Uchimura, the great lesson from the two great wars modern Japan experienced. Uchimura showed that his nation had begun to lose its sense of respect for human life. He was terribly frightened by how excited the Japanese got about their military triumph and how enthusiastic they were about the great number of enemy soldiers killed by their military. On the other hand, they easily forgot about their own war casualties and the miserable state of the families of the fallen soldiers.

> The war has made us so immoral and dishonest. If the morality of people is worth something — I believe it will be — the great loss of people's morality cannot be compensated by the tiny amount of territories and interests that the victory of war produces.
>
> "We have won. We have beaten our foes." The news made us completely forget about our fellows' sufferings. War makes people not only irrational but also inhuman. People become hostile to their enemy and ignore their fellow citizens. Nothing is so inhuman and destructive to a community as war. War makes people animal. (13:403)

The victory of war paralyzes people's conscience and degrades their character. Uchimura was determined not to justify any war anymore.

The Principle of Nonresistance

The root of war is one's hatred of the enemy. Therefore, Uchimura thought it imperative for people to get rid of this hatred that persistently hardens human hearts. That conviction also derived from his personal experience: "My personal experience testifies: I was severely criticized by a group of people a few years ago. Then, one of my friends advised me to be patient with them and not to resist them. As a result, I regained inner serenity so that my work was not damaged by their blame but also assisted by my new friends, who are very helpful. I then thoroughly found the contestation so thoroughly foolish and ugly. As this experience shows, my work would have been much damaged and I would have been miserable if I had retaliated against their insult" (12:424).

The principle of nonresistance correlates with why Uchimura was not eager to lead or participate in political movements. The nonresistance theory presents his meticulous thinking. Uchimura refers to the famous words of Jesus Christ in Matthew 5:32-42,[2] telling that this is precisely the biblical basis of nonresistance policy. He questions whether Jesus admonishes his followers to practice it literally because it is difficult for anyone to put it into practice. And he says yes. For Uchimura it does not matter whether it is difficult to do or not.

Certainly, since Christianity on the whole exhorts us to practice the highest moral values, the difficulties of this practice testify to the super-natural character of the religion. It is very easy for us to follow the teachings of human-made religion. On the other hand, it is very hard for us to follow the divine teachings. . . . Although the teaching in

2. "But I say unto you, That whosoever shall put away his wife, saving for the cause of fornication, causeth her to commit adultery: and whosoever shall marry her that is divorced committeth adultery. Again, ye have heard that it hath been said by them of old time, Thou shalt not forswear thyself, but shalt perform unto the Lord thine oaths: But I say unto you, Swear not at all; neither by heaven; for it is God's throne: Nor by the earth; for it is his footstool: neither by Jerusalem; for it is the city of the great King. Neither shalt thou swear by thy head, because thou canst not make one hair white or black. But let your communication be, Yea, yea; Nay, nay: for whatsoever is more than these cometh of evil. Ye have heard that it hath been said, An eye for an eye, and a tooth for a tooth: But I say unto you, That ye resist not evil: but whosoever shall smite thee on thy right cheek, turn to him the other also. And if any man will sue thee at the law, and take away thy coat, let him have thy cloak also. And whosoever shall compel thee to go a mile, go with him twain. Give to him that asketh thee, and from him that would borrow of thee turn not thou away."

this respect might be difficult to practice, it is not impossible. Any moral action is under the control of human will. Where there is a will and courage, there is a way to achieve it. . . . Although Christianity requires the highest moral values of us, it does not punish us for failing in the demand. It provides us the supernatural power and motive to perform it. (12:168-69)

Uchimura tackles the tough issue of the application of nonresistance in international politics. How can he refute a hypothesis that "nonresistance theory can be applied to an interpersonal issue, not to an international conflict"? He says, "We cannot figure out whether this teaching (non-resistance policy) should be followed, unless it is actually practiced. We cannot realize that it is the best policy until it is actually practiced. . . . Which nation will have the honor of leading our world to apply the non-resistance policy to the international sphere?" (12:173-74).

Contemplation on the Human Heart

The principle of nonresistance reveals that the issue of war and peace inevitably correlates with the human heart or conscience. If one's heart leans to malice or vice, the situation in which one engages would produce such human vices as jealousy, conflict, and war. Uchimura reminds us to reconsider the problem of the human heart in order to address issues of war and peace.

Truly, the human being has a great heart. If one has it, he or she should be satisfied with any situation no matter that life is full of hardships. However, if one cannot be satisfied with one's heart, aspiring for something beyond oneself, such vices as complaint, contestation, and finally all kinds of detestable human relationships would tear one's character apart. One would get weary with oneself not only because of greedily aspiring to economic success, but also because of anxiety about gaining higher education to promote one's poor academic career, purchasing too many books to read and damaging one's eyesight and mind. In this situation, one cannot restrain one's ambition, which expands further and further, plunging one into an unhappy mental state full of distress, dissatisfaction, and jealousy. (16:304-5)

A Passive Attitude to Activism

Uchimura's practice of pacifism did not directly lead to a mass movement, although his pacifism does seek to integrate idea and practice. Generally, the practice of his pacifism focuses not on a direct social activism but on evangelism, through preaching at Sunday service and publishing a small magazine on biblical study.[3] His antiwar policy was proclaimed by means of his lectures on biblical studies; he was not an outstandingly heroic leader of an antiwar movement. However, his pacifism has continued to run deep and silent in the minds of conscientious Japanese citizens.[4]

Dialogue with Other Pacifists in the Modern World

Nonresistance and Civil Disobedience

Uchimura's pacifism correlates with his inner spiritual experience, leading him to nonresistance. The word "nonresistance" inevitably reminds us of the famous notion of "civil disobedience" or "civil resistance" in the thought of Mohandas Karamchand Gandhi and Dr. Martin Luther King Jr. According to Gandhi, the notion of "civil disobedience" or "civil resistance" is a public application of *satyagraha*. He says, "'*Satyagraha*' differs from Passive Resistance as the North Pole from the South. The latter has been conceived as a weapon of the weak and does not exclude the use of physical force or violence for the purpose of gaining one's end, whereas the former has been conceived as a weapon of the strongest and excludes the use of violence in any shape or form."[5]

A civil resister ever obeys the laws of the state to which he belongs, not out of fear of the sanctions, but because he considers them to be good

---

3. Uchimura's pacifist teachings and writings were so inspiring that a Japanese naval officer was deeply moved by them and dove into the sea from his battleship to save drowning Russian sailors in the midst of the Battle of Tsushima during the Russo-Japanese War. Masaike Jin, *Uchimura Kanzo Den* (Tokyo: Kyobunkan Publishers, 1977), 410.

4. Uchimura's followers such as Yanaihara Tadao, Suzuki Sukeyoshi, Asami Sensaku went further from their mentor's position, engaged in resistance to Japanese militarism, and were persecuted by the military regime during WWII.

5. *Gandhi: Selected Writings*, ed. Ronald Duncan (Mineola, N.Y.: Dover Publications, 2005), 73.

for the welfare of society. But there come occasions, generally rare, when he considers certain laws to be so unjust as to render obedience to them a dishonor. He then openly and civilly breaks them and quietly suffers the penalty for their breach. And in order for the resister to make his protest against the action of the law-givers, it is open for him to withdraw his co-operation from the state by disobeying such other laws whose breach does not involve moral turpitude.[6]

Uchimura's notion of nonresistance seems to be different from the notion of "civil disobedience" or "civil resistance" in Gandhi's thought. Nevertheless, Uchimura's understanding of nonresistance does not indicate a passive or servile attitude toward an evildoer or a demonic authority.

First, "Do not resist an evildoer" does not mean that it is prohibited to criticize a vicious act as evil by rational speech. When an evildoer bears toward us, we should be kind enough to articulate the cause of evil to him or her. . . . Second, we should not welcome and surrender to an evildoer. We should identify a vicious act as evil. Not to resist an evildoer does not mean concession to him. We have no intention to kill evil people; however, we might be killed by them due to our accusation. Third, we should use our wisdom to deal with an evildoer. The teaching "so be wise as serpents and innocent as doves" is a good lesson in this case. We should avoid a vicious act before resisting it. (12:174)

Although there is a clear difference between Uchimura's nonresistance and Gandhi's civil disobedience as a method of achieving social justice, Uchimura's nonresistance can be understood to be harmonious in spirit with Gandhi's understanding of nonviolence. Uchimura also appreciated Gandhi's practice of nonviolent resistance.

"Socially Oriented Conversion"

Uchimura's conversion to pacifism can also be compared to those of modern pacifists. Dr. Martin Luther King Jr. went through a similar experience. King is well known for his leadership in the civil rights movement in the 1960s. He adopted a peaceful method of nonviolent resistance against the

---

6. *Gandhi: Selected Writings*, 73-74.

segregation system in the United States. King won the Nobel Peace Prize for helping to abolish the social evil that had oppressed African Americans for a century. Although we tend to focus on King's magnificent achievement as a leader of the civil rights movement, another aspect of his contribution to modern pacifism should be given more attention, namely, King's decision to oppose the Vietnam War.

King kept silent about the deterioration of the Vietnam War in the midst of the upheaval of the civil rights struggle. Although President Lyndon Johnson was advancing the war policy, he was very sympathetic with the civil rights movement, energetically lobbying for the enactment of the Civil Rights Act. If King had begun to criticize the Johnson administration's Vietnam policy, he would have betrayed an important supporter of the civil rights movement. King could have been silent on the war issue because of his primary concern for the domestic issue of desegregation. He came to express his view of the war, however, because of his battle for desegregation, in which he persuaded young, militant black men in the ghettos to resist injustice in a nonviolent manner.

> As I have walked among the desperate, rejected, angry young men, I have told them that Molotov cocktails and rifles would not solve their problems. I have tried to offer them my deepest compassion, while maintaining my conviction that social change comes most meaningfully through nonviolent action. But they asked, and rightly so, what about Vietnam? They asked if our own nation wasn't using massive doses of violence to solve its problems, to bring about the changes it wanted. Their questions hit home, and I knew that I could never again raise my voice against the violence of the oppressed in the ghettos without first having spoken clearly to the greatest purveyor of violence in the world today: my own government. For the sake of those boys, for the sake of the government, for the sake of the hundreds of thousands trembling under our violence, I cannot be silent.[7]

King's conversion to an antiwar stance became so intense that he released a series of antiwar speeches. This conversion derives from the same kind of renewed social awareness that Uchimura underwent when he came to regret justifying the Sino-Japanese War. Both King and Uchimura went

---

7. Martin Luther King Jr., "A Time to Break Silence," in *A Testament of Hope: The Essential Writings and Speeches of Martin Luther King, Jr.* (New York: HarperCollins, 1991), 233.

through a socially oriented conversion to proclaim their own pacifism inspired by the new vision of the world. King calls the new vision "a radical revolution of values" or "a true revolution of values."

> A true revolution of values will soon cause us to question the fairness and justice of many of our past and present policies. . . . A true revolution of values will soon look uneasily on the glaring contrast of poverty and wealth. With righteous indignation, it will look across the seas and see individual capitalists of the West investing huge sums of money in Asia, Africa, and South America, only to take the profits out with no concern for the social betterment of the countries, and say: "This is not just." It will look at our alliance with the landed gentry of Latin America and say: "This is not just." The Western arrogance of feeling that it has everything to teach others and nothing to learn from them is not just. A true revolution of values will lay hands on the world order and say of war: "This way of settling differences is not just."[8]

Although King severely criticizes modern America with the phrase "the Western arrogance," he still hopes for the noble mission for his own country: "America, the richest and most powerful nation in the world, can well lead the way in this revolution of values." King's prophetic voice to his nation also resounds with Uchimura's notion of "Japan's mission." Both of them prove to be expressions of prophetic patriotism to their nations.

Conclusion

Uchimura Kanzō dedicated himself to proclaiming the gospel of Jesus Christ. By way of his personal spiritual experience, Uchimura rediscovered the life and teaching of Jesus Christ that could produce a new living faith of world peace. He witnessed a war that had warped people's minds and morality and had left the hearts of his nation deeply wounded by the endless vicious circle of modern Japan's war policies. He was very proud to be a descendant of a samurai warrior clan and sympathetic to the puritanical Christian faith compatible with the Anglo-American military heritage. However, he went through an inner spiritual transformation that led to a complete rejection of any war for any cause. "Peace is the major field of

---

8. King, "Time to Break Silence," 241.

Christian religion. That is why people in the world show respect for it" (12:150).

Yanaihara Tadao, a brilliant scholar and faithful disciple of Uchimura, outlines ten major battles in which Uchimura engaged. Yanaihara classifies the battles into two categories, outer battles and inner battles. The outer ones are fought for Uchimura's nonchurch theory, freedom in education, the environmental protection at the Ashio mine, antiwar policy, and Japanese immigration to the United States. The inner ones are against sin, misunderstanding and persecution, his unhappy life at home, poverty, and death. He writes,

> Mr. Uchimura is faithful to his policy: being courageous to fight every foe against God's truth and offering little resistance to his own rivals. . . . He fights as a servant of God. In the case of divine truth, he never gives up fighting for freedom and justice no matter what the opponents are, even if they are all Christian churches, all nations, all communities, all capitalists, all wealthy people and the whole world. He is truly a brave fighter. However, he is also meek when he is in anguish over his sin, is misunderstood by others, or faces the tears, poverty, illness or death of his family, and as far as his interest and honor are concerned. He is truly a brave and meek person.[9]

As Yanaihara explains, Uchimura's pacifism is a great heritage to our generation, which still strays off course in the passage to international peace and justice. Uchimura goes through a profound soul-searching that guides him to "a contrite heart and broken spirit" when he develops his pacifist thought. Nonresistance is the outcome of his brave and meek attitude to his public and private life. We have to realize that Uchimura's nonresistance is not sufficient to appeal for sociopolitical change on a massive scale compared with the notion of civil disobedience in Gandhi and King. The meek and humble attitude in Uchimura's personal relations, however, reveals much about the fundamental question of mass movement in the modern age.

Uchimura carefully avoids an inflammable fanaticism whenever he engages in any large-scale public activity. He knew that self-righteous social criticism might destroy the lives of those connected to him.[10] Sekine

9. Yanaihara Tadao, *Uchimura Kanzō to tomoni I* (Tokyo: UP Sensho, 1972), 124-25.

10. Uchimura once participated in a social protest against the environmental pollution

Masao, a notable biblical scholar and Uchimura's late disciple, comments on the meaning of social action for Uchimura.

> Mr. Uchimura has a sharp eye for the abyss of the human sin both in personal and social spheres. He has ultimate hope in the cross and the second coming of Jesus Christ. His basic behavior in social action inevitably points to eschatology. We need to consider his principles carefully when we look at his social actions. We should only undertake social action after we realize that any kind of social action in our time is exposed to a fundamental meaninglessness whether it derives from Christian or humane conscientious motivation. If we are blind to this recognition, we cannot be truly conscientious.[11]

It is not an exaggeration to say that Uchimura fought well for religious liberty, peace, and justice in the world during the era of imperialism. As he insisted that a Christian faith should be grafted onto the Bushidō *seishin* (spirit) (the traditional Japanese moral value for the samurai) in order to save the Japanese nation, pacifism in our age should both learn and gain some spiritual and intellectual lessons from the courageous spirit and way of life that Uchimura Kanzō exemplified.

---

caused by the Ashio Copper Mine Company. During the opposition, he witnessed the moral corruption of both the manager of the company and the victims of the disaster. After that he had an especially strong conviction that an individual's spiritual transformation should come first before a person engages in social action. Suzuki Norihisa, *Uchimura Kanzō* (Tokyo: Iwanami Shoten, 1984), 127.

11. Sekine Masao, "Uchimura sensei to seisho no kenkyū," in *Kaisō no Uchimura Kanzō,* 332.

Prophetic Nationalism:
Uchimura between God and Japan

YAGYU KUNICHIKA

There is an impressive passage in *How I Became a Christian,* a book Uchimura wrote in his early days, which goes, "I learned from Christ and his Apostles how to save my soul, but from the Prophets, *how to save my country*" (3:109E).[1]

Uchimura was a nationalist like many other young Japanese intellectuals of his day. Like his fellows, young Uchimura wished his nation to be "saved" from the threatening tusks of the Western powers and wished to see Japan become a leading nation in East Asia. However, *unlike* his fellow intellectuals, he also wished to see his nation "saved" from the ethical judgment of the transcendental God. Uchimura, who had already been baptized in Sapporo, was quite impressed when he read the Old Testament closely for the first time in America at the age of twenty-four. He had become convinced that every nation needed and continued to need prophets to teach the principles of righteousness to the people — even if these prophets did not use exactly the same words as Amos and Jeremiah — in order to avoid the fall of their nation. Uchimura's nationalism made him think passionately about the "mission" that he believed God must have given Japan. Uchimura wished to find out what this mission could be and wished to devote himself to it. Thus the man became a "nationalist" in a quite unique sense.[2]

---

1. Recently, John F. Howes has published his valuable book on Uchimura, *Japan's Modern Prophet: Uchimura Kanzō, 1861-1930* (Vancouver and Toronto: UBS Press, 2005). I only hope my essay contains some new observations on Uchimura as a prophet.

2. For Uchimura, God is not a God of an abstract universality but the God of history who gives individual life and historical characteristics to each nation (3:92). It was not exactly a natural love for the nation that was the ultimate motive force throughout Uchimura's

This way of thinking was especially characteristic of Uchimura in his thirties — when he worked as a journalist, and when he, like a prophet, criticized the policies of his government and stood against the opinion of many of his fellow citizens. At first glance, Uchimura's positions might seem somewhat contradictory to the usual meaning of nationalism, but they were all part of his unique nationalism. In spite of his passionate nationalism, he protested the Tennō (emperor)-worshiping nationalism (that is, the state's use of the Shintō religion to foster an extreme sense of nationalism). In spite of his wish to see Japan carry out its mission in eastern Asia, he criticized foreign policies of his government that rapidly became "imperialistic." In spite of his hope to see the commonweal of the Japanese nation increase, he criticized economic policies of the government that made the rapid growth of oligarchic capitalism possible. I should like to call the dialectical character of his nationalism prophetic nationalism.

Though the paradoxical character of his "nationalism" remained basically the same throughout his life, some important modulations took place during two periods: first when he was in his late thirties, and again when he was in his late fifties. In 1904, for example, Uchimura became more and more sensitive to the antagonism between the radical ethic of religious universal brotherhood and the use of the legitimized violence of the sovereign state. He confessed his newly acquired pacifism on the eve of the Russo-Japanese War (1904-5). Uchimura's earlier prophetic nationalism, which had allowed him to legitimize the use of military power in certain necessary cases, needed to be modified. He had to develop a new ideal for the nation.

The second major modification to his views came in his late fifties, after the outbreak of the First World War, and especially after the United States entered the war in 1917. This period brought Uchimura great disappointment. He could no longer believe in the overall progress of humanity — a philosophy of history that he trusted in for years. He became totally skeptical that there was some meaning to the whole of human history or

---

life; rather, it was this credo — a credo in which every nation has its own value and reason to exist, because its cultural individuality is the creation of God. Uchimura retained a belief in his "theology of nation" even after his theology became more "christocentric" during the First World War. Uchimura was concerned with four questions. (1) What was the positive, God-given legacy of traditional Japan? (2) How could Japanese make this legacy more suitable for God's use (that is, for the furtherance of God's purpose on earth)? (3) What should be done to change traditional Japan so that the nation could become the Japan that God wants? (4) What could be the mission of Japan in the cultural and political situation in the contemporary world? My essay here deals mainly with issues 3 and 4.

some significance in the development of civilization. In the end, Uchimura began to be convinced that human history would never reach perfection. That is, humanity could only be saved by the intervention of the transcendental God in the eschaton — through the second coming of Christ.

Those two modifications in Uchimura's fundamental religious thought significantly influenced his prophetic nationalism. Nevertheless, he believed that the prophetic ideals, criticisms, and warnings about political and social realities were still necessary — for any time in history, the judgment of God will be unavoidable for any nation engaged in wrongdoings. In such a context, Uchimura kept his eagerness to study and to interpret the books of the Old Testament prophets to the very end of his life.

In 1930 (two years before the establishment of the Empire of Manchuria under the "protection" of Japan) Uchimura died at the age of sixty-nine. After his death, Uchimura's ideals of prophetic nationalism were further developed by younger followers Nanbara Shigeru, Yanaihara Tadao, and others. Yanaihara's rather bulky book, *Uchimura Kanzō to Tomoni (Standing with Uchimura)*, tells us how much the young followers depended on Christian eschatology and Uchimura's prophetic logic in their bitter struggles against Japanese imperialism and fascism. They had learned both of these concepts from Uchimura.[3]

Uchimura's Life Experience and the Formation of Prophetic Nationalism

Boyhood and Youth

Uchimura, who was born in 1861, was six years old at the time of the Meiji Restoration; in his boyhood, he breathed the atmosphere of "Keishin-

---

3. Nanbara and Yanaihara attended Uchimura's Bible study meeting from their student days until Uchimura's death. Nanbara was a professor of the history of political theory at Tokyo Imperial University. His book, *Kokka to Shūkyō (State and Religion)* (Tokyo: Iwanami Shoten, 1942), sharply criticized Nazi ideology and the so-called *Tennō-sei* fascism of Japan's imperial system after 1930. Yanaihara was a professor of colonial policy at the same university who fought against the aggressive colonial policy of Japan and against the fascism. See his *Shoku-min Seisaku no Shin Kichō (New Keynote of Colonial Policy)* (Tokyo: Iwanami Shoten, 1927). Yanaihara's *Uchimura Kanzō to Tomoni* (Tokyo: Tokyo-Daigaku Shuppannkai, 1962) is a collection of his "Uchimura Lectures," which covers various issues of prophetic nationalism from 1932 to 1960.

Aikoku" (worship Shintō gods and be patriotic), which prevailed in Japan shortly after the Meiji Restoration. In 1868, the Restoration overthrew Japan's eight-hundred-year-old feudal system and established a sovereign state. Forming a sovereign state was necessary for the Japanese nation to confront the threat from the Western powers. The new state was established by the league of revolutionary samurais from four territorial states *(han)* of southwestern Japan (Satsuma, Chōshu, Tosa, and Hizen), which carried the imperial flag of Tennō. (According to the Shintō myths, the lineage of Tennō descended from the great goddess of the sun, Amaterasu Ōmikami.) The new government eagerly supported Shintō, because it was the only political theology that could give legitimacy to the sovereignty of the emperor and his government. It was only natural that young boy Uchimura, who had a strong religious sensibility throughout his childhood, would became a faithful adherent of Shintō shrines — though he never forgot his Confucian education.[4] However, when he was sixteen, Uchimura entered the gates of the Sapporo Agricultural College (the origin of Hokkaido Imperial University) and found that enrolled students were waiting to convert all the freshmen to Christianity. The existing students had become Christians under the influence of the charismatic former president, William S. Clark. Even the determined and unyielding Uchimura could not resist for very long, and he was persuaded to accept the gospel. The acceptance of a transcendental God freed Uchimura's mind from earlier taboos, and gave him an integrated religious self-identity.[5]

After graduating from college, he worked as a civil servant and soon met Asada Také, a modern, well-educated girl who had been baptized. The two married but quickly separated. Though Uchimura believed that his wife's careless behavior brought their marriage to this disastrous end, he

4. In his childhood, Uchimura Kanzō, like any other son of the samurai class in the Tokugawa period, was educated in Confucian ethics (that is, the ethic of loyalty and filial piety), which was not necessarily antagonistic to Shintō. However, as he grew older, Uchimura decided to learn newly introduced Western technological knowledge. The Meiji government was eager to introduce such technologies to "modernize" Japan. It was called "Wakon-Yōsai" (Japanese spirit and Western technology) policy.

5. Emancipation of the Japanese mind from the magical mentality had begun in the Jōdo-Shin and Zen Buddhism of the thirteenth century. However, as Max Weber had suggested, a process of remagicalization took place in the early seventeenth century when these Buddhist sects lost their genuine religious influences. (See his *Hinduismus und Buddhismus*.) See also, Robert Bellah, *Imagining Japan: The Japanese Tradition and Its Modern Interpretation* (Berkeley: University of California Press, 2003).

kept on blaming himself for his own immaturity (or "sinfulness") that prevented him from establishing an appropriate Christian home in a Japanese style. His experience with a collapsed marriage caused him to severely criticize himself. Thus, at the age of twenty-three, wishing to reconstruct his own identity (and at the same time improve his education at advanced universities in America and possibly in Europe), Uchimura followed the example of other Sapporo alumni and left for America.[6]

Reading Jeremiah

At the beginning of his stay in the United States, Uchimura was welcomed by several Americans, like Mrs. Harris, the wife of the minister who baptized him. Then he went to Elwyn, Pennsylvania, to see an institute for handicapped children (Pennsylvania Training School for Feeble-Minded Children). Uchimura stayed at the institute for eight months, serving the handicapped children and trying to make himself a truly humble Christian. However, life in the highly developed industrial society of America brought this young man from the Far East to the point of a severe identity crisis. Uchimura might have fallen into another pit of depression if he had not begun to read the book of Jeremiah. Here are his own words:

> But now with half curiosity and half fear, I peeped into Jeremiah . . . and lo! What a book! So human, so understandable; so little of future-telling in it, and so much of present warnings! Without a single incident of miracle working in the whole book, the man Jeremiah was presented to me in all the strength and weakness of humanity. "May not all great men be called prophets?" I said to myself. I recounted to myself all the great men of my own heathen land and weighed their words and conduct; and I came to the conclusion that the same God that spoke to Jeremiah did also speak to some of my own countrymen, though not so audibly as to him; that he did not leave us entirely without his light and guidance, but loved us and watched over us these long centuries as he did the most Christian of nations. The thought was inspiring beyond my power of expression. Patriotism that was quenched somewhat by accepting a

---

6. Among explanations by other analysts, Howes tried to explain the cause of Uchimura's departure to America with the psychological analysis of his marriage and separation in his *Japan's Modern Prophet.*

faith that was exotic in origin, now returned to me with hundredfold more vigor and impression. I looked at the map of my country, and wept and prayed over it. I compared Russia to Babylonia, and the Czar to Nebuchadnezzar, and my country to the helpless Judea to be saved only by owning the God of righteousness. (3:108E)

This introduction to the God of *world history* modified Uchimura's understanding of his Christian faith. Though he had accepted Christianity in Sapporo earlier in his life, his interest had been concentrated mostly on the New Testament. Now in America, Uchimura's eyes were opened to search for the traces of Providence in the history of every nation, including Japan. Uchimura came to understand that all the nations were the creation of Yahweh, that he must have guided all nations by sending prophets to each of them, and that these prophets would somehow reveal the basic norms of social life and the basic standard of governance. This new idea greatly encouraged Uchimura.

By looking at a distance from the land of my exile, my country ceased to be good-for-nothing. It began to appear superbly beautiful, — not the grotesque beauty of my heathen days, but the harmonic beauty of true *proportions,* occupying a definite space in the universe with its own historic individualities. Its existence as a nation was decreed by Heaven itself, and its mission to the world and human race was, and is being, distinctly announced. It was seen to be sacred reality, with purpose high and ambition noble, to be for the world and mankind. (3:92E)

Thus, Uchimura's wounded national identity was healed in a foreign country; in this way Uchimura's prophetic nationalism began to grow, not as miserably blind chauvinism, but as a way of believing that there must be reasons for the existence of his nation in the providence of God. In these early days, however, Uchimura's mature prophetic nationalism, the nationalism that could sharply assess the negative sides of his nation, was still underdeveloped. Naïve high spirits, inspired by his new conviction, overwhelmed him. Some may find that Uchimura's thought process was an example of what Nietzsche called "the transformation of resentment." However, in this case such an interpretation does not seem quite persuasive enough to explain its dynamism. His first long essay written in English, "Moral Traits of the 'Yamato-Damashī,'" and his first book in English, *Japan and the Japanese: Essays,* were both written with the sense of gratitude to heaven for the blessings God had given Japan by sending many prophets throughout the country's long history. In these early days, especially in his essays written for foreigners, Uchimura looked somewhat like a priest who praises the blessedness of his nation. Later, however, he came to look more like a prophet who takes a principled and critical stance against his nation.[7]

Uchimura's Philosophy of History

Another important factor in Uchimura's intellectual development in America ought to be mentioned for the formation of his theory of prophetic nationalism. After he became acquainted with the God of world history and prophets of the Old Testament, Uchimura found himself very much attracted to the study of world history. When he began his second college life at Amherst, he was greatly inspired by the lectures of Professor Anson D. Morse, a historian and a philosopher. Uchimura left a thick notebook with notes about Professor Morse's history lectures, and those notes tell us how Morse's first lecture began: "'History is the record of the progress of the human race.' He continued further, 'One nation rises up, does certain services to the whole human race, and dies. The new nation takes the place of the older one. . . . Really, however, the value of history lies in acquainting ourselves to the development of the race'" (40:97-181E).[8]

Morse gave rich lectures that covered the development of human civilization, starting with the civilizations of the ancient Orient and ending with the civilizations of modern Europe. Uchimura was greatly influenced

---

7. See "Moral Traits of the 'Yamato-Damashī'" (1:113-35). In this work, Uchimura summarized the "spirit" of Japan as a system of three virtues, namely, filial piety *(kō)*, loyalty to higher authorities *(chū-gi)*, and love for inferiors *(ji-hi)*. According to Uchimura, Japan's spirit was a blend of Shintō, Buddhism, and Confucianism. Some years later, Uchimura wrote his much better prepared book, *Japan and the Japanese: Essays* (Tokyo: Min-yū Sha, 1894); revised and published as *Representative Men of Japan* (Tokyo: Keisei-Sha, 1908). In this book, he presented as great thinkers the Buddhist preacher Nichiren (thirteenth century), Confucianism teacher Nakae Tōju (seventeenth century), virtuous lord Uesugi Yōzan (seventeenth century), syncretistic thinker Ninomiya Sontoku (nineteenth century), and the revolutionary samurai with Yang-Ming philosophy, Saigō Takamori (nineteenth century). In later years, however, the mature Uchimura wrote sharp critical analysis on the negative sides of traditional Japanese thoughts.

8. At Amherst, Uchimura learned Hebrew in addition to German, presumably because he wanted to read prophets. (Later, he learned Greek in order to enter Hartford Divinity School.)

by Morse's philosophy of historical evolution, which included a Hegelian taste of theism. The influences of Morse are clearly found in Uchimura's early books, such as *Chi-Jin Ron (Man and Earth)* and *Kō-koku Shi-Dan (Historical Observations on the Rise of Nations).*[9]

Inspired by the theistic philosophies of history, which he had learned in different ways from reading the prophets and from listening to Professor Morse, Uchimura begins to think of the historical role (not only the geographical role) of Japan in the world of his own era. He developed the idea of Japan as the "mediator of Eastern and Western civilizations." First, Uchimura hoped that future Japan would be able to contribute an Asian spirituality to the history of Christianity. Second, he imagined that the new stage of world history would start in Japan, as a result of such fusion of Asian and Western civilizations. Third, he thought that Japan had the responsibility to help modernization (or even revolution) in other East Asian nations, so that they might win political and economical independence from the yoke of Western colonialism.

Uchimura's Direct Encounter with Jesus Christ

We should not hasten too quickly through this part of Uchimura's life. There was another important experience in his life in America: Uchimura's authentic conversion to Christianity at Amherst (in contrast to his earlier, rather incomplete conversion in Sapporo). The Reverend M. C. Harris of the Methodist Church had already baptized sixteen-year-old Kanzō in Sapporo. However, in Amherst Uchimura became a Christian in a much deeper sense. This took place the year after he had been inspired by the book of Jeremiah. After eight months of hard work as a nurse in Elwyn, Uchimura realized that one of his main purposes for coming to America — namely, to reestablish his own identity as a person after the emotional turmoil caused by the failure of his earlier marriage — had not been realized. He had tried to overcome what he saw as his own selfishness and sinfulness by devoting himself to handicapped children, but still he found himself to be selfish and sinful. As a result, instead of choosing a course of advanced studies at the University of Pennsylvania or at Harvard, Uchimura applied to Amherst, a college in the genuine Puritan tradition that had been recommended by his older friend Niijima Jō, an Amherst

---

9. *Chi-Jin Ron* (Tokyo: Keisei-sha, 1897) and *Kō-koku Shi-Dan* (Tokyo: Keisei-sha, 1900).

alumnus. Uchimura was especially looking forward to attending the lectures of Julius H. Seelye, who was the professor of philosophy at Amherst while serving as college president. While still in Japan, Uchimura had heard already of Seelye's good reputation as a Christian and as a scholar. Seelye was an Amherst alumnus and had done advanced studies in Halle, Germany, where he had been influenced by the ethos of German pietism. Seeley advised Uchimura to rely totally on the salvation given by Christ on the cross, not on his own vain efforts to purify himself. This was a timely revelation for Uchimura, and some time later he wrote in his dairy:

> Sept. 13 [1886] — Evening was serene and beautiful. Just when I was going out to supper, thought came to me that devils cannot attack me when I am dead in the flesh. And this "death of sin" can be accomplished, not by looking into my sinful heart, but by looking up to Jesus crucified. I can be more than a conqueror through Him that loved me. The thought was extremely refreshing, and all the burdens of the day were entirely forgotten. Gratitude filled my heart, and I wished to commemorate the day by partaking [of] the Lord's Supper. So I pressed a little juice out of a cluster of wild grapes, and put it in a little porcelain dish. Also I cut a small piece of biscuit. I placed these upon a cleanly washed handkerchief, and I sat in front of them. After a thanksgiving and a prayer, I took the Lord's body and blood with very thankful heart. Extremely sanctifying. I must repeat this again and again during my life. (3:121-23E)

"Sacrilegious! Playing with a holy ordinance, the Church-ism and other Popish-isms will say to this," he wrote. However, a new life — *another* life within him — seems to have begun at Amherst in the summer of 1886, when he was twenty-five. Uchimura continued, "I am crucified with Christ: nevertheless I live; yet not I, but Christ liveth in me." Thus, as Uchimura expressed it, he learned "how to save my soul." His early book in Japanese, *Kirisutoshinto no Nagusame (Consolations of a Christian)*,[10] interpreted the fundamental character of Christianity as that of a religion beyond morality. Had Uchimura not experienced this direct encounter with Christ, his prophetic nationalism would not have been so strong.

It was the blending of those experiences that created Uchimura's unique nationalism. However, his prophetic nationalism still needed to pass through several trials in the wilderness.

10. *Kirisutoshinto no Nagusame* (Tokyo: Keisei-sha, 1893).

Dialectical Development of Uchimura's Prophetic Nationalism

Negative Experience — Lèse Majesté

When he was a thirty-year-old faculty member at Dai Ichi-Kōtō Gakkō (First National Higher Middle School), which was the preparatory school for Tokyo Imperial University, Uchimura caused what was called the *fukei-jiken* (*lèse majesté* incident). Uchimura found that a certain part of the school's official ceremony commemorating the promulgation of Kyōiku-Chokugo (Imperial Rescript on Education) contained reference to the godlike status of Tennō (the heavenly emperor). Uchimura refused to take a deep bow at the ceremony. He escaped prosecution for this *lèse majesté*, but he was forced to resign his position.[11]

To understand the full meaning of this affair, we should briefly review the distinctive character of the so-called *kindai tennō-sei kokka* (modern Tennō state), also known as the Meiji *kokka* (Meiji state). In 1889 Emperor Meiji promulgated the Dai Nihon-Teikoku Kenpō (the Constitution of the Empire of Japan), also called the Meiji Kenpō (the Meiji Constitution). The Imperial Rescript on Education (Kyōiku-Chokugo) was promulgated the next year. Both documents — the constitution and the rescript — were carefully prepared by key officials of the Meiji government and were designed to withstand radical appeals for further democratization by Jiyu Minken-Ha (supporters of the movement for freedom and civil rights). They introduced the Prussian-style constitution; in the Prussian model, the power of the kaiser and his officials was great and the power of the Reichstag, or parliament, was limited. Tennō's Rescript on Education was promulgated to indoctrinate ordinary people in the behavior appropriate to obedient and conscientious subjects of the emperor, and assumed that the emperor's subjects would be devoted to his wars. The constitution was signed by the emperor himself and by all members of his cabinet. The rescript, however, had only the emperor's signature and seal. The rescript was a permanent set of instructions on ethics given for his subjects by the holy sovereign himself. The copies, on which was the original signature *(Goshin-pitsu)* of the emperor, were considered invaluable.

---

11. On the affair, see Howes, *Japan's Modern Prophet*, 72. The Meiji government declared that Shintō was *not* a religion but a *mere* "rite of the state" because Shintō had no teachings at all on the life of the individual — unlike the doctrines of Buddhism or Christianity. Following this logic, the Meiji state could officially depend on state Shintō without admitting that it trampled on the principle of the separation of church and state.

One such copy of the rescript was given to the First National Higher Middle School where Uchimura was teaching. On January 9, 1891, the school carried out a special ceremony to mark the occasion of this great honor. On that day, the vice principal of the school asked each professor to proceed to the table before the portrait of the emperor, on which the document lay, and to make a very deep bow to the original signature of Emperor Meiji. Uchimura could not, in good conscience, take such a bow of "worship," neither for the emperor or the imperial signature. He went to the table, but he bowed only slightly. Right-wing professors and students assumed that Uchimura had refused to bow, and the next morning a newspaper reported the incident. Soon, accusations of Uchimura's "blasphemy" spread throughout the land.[12]

Many people called on Uchimura to accuse him of blasphemy. Some of them were quite rude. He was already ill, and continuous "attacks" turned his influenza into pneumonia. After discussing the matter with four Christian friends, Uchimura accepted a compromise plan proposed by the principal — he would perform a proper bow before the imperial signature, with the mutual understanding that the action had no religious meaning at all. Because Uchimura was still sick in bed, a colleague executed the bow in his place. Nevertheless, as Uchimura soon learned from the newspaper, he was deprived of his job. After weeks of emotional and physical stress, his second wife, Kazuko (whom he had married after his return from America), died of pneumonia.[13]

According to Masaike Megumi's *Uchimura Kanzō Den (Biography of Uchimura Kanzō),*[14] 128 articles and essays about the event had appeared in newspapers and magazines by the end of 1891. At least thirty books were published concerning the affair. The vast majority of these articles (including those written in bulletins of Buddhist denominations) were accusatory. The articles proclaimed that Christianity was not compatible with the traditional Japanese way of life, and that Christianity was especially incompatible with the tradition of loyalty to a sacred emperor.

As a nationalist, Uchimura, like many of his contemporaries, looked with much favor on the Tennō dynasty, at least up to this time. Neverthe-

12. This "worship" of the signature had not been ordered by the government. However, later the ceremony related to the Imperial Rescript on Education took place on national holidays at every school and itself became a quasi-religious ceremony.

13. Uchimura told his followers that someday the true history of education in the Meiji era should be written and the death of his second wife would be remembered.

14. Masaike Megumu, *Uchimura Kanzō Den,* 2nd ed. (Tokyo, 1977).

less, he refused to deify Tennō or his dynasty. Uchimura's action at the ceremony and the philosophy behind the action were unacceptable for those people who would not (and could not) separate politics and religion. The worship of the emperor in the Meiji state was an example of what Eric Voegelin called "this-worldly type political religion."[15]

Subjectively, Uchimura's action in this affair was caused by the "transcendental and vertical moment" (Paul Tillich) in his ethos. He had to refuse practices that he considered idolatrous, as had the prophets and Puritans before him. *Objectively*, Uchimura's prophetic action demanded the undeification or the secularization of the Meiji state.[16]

The German Protestant theologian Ernst Troeltsch pointed out that the modern Western state is a *secular state* that had abandoned the ambition to dominate the inner sphere of human life. This secular state was the product of a culture that had experienced a long struggle between ecclesiastical and political power.[17] Though the Meiji government allowed legally the "freedom" of religion under the Meiji Constitution of 1889, the government nevertheless began to inculcate the ethos of state Shintō, especially through the Chokugo Hōdoku-shiki (a quasi-religious ceremony in which the principals solemnly read the Imperial Rescript on Education to the teachers and students) on public holidays. In primary and middle schools, classes on ethics and morality interpreted the "national ethics" taught in the rescript.

In 1924, long after the bowing incident (when Taishō Tennō, the son of Meiji Tennō, had died, and Shōwa Tennō had ascended to the throne), sixty-five-year-old Uchimura explained to one of his followers: "What do you think is the reason that everything is turning rotten in our country, and education and politics are now facing a dead end? There could be, of course, other reasons for these results. Nevertheless, the main cause is the deification of human being that is directed by the government. People are

---

15. Eric Voegelin, *Die Politischen Religionen* (Munich: Fink, 1993). See also, Masao Maruyama, *Denken in Japan*, trans. W. Schamoni and W. Seifert (Frankfurt am Main: Suhrkamp, 1988); Carol Gluck, *Japan's Modern Myths: Ideology in the Late Meiji Period* (Princeton: Princeton University Press, 1985).

16. Later, Uchimura confessed that one of the causes that made him refuse to bow was the influence of Thomas Carlyle's *Oliver Cromwell's Letters and Speeches* (London: Chapman and Hall, 1873). Though Uchimura was influenced by Seelye's pietism, he also had much sympathy for puritanism. See "Jiyū no Kami" ("God of Freedom"), 6:76.

17. Ernst Troeltsch, "Wesen des modernen Geistes," in *Ernst Troeltsch Gesammelte Schriften*, vol. 2 (Munich: Mohl, 1961).

led to worship a human being as God. Idolatry could mean a quite horrible thing. It is the root of all the hypocrisies."[18]

For Uchimura, the bowing episode was a pivotal experience, in which he faced up to the traditional ideas of nationalism that clashed with his own views on nationalism. Through this negative experience, he found his own identity more clearly. However, Uchimura did not have to face the more severe challenges of the implementation of state Shintō, which came shortly after his death.

Uchimura's Mistake — Justification of the First Sino-Japanese War

In the late 1890s, Uchimura experienced another trial in the wilderness. After studying the book of Jeremiah, and influenced by Professor Morse's lectures, Uchimura began to consider the possible mission (missions) of his nation — that is, the mission God had given Japan in the contemporary world. In 1892, Uchimura outlined his conclusions in "Japan's Future as Conceived by a Japanese," an article for the *Japan Mail* (a newspaper published in Yokohama). He broadly suggested that Japan should become the *matchmaker* of Western and Eastern civilizations:

> Japan is located in between the republicanism of the western world and the monarchial China, between the Christian America and the Buddhist Asia. . . . Therefore, we should take legislations, religion and politics of the west and develop them in our Asian soil, and then hand them over immediately to our neighboring Asian nations. Our neighbors also should get the profit of using them. However, we should have good enough courage, in case it should be necessary, to lead the weak Asia and topple the haughtiness of the Western nations. . . . Let thy light shine to the east and to the west, reflect the light to the west and brighten Asia. O, ye the Empire of the Rising Sun! (1:243E)

Uchimura introduced the last part of his cultural-geographical theory of world history in his book *Chi-Jin Ron (Man and Earth)*. Uchimura thought it a great blessing that, under God's direction, Japan had escaped the threatening tusks of the Western powers and had established a sover-

---

18. Isihara Hyōe, *Mi-jika ni sesshita Uchimura Kanzō (Uchimura Kanzō I Knew Personally)* (Tokyo: Kyōbunkan, 1972).

eign state of its own. Uchimura believed that God had initiated this process, so that Japan could help other Asian nations establish their own independence, separate from imperial Western powers. Uchimura's political essay "Justification of the Corean War," which he wrote at the onset of the First Sino-Japanese War (1894-95), was based on his cultural-geographical theory of world history.

Though he was by no means a jingoistic "nationalist" seeking only for the glory and profit of his nation, he insisted that Japan should engage in hostilities against China's Qing Empire. Uchimura saw that the political control of Qing over the Korean Peninsula prevented Koreans from establishing their independent state. He also thought Qing was preventing the modernization of Korea. If Korea remained a weak and subordinate nation to the Qing (though a declining empire), Russia might well invade the Korean Peninsula. The peninsula was located close to Japan, so why could not Japan rise to protect the Koreans, help them realize their political independence, and assist in the modernization of their country? Besides, had not the Qing Empire been quite rude and arrogant to Japan in recent years? "Justification of the Corean War" appeared in the liberal national magazine *Kokumin no Tomo (Companion of the Nation)* in August 1894. This article brought Uchimura national and even international fame (3:38E).[19]

However, shortly after Japan's victory in the First Sino-Japanese War, Uchimura realized that the war had been fought for the profit of Japan. The war had not been fought for its officially announced war purpose, which was more or less in accordance with Uchimura's own argument that it was necessary to protect Koreans from the evil rule of the Qing Empire. The hypocrisy of Japanese actions in East Asia became evident, and Uchimura turned his attention to criticizing such deception by the Japanese government. He repented the "foolish" article he had written earlier.

As a result of the war, Japan gained Taiwan and the Liaodong Peninsula. (Japan, however, was asked to abandon the Liaodong Peninsula by Russia, Germany, and France and received 300 million ryō in reparations for this from Qing.) Japanese capitalism grew rapidly in the period that followed, built on the Chinese reparation and on the wealth (mainly sugar industry) exploited in Taiwan. Later, Japan moved further away from its

---

19. Written first in English, the article's original title was "Justification for the Corean War." A Japanese version appeared in the next month in the same magazine. Tokutomi Sohō, the editor of *Kokumin no Tomo,* who asked Uchimura to write for the magazine, was a democrat and an antimilitarist until the end of the First Sino-Japanese War. However, Sohō became a prominent right-wing ideologue after the war.

stated goals, and the Korean Peninsula officially became a colony of Japan. When crowds of people in Japanese cities rejoiced wildly at the outcome of the war, and sang a popular song praising the army and navy, Uchimura was astonished to learn that the war and the outcome of the war caused a marked lowering of governmental and popular ethical standards. The miserable experience of making this mistake (that is, his original support for what he concluded was unethical war) was necessary for Uchimura to learn about the world and to sharpen his theory of prophetic nationalism.

Uchimura's grief and anger burned even more when Binhi (the anti-Japan consort of Korea, who was inclined to depend on Russia) was murdered in Seoul in October 1895. It was an intrigue of a Japanese minister in Korea. Uchimura wrote a long and sharp essay, "Jisei no Kansatsu" ("Observations on the Trend of the Day"). Sixteen thousand copies of the periodical in which this essay appeared *(Kokumin no Tomo)* were sold in one day, and by the next day, the price for a copy had tripled (3:226E).[20]

Uchimura as a Writer on Prophetic Nationalism

After the First Sino-Japanese War, Kuroiwa Ruikō, the publisher of a yellow newspaper, *Yorozu Chōhō (All the News for Morning)*, wanted to transform his paper into a quality periodical. In his newly formatted newspaper, Kuroiwa dared to introduce a group of critics such as Uchimura and early socialists Kōtoku Shūsui and Sakai Kosen as editorial writers. Kuroiwa was particularly eager to recruit Uchimura as his chief writer of English editorials; by this time he was known as a good English writer and a unique man of Christian virtue. In 1897, Uchimura began to write his articles on political and social problems, mostly in English but often in Japanese. Uchimura's pointed articles were welcomed by intellectuals, including students in higher educational institutions. His basic observation of the country at the turn of the century was as follows:

Not a single philosopher we find who could give us a lecture on the great harmony of the universe. Yet we see weapons of thirteen divisions glittering in every portion of the land. Not a single poet we see healing the gloom of the people. Yet we see 260,000 tons of warships serenely

20. In this essay, the critical character of Uchimura's prophetic nationalism became quite clear.

making waves like huge whales going over the ocean. Inside the houses messes are going on. Fathers and sons hating each other, brothers blaming each other, mothers and daughters contempting each other. And yet the nation takes pride in being flattered from foreigners as the noble nation in the east, the nation of virtue. These are the realities of [our] empire and [our] imperialism. (9:118)[21]

To confront the economic and political pressures of the Western powers, the Meiji government milked the countryside of its resources — and this in an era when the farming population amounted to more than half of the nation. The government then poured these funds into the modernization and Westernization of Japan's industries, especially of military industries and export industries like textiles. After 1893, as a result of these policies, the percentage of Japan's tenant farmers increased rapidly (to more than 60 percent of the total number of farmers). The permanent duration of poverty of the tenant farmer families enabled industries in the cities to recruit low-wage workers for factories that produced goods for export, while at the same time Japan's domestic market remained quite limited. This structure remained fundamental to capitalism in Japan up to the end of the Second World War. Uchimura addressed these issues in the following comments: "I have traveled to a naval port to preach the gospel, and have seen a gigantic warship that has just been completed. Looking up at it I said, 'How glorious is our navy!' I have traveled to the countryside to preach the gospel, and have seen so many dilapidated houses. Looking at them I said, 'How pitiful are our people!' Watching such a nation building such a warship, we realize that the boost of national prestige is not necessarily a sign of the happiness of the people" (15:180).

After the Restoration, well-funded traditional trader families like Mitsui and Sumitomo, and the newly developed like Iwasaki (Mitsubisi), maintained close, informal political relations with the influential officials in the Meiji government. These economic factions led Japan's industrial

---

21. Introduction to *Teikoku-shugi (Imperialism)*, by Kōtoku Shūsui. Kōtoku was a socialist who was executed in 1901 for his commitment to a plan of the socialists to assassinate the emperor. (However, it is known today that the whole story was fabricated by the government.) Uchimura had a rather favorable opinion of socialism, so long as it did not deny religion or advocate violence. However, he was convinced that unless the minds of people were changed by Christianity, all social-reform movements (including socialism) might not have positive results. "Kirisuto-kyō to Shakai-shugi" ("Christianity and Socialism") (11:193).

development by buying imported factories and new technologies from the Japanese government at the cheapest prices. These were called *Sei-shō* (privileged *political tradesman*), and they were the origins of huge, influential combines (the *Zai-batsu*) that were dissolved after the Second World War. On the whole, the development of capitalism in Meiji Japan was not accompanied by the development of a sound and modern civil society. In this context Uchimura used a paragraph from the Old Testament to criticize the political and social realities of Meiji Japan:

> *But let judgment run down as waters, and righteousness as a mighty stream.*
>
> Building the warships would bring us not much benefit. It would be meaningless even if we prepare for the attack from the sea with them. . . . Let the poor lead at least a bit better life. Let the people have honest and trustworthy educations. Make the tax rates be fair ones. Avoid purveyors. Don't let flatterers come around the government. Revise the regulations for the assignment of the government officials. Eradicate the corruption and the bribes. "And ye shall live." (3:163)

Uchimura keenly criticized the "anticivic" and "semifeudal" character of the privileged *Sei-shō* capitalists. One such entrepreneur, Furukawa Ichibei, who established the Furukawa Conglomerate, "improved" the production of the Ashio Copper Mine in Tochigi Prefecture. About 100,000 hectares of soil along the two rivers, Watarase and Tone, were polluted because of the new mining method. Farmers vainly petitioned the government for the suspension of the mine's operation. In 1903, promoted by Kuroiwa, Uchimura and other journalists like Kinoshita Naoe, a Christian, and Kōtoku Shūsui and Sakai Kosen (socialists in their early days in Japan) formed a society named Risō-dan ("Association for Ideals") and began campaigns for social reforms, including those associated with the Ashio Mine problem. In this work, the group cooperated with the congressman Tanaka Shōzo, who zealously fought for the rights of the farmers. Years later, however, during the First World War, the government forcibly introduced a new flood control system on the Watarase and Tone Rivers. The whole area was artificially changed into a huge marsh, and the residents had to be removed. The problem of the Ashio Mine was solved in a negative way both for the farmers and Risō-dan.

Uchimura's political opinion in the era between the Korean war and the Russo-Japanese War could be summarized as follows.

The minimum reforms I now wish to crave for are these. 1. Reduce armaments, expand and improve the education system. 2. Abolish the status system of peers, including Shi-zoku (the status of the former samurai class), and call all people Shitizun (citizens). 3. Abolish all national orders of merit and rank, except for the military. 4. Establish perfect local autonomy. Let the governor of prefectures and counties be elected directly by the people. 5. Eliminate the restrictions on political rights that are conditioned by the amount of property. 6. Revamp the house of peers by excluding those who lack common sense. 7. Eliminate the remaining of the "Han-batsu" (political clique — former samurai members of Satsuma and three other "Han" of south-eastern Japan — which held the real powers of the government in their hands) from the government. (6:199)

Pacifism and a New Vision for the Nation — the Russo-Japanese War

After the First Sino-Japanese War, Russia, cooperating with France and Germany, hindered Japan from taking the Liaodong Peninsula from the Qing. As early as 1896, however, Russia had already acquired the rights from the Qing government to construct a railroad on the peninsula. In 1898, the Chinese government leased the peninsula to Russia, which created a dangerous situation for Korea. Russia's policy of southern expansion became a menace for Japan, which was itself preparing to colonize Korea and to expand the Japanese empire. In 1902, Japan signed a military alliance with the British government, which wanted to use Japan as a military safety valve in northeast Asia. Ultimately, war broke out between Japan and Russia in 1904.

This time, Uchimura did not write an article to justify Japan's war goals. Political leaders, leading intellectuals, and even the leaders of Christian churches — like Uemura Masahisa, who supported Uchimura in the rescript affair — supported Japanese hostility against Russia.[22] However, Uchimura, who had become a pacifist shortly before, refused to join the national zealotry for the war. The important point here is that he was dissenting not only from *this* war but from *all* wars: "It is quite obvious that the most influential cause that made me a pacifist is the Bible, the New Testament specifically. As

---

22. See Suzuki Norihisa, *Uchimura Kanzō Nichi-roku (Life of Uchimura Kanzō by His Diary)* (Tokyo: Kyōbunkan, 1994), vol. 6; also, see Masaike, *Uchimura Kanzō Den*, chapter 7.

I studied the Bible more and more . . . I came to the understanding that it is the spirit of the New Testament as a whole, not the specific words we read here and there, that tells us to regard warfare, including the war between states, as wrongdoing. I have come to think that the warfare should not be justified so long as the Gospel and the Cross exist" (12:423). Uchimura also wrote, "I am not only dissenting against the argument for Japan-Russo War, but I am also insisting that it is necessary to abolish all wars. War is killing. Killing of human beings is a great sin. No man or state could gain long lasting profit by committing such a great sin" (11:296).

Those words of Uchimura may have the tone of what Max Weber called "the *rejection of this-worldliness (die religiöse Weltablehnung)* for the sake of radical religious brotherhood."[23] I will address this issue shortly. Nevertheless, the paragraphs I introduce below show us that Uchimura had also quite a realistic viewpoint when he observed the political situation.

> The Russo-Japan War is still at an early stage. However, even if Russia should give up in the not-very-distant future, the warfare would still not have been concluded by a single victory of Japan. Many historians tell us today that this war is only Act Two of the drama "Division of China." Therefore, they say, one war after another will continue until the destiny of China is ultimately settled. If this theory is true, we must say that it is much too early to say anything about the total result of the war. The inevitable next war could be many times more disastrous than the one we are observing now. Only God knows whether millions must throw their lives away before the peoples of four hundred counties in China will be relieved, or whether there will be some other development in this part of the world. (13:112)

> We Japanese, who encouraged our soldiers to attack Qing forces [in the First Sino-Japanese War], have greatly suffered because of these soldiers for ten years after that war. The wealth of our nation has been almost totally spent to raise more soldiers. How much greater their claim on us would be, if we let our soldiers attack Russia now. We can foresee the result quite clearly. The small amount of liberty still remaining in our hands will be burnt to ashes, together with our constitution. The whole of Japan will turn into a huge military barracks. (11:419)

23. Max Weber, *Politics as a Vocation*, in *The Vocation Lectures* (Indianapolis: Hackett, 2004).

Japan, however, gained its "victory" by receiving over half of Sakhalin Island from Russia and the rights to operate the Southern Manchurian Railroad. These railroad rights allowed Japan to deploy an army, with the approval of the Qing government, in areas contiguous to the railroad. Japan also made Korea a protectorate (later, a colony) of Japan, thereby eliminating Russia as a power on the Korean Peninsula. All these results were seen as vital to the national interest by the "realists" in Japan. The "destiny of China" was left floating in the rough sea. In 1932, Japan established a puppet state in Manchuria, and in 1937 Japan invaded mainland China even further. These developments led Japan ultimately to the "Asia-Pacific War" (Second World War). After 1938, the whole of Japan became a "huge military barracks" under the military dictatorship in which most human rights were not protected. Uchimura had shown sharp prophetic insights into the future.

However, at the turn of the twentieth century, Uchimura's opposition to the opening of hostilities against Russia was not based on such insights into the future of Japan. Rather, his opposition was based more on his conviction — his relatively new conviction — that war in general was wrong and sinful.

Uchimura was not exactly a pacifist until 1902. Certain experiences led a hesitant Uchimura to pacifism; these included a deeper reading of the New Testament; anger about recent wars of imperialism like the Korean War, the Spanish-American War, and the Boer War; and the influence of Uchimura's Quaker friends.[24] Tolstoy's pacifism also greatly influenced Uchimura, though he remained severely critical of Tolstoy's unitarian understanding of the gospel. It is well known that Max Weber criticized Tolstoy's pacifism in *Politics as a Vocation,* pointing out that pacifism is doomed, objectively, to bring about brutal consequences. The American theologian Reinhold Niebuhr criticized pacifism (though he was not a non-Christian realist like Weber), and advised people to be more politically responsible.[25] If the *Realpolitiker* Weber had read Uchimura's articles on the Russo-Japanese War, he might have called Uchimura's attitude too naïve to confront the political intentions of Russia. Niebuhr, however, might have said something a little more supportive of Uchimura, if he had

---

24. For example, Wister Morris and his wife — who treated young Uchimura kindly in America and kept in contact with him throughout his life — were Quakers.

25. See Weber, *Politics as a Vocation.* Reinhold Niebuhr's criticism of pacifism is shown in *The Nature and Destiny of Man,* vol. 2 (New York: Charles Scribner's Sons, 1943).

read these comments of Uchimura: "After all, those who love the land most will be the owner of the land in the end. Those who love Manchuria most will win Manchuria in the end. Land cannot be taken either with sword or political tactics." Still, Niebuhr would probably have criticized Uchimura's fundamental pacifism. Nevertheless, we should remember that it was necessary for modern Japan to have, at least once, a prophet who would openly declare his genuine pacifism, deny the justness of war, and proclaim all killings deeply sinful. It is only after having such proclamation of the *absolute* ethic of pacifism based on the transcendental religious brotherhood that people could not only make the ultimate choice between the ethic of religious conviction and the ethic of secular responsibility, but also begin to think of lesser-evil choices in politics.

Be that as it may, we should next ask these questions — what was the influence of Uchimura's new pacifist point of view on his prophetic nationalism? Had Uchimura discarded nationalism altogether?

Even before he became a pacifist, Uchimura was convinced that the strength of a nation should be judged neither by the amount of its military equipment nor by the prosperity of the *Sei-shō* businesses and landowners. Uchimura believed that the criterion of a nation's success was the living standard of ordinary people. "The real substance of strength of a nation is made only by the hands of farmers and merchants." Now that he had become a pacifist, Uchimura began to suggest even more that a policy of "expansion *within* the country" would bring about better results for Japan's economic development than would an "expansion *to* the outside." Uchimura's vision of ideal national development is shown most symbolically in his well-known booklet *Denmaruku-koku no Hanashi (The Story of the Danish Nation)*. This work was published in 1911, a year after the annexation of Korea by the empire of Japan. Uchimura wrote that the "Danes saved their nation without using military forces, without invading anywhere, but only by the afforestation of the land and faith" (18:381). Danes lost their former territories on German soil after the Schleswig-Holstein War. However, according to Uchimura, Danes had great success reconstructing their national economy by the afforestation of Jutland and by the agricultural industries connected with it under the leadership of a "descendant of a Huguenot," Enrico Mylius Dulgus.

Uchimura's piece on Denmark may well have been an introduction of his new vision, or his ideal of Japan in the context of his new pacifism. However, it remained only a sketch. After this, Uchimura began to concentrate on the study of the Bible. Further development of Uchimura's "prophetic nationalism" was handed over to the next generation of *mukyōkai* Christians, who could draw from greater professional knowledge of political science and economics (18:304).[26]

Eschatology and Prophetic Nationalism — First World War

The outbreak of the First World War, and especially the 1917 entrance of the United States into the war, was shocking to Uchimura, who at that time was approaching sixty. For Uchimura, America was a nation representing the newest stage of human progress, though he often furiously criticized the negative side of U.S. modernity, including "American mammonism." Even after the Spanish-American War, which Uchimura called a war of American imperialism, America was, to Uchimura, at least, not like the brutally aggressive European states that had ignited the world war.

At Amherst College Uchimura was impressed with Professor Morse's vision of human history, and world history was for Uchimura basically the record of human progress. His trust in divine providence and his trust in evolutional and yet idealistic philosophy of history were harmoniously united in his mind. However, the outbreak of the modern and brutal First World War, and especially the entry of America into the war, had thrown him into a profound state of skepticism about the idea of the progress of human history and even about the idea of a God of world history. Uchimura confessed later that during this period he was really facing a severe predicament of faith. It was only through a fundamental reexamination of his earlier thoughts and theories that he could overcome this predicament.

Uchimura abandoned the idea of history as a record of human progress that in the end would fulfill the purpose of divine creation. Only by separating human progress from divine providence was Uchimura able to break through his spiritual predicament. At this crucial moment he reconsidered the doctrine of the parousia (the second coming of Christ). Uchimura was encouraged by this doctrine, which included the idea that

---

26. Uchimura's vision of a development of national economy encouraged Yanaihara to develop his *Shoku-min oyobi Shoku-min Seisaku (Colonization and Colonial Policy)* (Tokyo: Iwanami Shoten, 1927). Also, economic historian Ōtsuka Hisao created a significant theory of "national economy." Ōtsuka Hisao, *Kokumin Keizai (National Economy)* (Tokyo: Kōbundō, 1965). Uchimura's vision of an ideal Japan encouraged his followers after the Second World War to support Japan's postwar constitution, which includes article 9 — which prohibits the act of war by the Japanese state.

the purpose for the creation of human beings will be accomplished only by God himself, through the second coming of Christ. Uchimura had already written somewhat on this doctrine before, but his new thoughts were, nevertheless, a new revelation for him. In January 1918, he began lectures on the parousia in Tokyo, Osaka, Kyoto, Kobe, and other big cities. He was joined by Rev. Nakada Jūji (Japan Holiness Church) and Rev. Kimura Seimatsu (Congregational Church). Two or three thousand persons gathered to hear every lecture. In spite of his belief in the parousia, however, Uchimura was not a fanatic eschatologist and he never prophesied exactly when and how the Lord would return. The important thing is that by the reassessment of the doctrine of the parousia, Uchimura's theology became almost totally centered on Christology.[27]

Throughout 1920 and 1921, Uchimura gave a series of sixty lectures in Tokyo on his new christocentric understanding of the theology of Paul's epistle to the Romans. Probably his greatest contribution to the history of Christianity in Japan was publishing *Roma-sho no Kenkyū (Study of Paul's Epistle to the Romans)* after he completed the lecture series.[28]

Uchimura's disappointment, and even despair, in human progress through history influenced his attitudes on political and social innovation. Uchimura denied neither the significance of the ideal of the League of Nations nor the efforts of Woodrow Wilson to establish that body. But he feared that the league might end up as another tower of Babel, for it would not succeed in institutionalizing eternal world peace; at best, he thought, the league would only prevent the next brutal war. He was also skeptical about the outcome of the Russian Revolution. It was now Uchimura's conviction that human efforts to improve the outcome of history would always be limited while sin was not totally eliminated from the world. According to Uchimura, the substance of *sin* is the self-separation of mankind from God

---

27. At last, Uchimura's theology of prophecy was firmly (almost totally) integrated to his Christology. However, not a few Japanese theologians at the time criticized Uchimura for his "irrational" faith in the parousia.

28. *Roma-sho no Kenkyū (Study of Paul's Epistle to the Romans)* (Tokyo: Iwanami, 1922), found at 24:16-448. It is well known that in Europe, young Christian theologians, such as Karl Barth and Emil Brunner, confronted their own, similar crisis of Christian faith during the First World War: these men established a new theology called the "theology of crisis," which contains a strong eschatological tendency. Uchimura, who belonged to the older generation, like Barth's teachers, formed a similar theology, though at the time Uchimura knew almost nothing of the "theology of crisis," except for some knowledge of the movement's pioneer, Kierkegaard.

the Creator: this causes discord between God and mankind, among human beings — and even more, between God and his creation.[29]

However, Uchimura did not abandon his prophetic nationalism. Even if the advice and warnings of prophets are bound to be ignored, it is still necessary for a nation to have prophets. The ideals of a nation and a sharp diagnosis of its problems ought to be stated clearly, so that people may choose to heed the warnings of the prophets or to reject their advice. After all, in the prophecy of the coming of the kingdom of God lies a great social vision as well as much social and political criticism.

Uchimura's Successors and Prophetic Nationalism

In the context of such thinking, Uchimura wrote: "Only among Christians were the authentic patriots found. Think about Luther, Milton and Cromwell. Profound patriotism is something a man could not hold without the knowledge of God." Uchimura also wrote, "The purest model of true patriotism is found among the prophets of the Old Testament." Uchimura's last lectures, on the book of Isaiah, directly addressed this issue (26:336-38). After Uchimura's death, the idea of prophetic nationalism was developed further by social scientists among his followers. These included Nanbara Shigeru and Yanaihara Tadao, both of whom risked their positions, and sometimes even their lives, in support of their beliefs. Yanaihara lost the position of professorship and was banished from Tokyo Imperial University in 1938 for his criticism of the Japanese imperialism and so-called *Tennō-sei* fascism of Japan's imperial system. He later wrote, "Christian faith and social science were rolled together to make a strong rope. It gave me power."[30]

29. It seems that Uchimura had gradually become conservative as he got older. However, we find Uchimura's prophetic nationalism still living in his lectures on Paul's argument about the state. See Miyata Mitsuo, *Authority and Obedience: Romans 13:1-7 in Modern Japan*, trans. G. Vanderbilt (New York: Peter Lang, 2009).

30. On Nanbara, see Andrew Barshay, *Public Man in Crisis* (Berkeley: University of California Press, 1988). On Yanaihara, see Susan C. Townsend, *Yanaihara Tadao and Japanese Colonial Policy* (Richmond, Va.: Curzon Press, 2000). Yanaihara's earlier book, *Marukusu Shugi to Kirisuto Kyō (Marxism and Christianity)* (Nagoya: Ichiryū-sha, 1932), was a kind of theology of social science (rather than a theology of socialism) that enabled him to advance the prophetic nationalism of Uchimura in a new era. State Shintō and the deification of Tennō were for Nanbara and Yanaihara the crucial and risky point of their argument on the problems of the empire.

The Legacy of Uchimura Kanzō's Patriotism: Tsukamoto Toraji and Yanaihara Tadao

Shogimen Takashi

Uchimura Kanzō's *mukyōkai* Christianity opposed the institutionalization of Christian faith; however, this does not mean that *mukyōkai* Christianity did not entail any organization or structure at all. In his lifetime and beyond, a number of regional voluntary associations sprang up. In 1905 the subscribers of Uchimura's newsletter, *Seisho no Kenkyū (The Biblical Study)*, organized a society called Kyōyūkai in various regions of Japan, which was followed by the founding of Tokyo Kyōyūkai in the capital where Uchimura was based. In 1909, *mukyōkai* Christian students of the First High School and Tokyo Imperial University were collectively named "Kashiwakai" by Uchimura. A number of other Bible study groups were subsequently organized by followers of Uchimura, but by the end of Uchimura's life *mukyōkai* believers had agreed that all the groups would be disestablished after the leader died. Hence, there were no official "successors" to Uchimura. However, Uchimura's Bible study groups incubated independent preachers, who subsequently emerged as leaders of "second generation" *mukyōkai* Christianity. They included Azegami Kenzō (1884-1938), Fujii Takeshi (1888-1930), Tsukamoto Toraji (1885-1973), Kanazawa Tsuneo (1892-1958), and Kurosaki Kōkichi (1886-1970). While they professionalized their Christian mission, there were others who were heavily involved in the *mukyōkai* mission while maintaining secular professions, including Yanaihara Tadao (1893-1961) and Ebara Banri (1890-1933).

I am grateful to Paula Hasler and Stephen Conway for their help during the preparation of this essay.

93

The present chapter addresses the reception of Uchimura's Christian political ideas by his disciples. More specifically, it seeks to explore Uchimura's idea of patriotism and the ways in which his patriotism was inherited by two of his leading disciples: Tsukamoto Toraji and Yanaihara Tadao.

As we shall see, patriotism was one of the defining features of Uchimura's literary output. Nonetheless, Uchimura's patriotism has not enjoyed much scholarly interest until recent years. The latest surveys of the history of modern Japanese political thought include some brief accounts of Uchimura's patriotism (or rather, his critique of it).[1] Probably in response to the recent upsurge of interest in patriotism in the public arena, Uchimura's writings on patriotism are now readily available as an edited volume.[2] In 2008 Kikukawa Miyoko produced the first article on Uchimura's patriotism, which focuses on the reason why he steered away from "nationalistic" patriotism.[3] If scholarly investigations into Uchimura's patriotism are a fairly recent phenomenon, its reception (or rejection) by his pupils has escaped academic investigation almost entirely. For example, the two-volume study of the "second generation" of *mukyōkai* Christianity, conducted under the leadership of Fujita Wakao, hardly touched upon patriotism.[4]

The present chapter seeks to fill this lacuna in modern scholarship.[5] I shall first examine Uchimura's discourse on patriotism in the contemporary political and social context. After that I will compare and contrast the ways in which Tsukamoto and Yanaihara assimilated or rejected Uchi-

---

1. See, for example, Kevin M. Doak, *A History of Nationalism in Modern Japan* (Leiden: Brill, 2007), and Yonehara Ken, *Nihon Seiji Shisō (Japanese Political Thought)* (Kyoto: Minerva Shobō, 2007).

2. Uchimura Kanzō, *Aikokushin wo megutte: Huhen no Ai to Kobetsu no Ai (On Patriotism: Universal Love and Particular Love)* (Tokyo: Shoshi Shinsui, 2006).

3. Kikukawa Miyoko, "Uchimura Kanzō no Aikokushin," *Asia, Kirisutokyō, Tagensei (Asia, Christianity, Plurality)*, no. 6 (March 2008): 73-86.

4. Fujita Wakao, ed., *Uchimura Kanzō wo Keishō shita Hitobito (Uchimura Kanzō's Successors)*, 2 vols. (Tokyo: Bokutakusha, 1977).

5. I have recently offered an account of patriotism in the wartime writings of Tsukamoto Toraji and Yanaihara Tadao, thereby presenting "another" patriotism, an alternative to the mainstream chauvinistic patriotism incubated by state Shintō. See Shogimen Takashi, "'Another' Patriotism in Early Showa Japan (1930-1945)," *Journal of the History of Ideas*, no. 71 (January 2010): 139-60. The article, however, did not discuss Tsukamoto's and Yanaihara's indebtedness to Uchimura in terms of the idea of patriotism. The present chapter also intends to fill the gap.

mura's idea of patriotism in their own contexts. This historical inquiry will reveal that Uchimura's patriotism, despite its axiomatic status in his thought, was not uniformly embraced by his disciples. Tsukamoto did not inherit Uchimura's "prophetic" patriotism; however, it found a loyal heir in Yanaihara. This contrast, I shall argue, stems mainly from two factors: the two thinkers' ways of wrestling with contemporary political realities, and their attitude toward the Old Testament, in particular the books of Jeremiah and Isaiah. Tsukamoto undercut Uchimura's patriotism only to acquiesce in the mainstream "nationalistic" patriotism, while Yanaihara not only embraced but also developed Uchimura's new idea of patriotism in his dissent from the contemporary militaristic and chauvinistic government policies.

Uchimura Kanzō and Patriotism

Uchimura discussed patriotism in two separate periods: from the mid-1890s to 1910, and in the 1920s, that is, the final decade of his life. The social contexts in which he wrote on patriotism differed significantly. From the mid-1890s to 1910, Uchimura was involved in journalism through *Yorozu Chōhō*, the newspaper founded by Kuroiwa Ruikō. The majority of the articles in which Uchimura touched upon patriotism in this period were written for the readers of *Yorozu Chōhō*. Thus, Uchimura's discussions of patriotism were presented in response to public issues such as Japan's place in the global community, its society and culture in general, and, perhaps most significantly, the ideal of the rejection of wars *(hisenron)*, which was shared by fellow contributors to *Yorozu Chōhō*: Kōtoku Shūsui and Sakai Toshihiko (Kosen). In the 1920s, by contrast, Uchimura wrote on patriotism almost exclusively in his own newsletter, *Seisho no Kenkyū*. Clearly, Uchimura's writings on patriotism in the 1920s were intended for a Christian audience, more specifically, the followers of his faith in *mukyōkai* Christianity. However, this is not to suggest that Uchimura's idea of patriotism was divorced from contemporary affairs; on the contrary, his writings on patriotism were prompted to a significant extent by the U.S. Immigration Act of 1924, which banned immigration from Japan.[6]

6. On Uchimura's (and other Christian leaders') response to the U.S. Immigration Act of 1924, see Lee Arne Makela, "Japanese Attitude towards the United States Immigration Act of 1924" (Ph.D. diss., Stanford University, 1973), 224-28.

Patriotism remained one of the key themes Uchimura explored from the start of his literary career. The first debate on patriotism Uchimura was involved in stemmed from the Imperial Rescript on Education (1890), which laid out the government policy on education in the Japanese empire under the sovereign rule of the emperor Meiji. It manifests sixteen virtues such as loyalty and filial piety in as little as 315 characters. While this was distributed to every school as the guiding principles of education, its brevity required a guidebook, which helped schoolteachers to instruct their students in the spirit underpinning the rescript. Thus the philosopher Inoue Tetsujirō, together with Inoue Masanao, edited a guidebook, *Chokugo Engi (A Commentary on the Imperial Rescript)*, in 1891.[7]

Chokugo Engi deserves special attention for two reasons: first, it introduced the idea of patriotism to expand on the spirit of the rescript, and second, one of the editors, Inoue Tetsujirō, would be a leading opponent of Uchimura in the public debate on religion and education. *Chokugo Engi* asserts that the essential message of the rescript is to "consolidate the foundation of the state by practicing the Confucian virtue of *kōteishūshin* (loyalty and filial piety) and to prepare for emergencies by nourishing the righteous mind of *kyōdō aikoku* (communal patriotism)." While the editors reassert the traditional virtues of loyalty and filial piety, they also introduce a new idea of "communal patriotism": a doctrine that, according to the two Inoues, had been practiced in both East and West throughout human history from ancient times to the present.[8] What they meant by "communal patriotism" was nothing other than "dying for one's country": "One must have the mind of public justice which enables one to give up one's life bravely, as if it were no more than dust."

Meanwhile, Inoue Tetsujirō was directly involved in the public debate over Uchimura's "*lèse majesté* incident," in which he refused to bow deeply to the rescript at the First High School, Tokyo, in 1891. Uchimura's action resulted in public condemnation in the mass media, which prompted Inoue to problematize the relationship between religion and education and to criticize Christianity for being "cosmopolitan, not nationalistic, and far too egalitarian," thus being disrespectful of the traditional virtues of loyal and filial piety. This incident and the subsequent attack from

7. http://kindai.ndl.go.jp/info:ndljp/pid/759403.
8. Fujita Masashi, *Gakkō Kyōiku to Aikokushin: Senzen Sengo no "Aikokushin" Kyōiku no Kiseki (School Education and Patriotism: The Trails of the Education on Patriotism during and after the War)* (Tokyo: Gakushū no Tomo Sha, 2008), 52-53.

Inoue were, as Uchimura recalled in 1909, a massive blow to his patriotism, to such an extent that he was "no longer able to love [his] fatherland,"[9] but eventually he felt compelled to respond to the newly emerging discourse on patriotism in the media.

Uchimura's earliest discussion of patriotism can be found in his 1893 work *Consolations of a Christian (Kirisutoshinto no Nagusame)*. The book, which consists of six chapters, each discussing the suffering of and consolation for Christians in six different situations, includes an account of a person being betrayed by the person's nation. For Uchimura, patriotism is "a manifestation of utmost sincerity in human nature"; one does not love one's country because one is forced to, but one cannot help but loving it. Hence, teaching patriotism at school is, for him, problematic: "The nation which is obliged to subscribe to patriotism is the nation which is losing patriotism. . . . I prefer being a man who actually loves the country rather than being someone who preaches patriotism" (2:17). At this stage, Uchimura attacked patriotism as a doctrine imposed on the nation through public education. He did not offer any account of what it means to love one's country, apart from stressing its emotive aspect as "an integral part of the spirit of an individual" as a member of his or her nation (2:17).

Likewise, Uchimura's rejoinder to Inoue on "the conflict between religion and education" raised the issue of patriotism because Inoue accused Japanese Christians of lacking patriotism as they were patronized by foreign missionaries (2:129). Uchimura did not examine or question Inoue's idea of patriotism per se; instead, he countered Inoue by criticizing his pretense to monopolize patriotism; thus, Uchimura suspected that those who preached patriotism such as Inoue were patronized by the government so that the motivation of preaching patriotism may be no more than flattery to government officials (2:130). Once again, Uchimura's interest in, and concern with, the idea of patriotism is manifest, yet his discussion does not go beyond polemics against his opponents.

The circumstance that drove Uchimura to reconsider patriotism more theoretically was the rise of Japanese imperialism. Indeed, after his dispute with Inoue, Uchimura witnessed Japan's military victories in the First Sino-Japanese War (1894-95) and the Russo-Japanese War (1904-5). The two wars triggered the explosive expansion of public discourse on patriotism. The socialist Kōtoku Shūsui's 1901 work *Nijusseiki no Kaibutsu Teiko-*

---

9. In *Complete Works of Uchimura Kanzō*, 40 vols. (Tokyo: Iwanami Shoten, 1980-84), 16:510. As elsewhere in the book, references to the *Works* are placed in the text.

kushugi (Imperialism, the Monster of the Twentieth Century), for example, presented a trenchant critique of imperialism, in which he analogized imperialism with textiles: the warp of "the so-called patriotism" and the woof of "militarism." Drawing on John M. Robertson, *Patriotism and Empire* (1899), Kōtoku rejected patriotism as "beastly instinct and belligerence."[10] The grave significance of the contemporary idea of Japanese patriotism was felt by a Japanese intellectual who lived outside Japan: Asakawa Kan'ichi. He lectured on Japanese history at Yale University and proposed to a Japanese general audience in his sole book in Japanese, *Nihon no Kaki (Japan's Possible Calamities*, 1909), that they reconsider how Japanese patriotism ought to be conceptualized. Asakawa observes that Japanese patriotism is under the influence of Bushidō, and explores some Bushidō virtues that the Japanese need to cultivate or critically reconsider.[11] Nitobe Inazō's short book in English, *Bushidō* (1899),[12] may also be understood as a work that defends Japanese patriotism to English-language readers.

Uchimura's discussion of patriotism at this stage of his career around 1900 may be seen as a Christian response to the debate on Japanese imperialism. In his essay on "Jesus' patriotism," he proposed two ideas of patriotism: one is the "so-called patriotism" *(yo ni iu tokoro no aikokushin)*, and the other is Christian patriotism, which can be discerned in Jesus Christ. In response to the popular view that Christianity lacks patriotic sentiment, Uchimura asserts that "Christianity does not entail the 'so-called' patriotism," which, he explains, is patriotism that "is proud of one's country, hates foreign enemies, and discounts justice or humanitarian considerations for the interests of one's state" (17:306-7). This type of "patriotism" is "no more than the projection of self-interest onto the state, which should never be enshrined."

Uchimura asserts that patriotism exists in Christianity — in Jesus Christ and his followers; however, the way in which Jesus loved his country in this world differed from the aspiration for "political" independence. Indeed, Christ's "political and military disservice" to his country was one reason he was crucified. What Christ desired, Uchimura argues, was not the "political" but the "spiritual" independence of his fellow countrymen. Christ did not attempt to expel external enemies but strove to destroy "in-

---

10. Itō Sei, ed., *Kōtoku Shūsui* (Tokyo: Chūō Kōronsha, 1984), 91.

11. Asakawa Kan'ichi, *Nihon no Kaki (Japan's Possible Calamities)* (Tokyo: Kōdansha, 1987).

12. Nitobe Inazō, *Bushidō*, trans. Yanaihara Tadao (Tokyo: Iwanami Shoten, 1938).

ner" enemies; that is, one ought to be courageous enough to criticize sophists and Pharisees and to rescue one's country by means of "not sword but righteousness." Thus, Uchimura concludes, the followers of Christ should not abandon but sanctify patriotism. In short, Uchimura replaces the "so-called" patriotism, which is xenophobic, belligerent, and nationalistic, with "Christian" patriotism, which attacks the sinfulness of one's own nation by virtues of Christian faith. Clearly Uchimura's patriotism is inseparable from Christian ideals.

Uchimura's proposal of "another" patriotism entails four ramifications. First, he clearly understood the "so-called" patriotism as a desire for military conquest, which he flatly rejected, thereby inferring that the alternative patriotism was not incompatible with pacifism. This is implied in his contrast between the "so-called" patriotism, which appeals to the means of the "sword," and "Christian" patriotism, which has resort to "love" (17:309). Second, Uchimura's rejection of "political" patriotism did not mean any indifference to one's this-worldly country; on the contrary, he asserted that an individual is worthless without a country to which to belong. "God gave each individual one country in which to live, so that he would love it and grow with it" (17:309). Uchimura's depoliticization of patriotism therefore proposed another way of loving one's country, not its rejection. Third, and as a corollary of the second ramification, Uchimura stepped outside of the contemporary paradigm of debate, which concerned either acceptance or rejection of (what Uchimura called the "so-called") patriotism. For example, Kōtoku Shūsui simply attacked patriotism in general, which he considered an integral part of imperialism, thus proposing no alternative form of patriotism, whereas Uchimura proposed another patriotism that was not but ought to have been embraced by the contemporary Japanese. Fourth, and finally, Uchimura's patriotism was premised on the teleological worldview that a part serves a greater whole. Hence, Japan exists for the sake of the world and not the other way around (3:260-64). Indeed, as his epitaph reads: "I for Japan. Japan for the World; the World for Christ; and All for God." Hence, Uchimura's patriotism is an instrument for the spiritual betterment of the world.

Although I have so far examined Uchimura's patriotism before 1910, he in fact did not discuss patriotism *as such*. On the contrary, his essays hardly ever included the word "patriotism" in the titles. In most cases, he merely touched upon the subject in passing in his discussions of Japanese society and culture and the place of Japan in the international context. Patriotism did not come to the fore of Uchimura's writings until the last decade of his life, especially after the U.S. Immigration Act of 1924 banned immigration from Japan.

Uchimura had been expressing serious interest in the United States' increasing exclusion of immigrants since early in the decade 1910-20, and he exploded in anger over the Immigration Act of 1924: he started to campaign against the United States, not only by writing in his newsletter but also, for example, by publishing an essay on "the harm of receiving money from the Americans" and many others in *Kokumin Shimbun*, the newspaper edited by Tokutomi Sohō.[13] Writing for *Kokumin Shimbun* meant the reunion of Tokutomi and Uchimura in journalism for the first time since 1897 when Uchimura criticized Tokutomi's departure from *heimin-shugi* (populism) (4:443). The magnitude of Uchimura's fury can also be gauged by his (not entirely successful) attempt, in alliance with the leaders of Protestant churches in Japan, to declare the independence of Japanese Protestants from the American Protestant churches (29:278-80). Despite his numerous literary responses to America's anti-Japanese immigration policy, Uchimura's writings on patriotism in particular were significantly removed from the general readership. While he attacked U.S. immigration policy openly in newspapers, he restricted his writings on patriotism to his own biblical journal, the *Biblical Study*. Uchimura's remark that his patriotism was not so passionate as twenty years earlier (29:141) is perhaps not irrelevant to his withdrawal from the public forum on this particular issue.

A distinctive feature of Uchimura's discussion of patriotism in the 1920s was that it was anchored in his study of the books of Isaiah and Jeremiah. Of course, Uchimura discussed the two Old Testament books repeatedly throughout his career as a Christian preacher; however, he did not present the two prophets emphatically as patriots until the final years of his life. Isaiah emerges as a patriot in his *Izayasho no Kenkyū* (*Study of the Book of Isaiah*, 1928), while Jeremiah is presented as a patriot in his *Eremiyaden Kenkyū* (*Study of the Book of Jeremiah*, 1926). The link between patriotism and the Old Testament is evident in the fact that Uchimura's commentary on the book of Jeremiah was coupled with the essay "On My Patriotism," while the first essay of the *Study of the Book of Isaiah* was published in his biblical journal together with the essay "Patriotism and Faith." Indeed, already in 1909, Uchimura had been unequivocal in criticizing the

---

13. The polemical (and mostly anti-American) essays published in *Kokumin Shimbun* in 1924 are found in 28:224-25, 228-30, 285, 315, 316, 322, 325-27, 348-50, 376-78. He did not write for *Kokumin Shimbun* after 1924.

Japanese partiality for the New Testament. He declared that the Old Testament was no less important than the New Testament, partly because the former was "indispensable in nourishing patriotism." For Uchimura, the Old Testament was "the greatest source of patriotism." Conversely, the neglect of the Old Testament, according to Uchimura, made Japanese Christianity too "individualistic" to pay due care to the salvation of the nation (16:306-8).

Uchimura found in Jeremiah the culmination of the prophetic spirit. While Jerusalem was in a state of confusion, Jeremiah continued to preach the word of God. In the end, he proposed the policy of being subject to Babylon, as he judged there were no other options. This was the reason why he was persecuted, being labeled a traitor. Uchimura's Jeremiah the patriot is filled with sorrow because of the spiritually (as opposed to politically) impoverished state of his fellow countrymen (29:360). Commenting on Jeremiah 9:1-3, Uchimura writes: "This is the voice of Jeremiah's grief, a patriot's sorrow. Who has ever shed tears for one's own country with such grave grief?" (29:397).

Uchimura's reading of prophets including Isaiah, Jeremiah, Ezekiel, and Daniel as patriots was also extended to Jesus Christ. Uchimura's 1925 book, *Jūjika no Michi (The Road of the Cross)*, has a chapter on Jesus' patriotism, which is based on Matthew 23:37-39, Luke 13:34-35, and Luke 19:41-44. Uchimura is unequivocal in asserting that Jesus was a patriot. He was no "individualist" who cared about himself alone; he loved his country. Uchimura maintained that the love of Jerusalem, manifested in Psalm 137, provided the model for the Christian's love of heaven. Jesus was deeply saddened by the state of Jerusalem, which turned out to be a "city of thieves." Jesus' prophecy of the fall of Jerusalem resulted in his crucifixion. Jesus' patriotism was represented by the tears he shed in the face of his fellow countrymen's unwillingness to be saved. Uchimura adds that Jesus as a patriot loved Jerusalem, and at the same time he loved the whole of humanity. "Patriotism," Uchimura asserts, "is the essential sentiment of humans." "It makes a human human. One's patriotism does not lessen one's love for humanity. On the contrary, those who love humanity passionately were those who embraced patriotism" (29:144). Uchimura discerns this sort of patriotism not only in Jesus and the prophets but also in Dante Alighieri, John Milton, and Oliver Cromwell.

To sum up: Uchimura's discussions of patriotism, which extend over two separate periods of his literary career, were prompted and dictated by contemporary circumstances such as the debate ensuing from the "*lèse majesté* incident," the public debate on patriotism in the context of Japanese military successes and the growth of Japanese imperialism, and the U.S. Immigration Act of 1924. Uchimura's thoughts on patriotism did not remain purely polemical but grew mature toward the end of his life. In his final decade, Uchimura not only proposed his "prophetic" idea of patriotism in opposition to the "so-called" patriotism but also anchored the idea in his reading of the prophets, Isaiah and Jeremiah in particular. The "prophetic" patriotism was conceptualized by Uchimura as a critical judgment of the spiritual conditions of one's nation in light of Christian faith. Thus, like Isaiah and Jeremiah, a "prophetic" patriot must be content with the fate of a "man of sorrow"; he would inevitably suffer persecution and exclusion by his nation: a theme that permeates Uchimura's writings on patriotism.

Tsukamoto Toraji

Tsukamoto Toraji's name has long fallen into oblivion; however, he was undoubtedly one of the most influential leaders of *mukyōkai* Christianity after Uchimura's death. A graduate in law from Tokyo Imperial University, Tsukamoto worked as a senior bureaucrat at the Ministry of Agriculture and Commerce until 1919, when he opted for the life of a Christian preacher. Tsukamoto was probably Uchimura's most beloved disciple. Tsukamoto joined Uchimura's Bible study group in 1909. He impressed Uchimura, who described him in a correspondence as "a very learned man, great Bible-scholar" (39:283). From 1923 Tsukamoto collaborated closely with Uchimura; he contributed to lectures at Uchimura's Bible meetings and interviewed, on behalf of his master, applicants who wished to join Uchimura's group. Uchimura was probably thinking of passing his group on to Tsukamoto; however, in 1929, due to serious disagreements, Uchimura demanded that Tsukamoto leave him and form his own group. Tsukamoto founded his Bible study group with 26 members, the vast majority of which were young women. Eventually, Tsukamoto turned out to be an immensely popular preacher; his Sunday Bible meeting, with about 300 members, was regarded as one of Tokyo's "special attractions" *(Tokyo Meibutsu)*.[14]

Tsukamoto was no journalist or public intellectual. He defined himself as nothing other than a Christian preacher. His literary output was

---

14. Fujita, ed., *Uchimura Kanzō wo Keishō shita Hitobito*, 2:104.

therefore restricted to essays on his faith, which were published mostly in his own biblical journal, *Seisho Chishiki (The Knowledge of the Bible)*. Founded in 1930, *Seisho Chishiki* enjoyed a subscription list of 2,000. The essays published in it were not always purely religious but included some commentaries on contemporary politics and society from the standpoint of his Christian faith. These writings are now available in his eighteen-volume *Collected Works*.[15]

He did not hesitate to say publicly that he did not comprehend anything about politics.[16] Indeed, his sermons at the Bible meetings made reference to, and were prompted by, contemporary circumstances in a purely abstract fashion. It is therefore futile to attempt to reconstruct the political context in which Tsukamoto opined on patriotism because, unlike Uchimura, he did not try to engage with any specific political issues. Indeed, in 1960, Tsukamoto, reflecting on what he had learned from Uchimura, wrote that the greatest difference between him and his master was his lack of interest in politics.[17]

Whereas Uchimura discussed patriotism repeatedly over two substantial periods in his career, Tsukamoto rarely wrote on patriotism per se. However, the idea of patriotism agonized Tsukamoto in the 1930s as Japan was marching toward total war. The 1930s opened with the Manchurian Incident (September 1931). In 1932, the "independence" of Manchuria was declared, while the liberal prime minister Inukai Tsuyoshi was assassinated. The following year Japan left the League of Nations, and in 1937 Japan declared war on China. In 1940 Japan signed the Tripartite Pact with Germany and Italy. At the end of the following year Japan attacked Pearl Harbor.

In 1934, Tsukamoto preached on the relationship between *mukyōkai* Christian faith and the salvation of the Japanese nation. He opened his sermon by declaring that he had abandoned the initial idea of relating Christian faith to current affairs because "in Japan today, no living truth is allowed to be mentioned publicly. If you mention it, you are in trouble. I had considered myself until yesterday as a patriotic preacher. I had hoped to save my beloved country. . . . I now realize, however, that I am not able to say

---

15. *Tsukamoto Toraji Chosakushū*, 10 vols. (Tokyo: Seisho Chishikisha, 1978-79); *Tsukamoto Toraji Chosakushū Zoku*, 8 vols. (Tokyo: Seisho Chishikisha, 1984-86); hereafter *Tsukamoto*, followed by volume and page numbers. In this chapter I refer only to the last eight volumes.

16. *Tsukamoto*, 3:53-54, 374; 4:33.

17. *Tsukamoto*, 1:502.

what God commands me to say in the way in which Jeremiah did."[18] Tsukamoto made it clear that he was no longer a "patriotic preacher" because he was not prepared to face "troubles," that is, persecution. Tsukamoto considered a "patriotic preacher" to be an individual like Jeremiah who would publicly say what God commanded him despite persecution. Although he recognized this, he could not embrace it. Tsukamoto's renunciation of "patriotism" is therefore motivated by the fear of persecution resulting from the public manifestation of divine truth in the "prophetic" fashion. We have already seen that Uchimura's patriotism was underpinned by the critical judgment of the spiritual state of one's nation in light of divine truth, which would inevitably result in a life of "sorrow" due to persecution by fellow countrymen. Clearly Tsukamoto was conscious of Uchimura's understanding of patriotism, and deliberately refused to inherit it.[19]

Tsukamoto's departure from Uchimura's patriotism, however, did not result in his wholesale rejection of patriotism. Tsukamoto failed to grasp Uchimura's distinction between the "so-called" patriotism and "Christian" or "prophetic" patriotism; consequently, he subscribed to a commonplace understanding of patriotism. After Uchimura's death in 1930, Tsukamoto wrote a number of essays, long and short, on Uchimura, which would be collected and published in 1961 under the title *Uchimura Kanzō Sensei to Watashi (Master Uchimura Kanzō and I)*. In it, Tsukamoto often referred to Uchimura as a patriot,[20] but he did not expand on his master's patriotism. Tsukamoto offered his only account of patriotism in response to the question "whether or not a Christian can be Japanese." For Tsukamoto, "a patriot is someone who lives exclusively for the sake of the country he belongs to, regardless of his honor, status, family or life."[21] Patriotism is first and foremost selfless service to one's country, and even self-sacrifice. This commonplace definition of patriotism explains not only why Tsukamoto believed military officers and statesmen are "of course" patriots, but also why he wrote in 1940 that he did not want to count Uchimura as one of the Japanese patriots.[22]

Instead of subscribing to Uchimura's "prophetic" patriotism, Tsuka-

---

18. *Tsukamoto*, 7:483-85.

19. Indeed, in 1948 when Tsukamoto discussed Uchimura along with Dante and Luther, he argued that these three were all great patriots whose love of the truth made their fellow countrymen their enemies. See *Tsukamoto*, 1:428.

20. *Tsukamoto*, 1:299, 355, 402, 418, 439.

21. *Tsukamoto*, 1:356.

22. *Tsukamoto*, 1:395.

moto attempted to reposition his understanding of patriotism within his Christian worldview. His views are elaborated in his essay "Warera no Aikoku" ("Our Patriotism"). Referring to a dictionary definition of patriotism as "the love of fatherland," Tsukamoto points out that Japanese *mukyōkai* Christians belong to "two cities": one is Japan and the other is the city of God. He questions whether the love of one city is identical to the love of the other. His answer is that "if the love of the earthly city is deep and great, it will be perfectly identical to the love of the city of God."[23] This idea was paraphrased by Tsukamoto as follows: "to love one's country is exactly the same as loving the City of God. Indeed, the better Japanese you are, the better Christian you are; and the better Christian you are, the better Japanese you are."[24] Such identification of the love of an earthly city and the love of the city of God is largely foreign to Uchimura's patriotism, which underscored the teleological relationship between the love of an earthly city (Japan) and the love of the whole world and beyond.[25] The love of Japan, according to Uchimura, was instrumental to the love of humanity, Christ, and ultimately God, and not the other way around. Tsukamoto, by contrast, claimed that the love of God could be reduced to the love of Japan.[26]

What lies beneath Tsukamoto's identification of Christian faith with patriotism is his worldview, which sees individuals, families, communities, states, and the city of God in continuum. Tsukamoto maintained that the problem of international relations could be reduced to the problem of a state, which in turn can be reduced to the problem of the family. It can ultimately be reduced to the problem of an individual. Hence, "the sins of a country are the sins of individual countrymen. . . . Sins do not belong to a country but to its individuals."[27] The solution to the problem of interna-

---

23. *Tsukamoto*, 7:507.

24. *Tsukamoto*, 7:508.

25. I say "*largely* foreign" because at times Uchimura expressed an idea that is not dissimilar to Tsukamoto's: for example, Uchimura wrote on October 1, 1910: "Faith is sacrificing oneself for God, while patriotism is sacrificing oneself for a country. Faith and patriotism share the idea of sacrificing oneself. *Yet I have not seen any believer in God who does not love his own country, nor have I known anyone who loves one's country but does not love God.* Patriotism can be acquired through faith. The enemy of God and the traitor of one's country are those who are dictated by self-love" (*Works*, 17:372, emphasis mine).

26. This is not to suggest that Tsukamoto did not understand Uchimura's view. Tsukamoto stated explicitly that for Uchimura the two "J's" — Japan and Jesus — were "not on a par but the former was subject to the latter." See *Tsukamoto*, 1:429.

27. *Tsukamoto*, 3:400.

tional relations was thus radically reduced to private individuals. This reductionism allowed Tsukamoto to see all public issues concerning politics, society, and diplomacy as questions of the sinfulness of private individuals. Thus, Tsukamoto demanded that his audience consider their "problem of the soul" *before* discussing public issues.[28] An implication of this is that the love of a country is also reduced to the matter of each individual's private faith.

If the problem of individual souls is at the root of all the problems ("humans' first and last problem"),[29] then the salvation of individuals would lead to the salvation of a community, which in turn would result in the salvation of a state, and ultimately the whole world. Tsukamoto declares: "I hope every one of you will not deceive yourself, stand in front of the living God and solve the problem of your relationship to Him; then, all other problems will be solved naturally."[30] The individual reductionism, which magnified the problem of individual sin, was diametrically opposed to any sense of optimism about public matters. Conversely, if individuals lived in a state of grace, public and societal problems would cease to exist. This explains Tsukamoto's weak engagement with political issues; public issues were, for Tsukamoto, to be resolved automatically as soon as the sins of individuals were redeemed.

Tsukamoto's reductionist worldview prioritized each individual's relationship to God, thus underestimating the "salvation of a country." Tsukamoto's "privatized" and "individualized" *mukyōkai* Christianity did not recognize any urgent necessity to confront the tension between ideals and reality on any level beyond the personal. Tsukamoto's individualist reductionism therefore undercut and departed from "prophetic" patriotism, which he inherited from Uchimura. Another possible reason for his lack of interest in "prophetic" patriotism is that his Christian faith was partial to the New Testament. His scholarly studies revolved around the New Testament. Tsukamoto produced no commentaries on any book of the Old Testament. He did not think reading the Old Testament was essential for acquiring faith.[31] Tsukamoto's partiality for the New Testament certainly lessened the significance of Uchimura's prophetic patriotism, which was anchored in his appreciation of the Old Testament as the fount of patriotism.

28. *Tsukamoto*, 4:177.
29. *Tsukamoto*, 4:177.
30. *Tsukamoto*, 7:492.
31. *Tsukamoto*, 2:87.

Yanaihara Tadao

Yanaihara Tadao joined Uchimura's Bible-reading group in 1911 when he was a student at the First High School in Tokyo. After studying law and politics at Tokyo Imperial University, Yanaihara worked for Sumitomo for three years before being invited to teach at Tokyo Imperial University in 1920, succeeding Nitobe Inazō. Upon appointment to the chair of colonial policy, Yanaihara was sent to Europe and America for research, returning to Tokyo in 1923. While Yanaihara organized Bible study meetings at Tokyo Imperial University from 1925, he hosted his own Bible study group; at first with others from 1929, and subsequently by himself from 1933. This, however, did not lead Yanaihara to live primarily as a Christian preacher. Unlike Tsukamoto, Yanaihara did not want to professionalize his Christian mission but insisted on being a layman. Although Yanaihara's pacifist dissent from the wartime government cost him the chair in 1937, his public profile was primarily academic: after being professor of colonial policy at Tokyo in the 1920s and 1930s, he was appointed director of the Institute of Social Sciences, and later, president of the University of Tokyo in the postwar years. Before, during, and after the Second World War, Yanaihara also remained active, whenever possible, as a public intellectual, contributing essays to newspapers and current affairs magazines. His literary output was diverse: he produced a mass of academic writings on Japanese colonial policy especially before 1937, and a number of essays on university education and administration after the war. He also wrote numerous essays on Japanese politics, economy, and society for a general audience, while he published his own biblical journals in order to disseminate his faith in *mukyōkai* Christianity.[32]

Yanaihara's relationship to Uchimura contrasted sharply with that of Tsukamoto. While Tsukamoto established a very personal relationship, Yanaihara abstained from approaching Uchimura privately. Yanaihara observed that those who sought a personal relationship with Uchimura often ended up clashing with him; this was an unfortunate situation that, Yanaihara believed, he could avoid by seeking only a public relationship between master and disciple.[33] Despite the "distance" between Uchimura and Yanaihara, or perhaps because of it, Yanaihara inherited the essence of Uchimura's prophetic patriotism.

---

32. Most of Yanaihara's works are collected in *Yanaihara Tadao Zenshū* (Tokyo: Iwanami Shoten, 1963-65); hereafter *Yanaihara*, followed by volume and page numbers.

33. *Yanaihara*, 24:495-96.

Yanaihara grappled with the idea of patriotism, like Tsukamoto, in the 1930s. However, the way in which he addressed the issue differed significantly from that of Tsukamoto. Yanaihara's view of patriotism was most clearly presented in his controversial 1937 article "Kokka no Risō" ("Ideals of a State"), which attacked the contemporary Japanese government's belligerent and expansionist policies. In it he wrote that a patriot was "not someone who ingratiates himself with the policies of the powers that be but the one who loves, and is loyal to, the ideals of the state."[34] "True patriotism does not consist in blind obedience to contemporary policies; rather, a prophet who resists blind obedience and criticizes the reality in the light of the ideals of the state is a patriot who leads the long-term policies of the state."[35] Since the article was written for a general audience, Yanaihara did not make himself clear about the source of the "ideals of a state"; however, he revealed in his essays for fellow *mukyōkai* believers that the source is nothing but God. Yanaihara's idea of patriotism was thus reiterated and expanded for a *mukyōkai* audience; in his biblical journal *Tsūshin (Correspondence)*, he wrote: "someone who loves the justice of God is a true patriot."[36] Again, "to love a country by means of Christianity is true patriotism."[37] "True patriotism is not expressed in such sentiments as 'my country is right.' It is what demands repentance of the nation and builds the state on the foundation of divine justice and morality. . . . Those who pray for the national interest, not for national morality, are not true patriots."[38]

From Yanaihara's accounts of "true patriotism" two things can be inferred: one is that Yanaihara clearly inherited Uchimura's two ideas of patriotism, thus dismissing the "so-called" patriotism and enshrining "prophetic" patriotism. Yanaihara rejected the view that blind obedience to the state is patriotism and redefined patriotism as the act of loving the ideals, not the reality, of a state. The other is that what Yanaihara regarded as "true patriotism" was modeled on the patriotism of prophets in the Old Testament, especially Isaiah and Jeremiah: the prophets in whom Uchimura discerned patriotism. Even in the "Ideals of a State," Yanaihara described a true patriot as "a *prophet* who resists blind obedience and criticizes the reality."[39] After his resignation from Tokyo Imperial University, Yanaihara wrote and

34. *Yanaihara*, 18:633.
35. *Yanaihara*, 18:642.
36. *Yanaihara*, 18:206.
37. *Yanaihara*, 18:218.
38. *Yanaihara*, 18:536-37.
39. *Yanaihara*, 18:642, emphasis mine.

published the two-volume *Yo no Sonkei suru Jinbutsu (The Men I Admire)*, in which he portrayed Isaiah and Jeremiah as patriots.[40]

Yanaihara's indebtedness to Uchimura in understanding patriotism can be gauged by Yanaihara's remarks on Uchimura's life and thought. Yanaihara wrote about his master's life, work, and belief on a number of occasions from 1930 to 1961. One defining feature of Uchimura's thought, according to Yanaihara, was patriotism. This observation was already obvious in one of his earliest essays on Uchimura; in 1932, when the first edition of the *Works of Uchimura Kanzō (Uchimura Kanzō Zenshū)* was published, Yanaihara depicted Uchimura as a man who "was reviled because of his love of his country, and accused of heresy because of his love of Christ."[41] Eight years later, Yanaihara argued that preaching Christianity was for Uchimura a matter of utmost urgency for Japan, which was bereft of social justice and political morality. Thus, Uchimura's departure from journalism and his devotion to the publication of his journal *The Biblical Study*, Yanaihara argued, represented "not retreat (from) but advance" toward patriotism: through his work on *The Biblical Study*, "Japan found the greatest patriot in [Uchimura]." Yanaihara thought identifying the task of saving Japan with the preaching of the Gospels underpinned Uchimura's patriotism: this observation remained constant before, during, and after the Second World War.[42]

Indeed, for Yanaihara, Uchimura's *mukyōkai* Christianity was not merely an expression of Christian faith opposed to an institutional priesthood but also a Christian faith anchored in patriotism. Patriotism was an integral part of *mukyōkai* Christianity, as Yanaihara declared: "*Mukyōkai* Christianity originates from prophetic spirit and patriotism."[43] Yanaihara was aware of the foreign missionaries' criticism that Uchimura and his disciples were excessively nationalistic, since Christianity was, according to these missionaries, global. In defense of Uchimura's position, Yanaihara asserts the necessary link between faith in Christ and passionate love of

---

40. *Yanaihara*, 24:7-45, 175-211.

41. *Yanaihara*, 24:445. This was reiterated in 1961: "Being reviled by pseudo prophets because of his love of Christ and attacked by pseudo patriots because of his love of Japan, that is the life and thought of Uchimura Kanzō" (*Yanaihara*, 24:577).

42. *Yanaihara*, 24:504-5.

43. *Yanaihara*, 24:349. Uchimura's "nationalism" was also characterized by Yanaihara as "prophetic." In the dialogue with the economic historian and a *mukyōkai* member, Ōtsuka Hisao, Yanaihara described Uchimura's nationalism as "prophetic nationalism," which belongs to the genealogy of Cromwellian nationalism, and added that "prophets were all patriots and in that sense nationalist" (*Yanaihara*, 24:599). See also chapter 4 in this volume.

country. Uchimura became more patriotic when he converted to Christianity than he had been as a son of a samurai. He learned to love his nation through the love of Christ.[44] Uchimura's patriotism was thus "the burning love of the Japanese nation which was mediated by the love of Christ."[45] To be sure, Uchimura's love of Japan is instrumental for the love of the world, and beyond. Hence, Uchimura's patriotism is remotely similar to the imperialist desire to conquer the world. This teleological worldview had already been manifested in one of the early essays: "first, love God. Second, love the world and humanity. Third, love your country and fellow countrymen. Fourth, love yourself and your family. If my love is offered in this order, I should be able to be in peace with everyone, my affairs should prosper, and my mind should always enjoy tranquility."[46] Patriotism was clearly not the love of the highest order, and yet, Yanaihara observed, it was an essential component of Uchimura's Christian faith.

Yanaihara's definitions of patriotism clearly suggest that he assimilated Uchimura's "prophetic" patriotism. However, Yanaihara was not a mere mouthpiece of Uchimura's patriotism, since he developed the idea of patriotism in a twofold way: one was to show an explicit link between patriotism and pacifism, and the other was to anchor patriotism in the "social-scientific" analysis of current affairs. The association between patriotism and pacifism was only implied but never expounded by Uchimura. Yanaihara, by contrast, asserted that the "ideals of a state" were "justice and peace," thereby attacking the chauvinistic and belligerent policies of the Japanese government. The source of such "ideals of a state" was the book of Isaiah;[47] indeed, Yanaihara's reading of Isaiah is also indebted to Uchimura's. Uchimura's interpretation of Isaiah clearly recognizes the ideal of peace.[48] However, Uchimura did not incorporate pacifism explicitly in his discourse on patriotism. He preached that patriotism was to love one's country by virtue of "justice," not "peace."[49] Since the popular understanding of patriotism enshrined self-sacrifice in defense of one's fatherland, belligerence was regarded as an integral component of patriotism. Yanaihara's inclusion of "peace" as an "ideal" that a patriot ought to uphold is clearly a noteworthy innovation.

44. *Yanaihara,* 24:570.
45. *Yanaihara,* 24:571.
46. As cited in *Yanaihara,* 24:521.
47. *Yanaihara,* 12:92-93.
48. *Yanaihara,* 23:285-86, 31, 35-41.
49. *Complete Works of Uchimura Kanzō,* 29:352.

Yanaihara also went further in underscoring the importance of empirical analysis in assessing contemporary politics and society. Yanaihara's patriotism as critical judgment of contemporary political and social reality of one's country required not merely the manifestation of "ideals" but also empirical analysis of "reality." In this context Yanaihara underlined the significance of his training in social science. Indeed, he recalled the time when he dissented from the militaristic government, saying that his "academic work and faith became one and the same" to confront the reality.[50] Yanaihara's academic research at Tokyo Imperial University was devoted to the economic theory of colonialism and case studies of Japanese colonialism in Manchuria, Taiwan, and the South Pacific. His critical analysis of Japanese colonial policy had revealed its economic irrationality and aggressive exploitation of the colonies. Uchimura lacked this academic training in social science; hence, his discourse on patriotism did not emphasize the analytical power of judgment based on social sciences. In this aspect too, Yanaihara took the patriotism he inherited from his master to a new level. In sum, Yanaihara elevated the ideal of Uchimura's prophetic patriotism by linking it with pacifism and armed the idea of patriotism with analytical power of judgment backed by his knowledge of, and insight into, political economy.

Conclusion

Although Tsukamoto understood the prophetic nature of Uchimura's patriotism, he abandoned that type of patriotism, which is illustrated by his acquiescence with the contemporary Japanese government's militaristic policy. Yanaihara, by contrast, inherited and translated into action Uchimura's prophetic patriotism. While Uchimura only shaped his patriotism in his final years in an explicitly prophetic fashion based on his reading of the books of Isaiah and Jeremiah, Yanaihara asserted that view repeatedly during and after the Second World War, which is manifest in his commentaries on the books of Isaiah and Jeremiah as well as in his biographical accounts of the two prophets.

Fifteen years following Uchimura's death in 1930 was the darkest period in modern Japanese history. The leaders of the "second generation" *mukyōkai* Christians were confronted by the question of patriotism in a

---

50. *Yanaihara,* 26:47.

context that was very different from that in which Uchimura developed his idea of patriotism. Tsukamoto and Yanaihara grappled with the idea of patriotism in contrasting ways, which may be attributable to a number of factors, including their personalities, and professional and academic backgrounds. However, two factors stand out: one is the way in which the two thinkers grasped the political reality, and the other is their attitude toward the Old Testament. From the political standpoint, Tsukamoto is characterized by a self-professed inability to analyze and comprehend the political reality, which was probably reinforced by his preoccupation with the sinfulness of private individuals. Yanaihara, by contrast, made the best use of his social-scientific knowledge and analytical skills to acquire the empirical understanding of, and to engage critically with, the political reality of the time. From a theological standpoint, Tsukamoto was clearly partial to the New Testament, and did not express any appreciation of Uchimura's interpretation of prophets in the Old Testament as patriots. Yanaihara, by contrast, inherited Uchimura's love of the Old Testament, especially the books of Isaiah and Jeremiah, and followed in the footsteps of Isaiah and Jeremiah as he and Uchimura understood them, thereby being content with the life of "sorrow" under the persecution of the contemporary government. Clearly Uchimura's idea of patriotism was open to diverse interpretative possibilities, let alone his *mukyōkai* Christian faith.

PART II

Biblical Studies and Theological Thought

The Biblical Research Method of Uchimura Kanzō

Miura Hiroshi

In 1918, Uchimura wrote, "Although I have had many work experiences since I became a Christian forty years ago, there has always been one thing which has never left my mind. That is the study of the Bible. My ambition has been to comprehend the Bible thoroughly by myself, and help others to their own understanding of it without depending on Bible commentaries" (24:56). Uchimura devoted himself to the study of the Bible in the latter half of his life, and made public the outcome of his research in his private monthly magazine, *Seisho no Kenkyū (The Biblical Study)*.[1] The first issue of his magazine was published in October 1900. The magazine continued publication until his death in 1930, a total of 357 issues. He also gave lectures on the Bible every Sunday. At first, those lectures were held at his residence in the outskirts of Tokyo; but in 1907, a lecture hall was built for him, funded by a donation, which he used for his Bible lectures until his death in 1930.[2] Uchimura's lectures greatly influenced many young men and women who attended them. A feature of his Bible study class was that he gave strict character tests to those who wanted to attend it. The number

1. The idea of publishing *Seisho no Kenkyū (The Biblical Study)* first came to Uchimura's mind when he was studying at Amherst College. Its eventual publication, therefore, was the realization of the plan he had cherished in his mind for the previous fifteen years. See "Honshi no hakkō ni tsuite" ("About the Publication of This Magazine"), 8:471-72.

2. Uchimura lived in Tsunohazu, now western Shinjuku, Tokyo, from 1899 to 1907. In 1907, he moved to Kashiwagi, also now in the Shinjuku area, where he lived for the following twenty-three years, until his death in 1930. Uchimura's Bible studies and lectures were mainly done while living in these two places. Kashiwagi in particular had a rich natural environment in Uchimura's time.

of people allowed to attend was limited. In its later years, his Bible study group produced well-known Japanese scholars, engineers, educators, and Bible researchers.

Uchimura argued that in order to know the Bible well one needs to study the Greek, Hebrew, English, and German languages, and Western history. However, the Bible was not written for today's Americans, Europeans, Chinese, or Japanese. The most recent part of the Bible was written about two thousand years ago and was written for Jews, Greeks, or Romans of that time in the common language of the eastern Roman Empire. Those people were different from the people who live in today's world in character, thinking, and surrounding environment. Therefore, it is no wonder that understanding the Bible is not easy for the people who live today; what is written in the Bible has very little connection with the world we now know (18:217). On the other hand, the Bible is a book of the inner affairs of the mind. Because of this, it is after all not too difficult to understand the Bible, for even people living today can relate their own internal experiences to those it describes (8:295).

How, then, did Uchimura study the Bible? That is the subject of this chapter.

Uchimura believed that the Bible was written by men but under the influence of God's Spirit. Therefore, those who do not recognize the existence of God or the Holy Spirit will have difficulty understanding the Bible.

As has been true since old times, some people consider the entire Bible to be the words of God. Therefore they must believe everything in the Bible exactly as it is written, in every detail. In such cases there is no room for research or interpretation. It is well known that such views are held by the Brethren, one of the Protestant denominations of Christianity. Uchimura, on the other hand, does not take this view of the Bible. His view is that it is to be studied but not worshiped (32:185). If the Bible is worshiped, it will become an idol and eventually a source of harm: "If the Bible had no truth in it, it would not deserve our esteem; however, the living truth is indeed working in it, and that is what gives it its worth. But even in spite of this special value which it has, we do not blindly worship it" (32:185). Uchimura also believed that Bible studies could reform this world fundamentally, and he himself engaged in such work, as already noted, by studying the Bible and publishing his findings in *Seisho no Kenkyū* (10:104-7).

For Uchimura, the Bible was the book of experience. For people who had a deep experience of life, therefore, the Bible was actually quite easy to understand. For example, to understand it well one should read it in its original language. But no degree of fluency in Hebrew or Greek, nor of understanding the history, geography, natural history, and archaeology of the Bible, will help a reader to understand what is written in John 3:16 in the New Testament. It is the truth that God directly reveals to the believer's heart. And it cannot be searched scientifically or philosophically. To understand Christ thoroughly, one has to have bitter experiences of life, suffering as he did, abandoned by his own countrymen and close friends, even including his own brother, and finally being hung on the cross along with the robbers.

The salvation of oneself, one's family, one's people, and the entire human race relies on Jesus. Everlasting life comes from him, and the objective of Bible studies is to know him (22:274).

"Why then do we need to know him? Because knowing him is life," Uchimura said (32:318). And to know Jesus, one needs to know the Bible: not only the New Testament but also the Old Testament.

According to Uchimura, knowing or not knowing Jesus makes a big difference. The Bible is called "the book of life" because it introduces Jesus, whose life was given to men, and who became the foundation of life. According to Uchimura, Bible studies are not merely research on an old book, but a means of gaining a life worthy of men for today (32:318). He also believed that the Bible is best understood if we focus on Jesus as the central figure when studying it (12:465-66).

Other factors affecting Uchimura's Bible studies are as follows.

Fact, Experience, Experiment

The most distinctive feature in Uchimura's Bible studies is the great importance he attaches to "the fact." This is related to his interest in science, an interest he developed in his childhood and maintained throughout his life, which led him to study the science of agriculture at Sapporo Agricultural College in his youth and start his career as a fishery scientist.

Uchimura placed great importance on fact, experience, and experiment in search of truth, both in his study of the Bible and in the practice of faith in this real world.

Here, the present writer investigates how these matters occupied Uchimura's mind and how he handled them.

Uchimura believed science is the observation of facts in the natural world, while religion is the observation of facts in the spiritual world.

Their common objective is to observe fact: they differ only in the area of observation. Science and religion are good brothers (15:446).

> My Christian faith is faith in facts, not faith in theory. It is also faith in experiments. (14:293)

> Religion is fact and also experiences. (2:228)

Uchimura claimed that his study of the science of agriculture at Sapporo Agricultural School, by training him to hold facts in high esteem, became his best guide in his Bible studies (14:293).

Uchimura compared the spirit of the scientist to the spirit of an infant. It believes in the facts of nature as they present themselves. Therefore, the miracles described in the Bible, for example, do not surprise Uchimura nor make him doubtful. He believes in them as written:

> My Christian faith until today is this. That is "the faith of fact," not "the faith of reason." It is also "the faith of experiment." I don't know why God exists. I only know that he does. I don't know why Christ is my savior. I only know my sins are taken away by Christ, and then I am able to have eyes to see God, and am able to think pure and righteous matters. (14:293)

> I don't know why the Bible is the words of God. I only know that they touch my heart as no mere words of men could do. Fish is fish, chicken is chicken, beast is beast, man is man, Christ is Christ. I believe in this way. (14:293)

Even before he changed the subject of his study from agricultural science to religion, Uchimura had never doubted the truth of religion. "If religion were not reality, I should immediately abandon it." "What the human body needs is real grains and meats, not political argument, economic discussion or sociology. Similarly, what the human soul needs is real Christ and spirit, not theological arguments or discussions about church or Bible studies" (14:293).

According to Uchimura, the best way to know nature is to experience nature. In the same way, the best way to know Christ is directly to experience the living Christ in our heart. The way of knowing them is the same in both cases. For Uchimura, the research method used in science is also the research method used in religion. "Faith is experiment," Uchimura said. The difference between science and religion is not in the method or the spirit of research, but only in the area of research (14:293). Conducting research on the matter of the earth is called earth science. Conducting research on the matter in the sky is called astronomy. Similarly, conducting research on the matter of the soul is called religion. For Uchimura, the study of religion means only that the field of study has moved from science to religion. That is to say, when Uchimura studied the Bible, he used the same method and spirit he had once used in fishery science, in his studies of abalone, herring, and salmon (14:290-94). Thus, it can be said that Uchimura applied the scientific method and its spirit to religious studies.

Suffering

To know Christianity, we study the Bible. However, Uchimura argued that it is impossible to know Christianity only through books. We sometimes have to suffer to know Christianity. Indeed, the experience of suffering is inevitable if we are to know Christianity truly. This means that we obtain biblical commentary through bitter experience and experiments in our own lives. That is to say, our experience of suffering provides us with commentary on the Bible of a different kind from that which we obtain from its actual words. In Scripture we find the words, "Ye have not yet resisted unto blood, striving against sin" (Heb. 12:4). "And not only so, but we glory in tribulations also: knowing that tribulation worketh patience; and patience, experience; and experience, hope" (Rom. 5:3-4). We will not be able to understand the full meaning of these Scriptures only by reading books and words of biblical commentary. The meaning of these words can only be known by enduring hardship in the name of Christ (14:249).

Uchimura also points out that the experience of persecution is difficult to bear but is nonetheless the most valuable experience we can have for understanding Christianity; indeed, it is the only way to understand Christianity completely, and therefore to be Christian in the full sense. To know who Christ is, and what Christianity is, one must have the experience of persecution for the Christian faith (21:197-98).

Uchimura himself had a bitter experience of this in what has been called the *"lèse majesté* incident," which took place in Tokyo in January 1891. It is a well-known event in the history of Japan and is described more fully in the introduction and in chapter 4.

Nature

Uchimura said that his faith stands on three foundations: the Bible, nature, and human history (11:201). He said that if even one of these three foundations is missing, it is impossible to maintain a healthy faith. All of them must be studied.

Here we will study one of Uchimura's three foundations: nature. "When I am weak," Uchimura writes, "I go to the mountain by myself. There I come in contact with Jehovah God who is my rock and my savior in prayer. Then, see what happens! I, who was weak when I entered the mountain, come out as a strong man. How great the mountain's power is, how immeasurable the effect of prayer! Having the mountain and the prayer, this world is not the valley of pain" (10:282-83). Uchimura also points out that a similar phrase can be found in the Bible: "I will lift up mine eyes unto the hills, from whence cometh my help. My help cometh from the Lord, which made heaven and earth" (Ps. 121:1-2). It is possible to learn what God's will is by observing nature, natural or physical phenomena. In the Old Testament, for example, the prophet Jeremiah was shown a boiling pot, and told by God what it meant. "And the word of the LORD came unto me the second time, saying, What seest thou? And I said, I see a seething pot; and the face thereof is toward the north. Then the LORD said unto me, Out of the north an evil shall break forth upon all the inhabitants of the land" (Jer. 1:13-14). In the New Testament, Jesus taught in parables using the birds in the sky — "Behold the fowls of the air: for they sow not, neither do they reap, nor gather into barns; yet your heavenly Father feedeth them" (Matt. 6:26) — and the lilies of the field: "And why take ye thought for raiment? Consider the lilies of the field, how they grow; they toil not, neither do they spin: And yet I say unto you, That even Solomon in all his glory was not arrayed like one of these. Wherefore, if God so clothe the grass of the field, which to-day is, and to-morrow is cast into the oven, shall he not much more clothe you, O ye of little faith?" (Matt. 6:28-30). Uchimura thought that loving nature should be a step toward reaching God. Men live in and with nature, and receive inspiration from it, and their minds are fostered by nature. Nature helps men to maintain their faith. But nature should not be treated as an altar to house God (16:321). If we do this, nature would become like Ashtoreth, the goddess of the Sidonians (1 Kings 11:33), and lead us to the sin of idolatry. Thus, Uchimura warned that people, by loving nature too deeply and too intensely, may be tempted to forget God and neglect their duty in this world. He thought that attending to God's words in the Bible and fulfilling one's duty in this world were more important than loving nature (16:321).

Nature had an important effect on Uchimura, mainly in the following three stages of his life. (1) In Takasaki, a town about sixty miles northwest of Tokyo, where he spent his childhood, he was keen on fishing in the Karasu and Usui Rivers when he was twelve years old. "What a happy time it was! My teacher and my father scolded me for not studying. But they did not understand what great learning I was involved in. What is the natural history? Learning in books and listening in classrooms are not the only way of studying nature. Obtaining true knowledge belongs with conducting experiment. My love of nature began by observing the natural things in both the Karasu and Usui Rivers" (7:227). (2) In Sapporo, Hokkaido, he was a student at Sapporo Agricultural College: "One could enter the virgin forest anywhere in the outskirts of Sapporo, without going far by riding a steam powered train. When I go out from the school gate, the flocks of snipes come to my foot running. I was grateful for having had this experience of breathing freedom. I ran around like a wild dog and ate the fish of the Ishikari River until I was full" (7:227). (3) Uchimura went to the United States in 1884, and entered Amherst College in Massachusetts in 1885. The natural scenery he came in contact with in and around Amherst had an important effect on him: "It was the time I had intimate relations with the fields and the mountains of the western continent when I searched for the footprints of ancient animals on the banks of the Connecticut River. Holding a hammer at my side, I looked at the meandering Milky Way, facing north from the top of Mt. Holyoke. Already familiar, this nature became even closer through the lectures of Professor Emerson" (3:91). Uchimura studied the science of agriculture at Sapporo Agricultural College. After graduating, he took a job as a fishery scientist in the government. The interest in science that he had in his youth remained with him throughout his life. However, he tried to attain his faith as a Christian at the same time.

It has generally been believed since old times that science and Christianity cannot be made to coexist. Is this true?

Uchimura believed that Christianity and science did not contradict each other and could coexist if both were well studied. He said, "If one wants to know the relations between Christianity and science, one has to study both of them deeply and from their foundations. Those who advocate the contradiction between them, do not usually study both deeply. They study only one side, and not the other" (14:272). Both science and

Christianity must be studied thoroughly and deeply; then they would be seen to support rather than contradict each other. Uchimura said that science without religion tends to become focused on worldly interests such as moneymaking and the pursuit of pleasure, and to be utilized solely for profit. Science pursued with this motivation cannot lead to true progress (6:97-98).

Scientific research on nature does not automatically lead to faith. Only those who have faith know that this universe, including nature, was made by God. Bible study is essential, for it is this that fosters faith (20:114-15).

History

For Uchimura, the study of history was as important as the study of the Bible itself or the study of nature. Uchimura thought that history was the record of human activities. World history comprises seeing the human race as a single unit, its development and advancement. History can also be said to be the drama played by the human race.

Anybody who does not know history will be narrow-minded, he said. Such a person does not understand that the human race in its entirety forms a single group. He may know the life of his own nation, but he does not know the life of the world or of the human race as a whole (3:277). Past events do not always repeat themselves in exactly the same way. But there has always been a rule working among the human race since ancient times, namely, that similar causes always bring similar end results. That is why the study of history is necessary and interesting (3:278).

Before Uchimura started concentrating on studying and lecturing on the Bible in the early 1900s, he had various work experiences such as schoolteaching, writing, and journalism. From such experiences he developed a sensitivity to "what is happening in the world." One can see where his interests were. He became involved in the Tennō (emperor) system in Japan, refusing to bow before the Imperial Rescript on Education as a teacher at the First Higher Middle School in Tokyo in December 1891, arguing publicly about the Sino-Japanese War, and quitting his job as a newspaper editor because of his antiwar conviction at the time of the Russo-Japanese War. He also expressed his opinion about the anti-Japanese movement in America in the 1920s. This shows that a fundamental conviction of Uchimura's was the need to observe the conditions of the contemporary world and directly or indirectly take an active part in its events. In other words, it can be said that Uchimura's faith was a living faith. It was also the attitude of the prophets of the Old Testament era such as Isaiah, Jeremiah, and Amos. They were not insensitive to the existing conditions of the world in their time.

According to Uchimura, the study of history leads one to the study of prophecy in the Bible because history is the fulfillment of predictions by the biblical prophets. Seen from a believer's standpoint, all histories are the fulfillments of God's will. And God foretells through his prophets about everything he does (32:339). By a full understanding of the words of the prophets, one can learn to understand history. And by studying history, one comes to understand how its meaning is revealed by the biblical prophets. However, according to Uchimura, Christians in his time, in spite of their beliefs, did not pay much attention to the study of prophecy (32:340). Most Christians at that time thought that faith was an individual matter that had nothing to do with the affairs of this world. Uchimura's view, however, was that the Bible clearly showed that the study of prophecy was necessary in order to foster one's faith. Christians in Uchimura's time maintained faith without prophecy. As a result, their faith was always weak and unstable. But the best way to consolidate and strengthen one's faith is by studying the prophecies; faith cannot prosper if this is neglected. God has sent many prophets to this world. A large part of the Bible is about prophecy, not only in the Old Testament but in the New Testament too.

The Afterlife as a Background to Bible Reading

How should we read the Bible? To understand it, we should read it with hope and fear of the next world in our minds. This can be deduced from Jesus' saying in the Sermon on the Mount (*Works*, 23:15): "Blessed are the poor in spirit: for theirs is the kingdom of heaven. Blessed are they that mourn: for they shall be comforted. Blessed are the meek: for they shall inherit the earth. Blessed are they which do hunger and thirst after righteousness: for they shall be filled" (Matt. 5:3-6).

According to Uchimura, all these words were spoken by Jesus in the expectation that there was a life after death (23:14-16). These are the words of the Son of God, who knows well what death and life after death are. As he said, "I am Alpha and Omega, the beginning and the ending, . . . which is, and which was, and which is to come, the Almighty" (Rev. 1:8).

Christians do not struggle without hope. They run the race for the joy set before them, and are not ashamed. God prepares a good city for them, and they go for the prize. Thus, by keeping the next world in mind while reading the Bible, we can recognize the deep and valuable meanings that this imparts to Jesus' words. Jesus clearly knew that there is life after death, as we know that tomorrow will surely come (23:15). Therefore, these words flowed out from his mouth: "Blessed are the poor in spirit: for theirs is the kingdom of heaven" (Matt. 5:3). The proclamations of the existence of life after death can be found not only in the Sermon on the Mount but throughout the Gospels. Let us see a few other places where the existence of life after death is shown: "For there is nothing covered, that shall not be revealed; neither hid, that shall not be known. Therefore whatever ye have spoken in darkness shall be heard in the light; and that which ye have spoken in the ear in closets shall be proclaimed upon the housetops" (Luke 12:2-3). These were the words Jesus spoke to his disciples, confirming that there is nothing hidden from people, and that everything will be made known publicly. Still another place where this is stated is the passage where the Sadducees, who said there was no resurrection, asked Jesus about the afterlife. Jesus answered: "The children of this world marry, and are given in marriage: But they which shall be accounted worthy to obtain that world, and the resurrection from the dead, neither marry, nor are given in marriage: Neither can they die any more: for they are equal unto the angels; and are the children of God, being the children of the resurrection" (Luke 20:34-36). What does this mean? It means that the Bible should be read with the existence of the next world always in the background of our thoughts. Uchimura believed that the Bible without the next world would become meaningless (*Works*, 23:21): "Blessed are the poor in spirit: for theirs is the kingdom of heaven" (Matt. 5:3). Seen with the eyes of the Almighty, those who are poor in spirit are, on the contrary, blessed. Those who are meek,[3] in contrast to their worldly state, will inherit the earth (23:15). From these statements, we can understand that reading these words in the Bible overturns a reader's sense of values. Since these words are the words of the Almighty, who can see the future, they are of enormous value. In Uchimura's view, they should not be considered simply as part of a sermon, but should be treated as prophecy (23:16).

The next world is also where people are judged by God. The apostle Paul said, "Knowing therefore the terror of the Lord, we persuade men" (2 Cor. 5:11). According to Uchimura, the Bible, especially the New Testa-

---

3. Meek means those who are treated with contempt.

ment, was written by men who were both yearning for and fearfully anticipating the life of the next world. Therefore, those who read it also have to have the same hope and fear.

Uchimura was greatly concerned with the state of Bible study in his own time, which nearly always failed to give proper consideration to the afterlife. Such an idea as God's judgment after death was generally ignored, as Uchimura thought, because people hated the idea. Bible scholars in Uchimura's time emphasized the love of God, but not the judgment of God. They did not accept Paul's words such as "For the wrath of God is revealed from heaven against all ungodliness and unrighteousness of men, who hold the truth in unrighteousness" (Rom. 1:18).

Thus, those who live in the present age offer only superficial cures for people's wounds, and say peace when there is no peace. They believe they will never face God's judgment after death. However, Uchimura did not agree with his contemporaries. He emphasized that we should fear God before learning about his love.

Study of the Bible was a lifeline for Uchimura in order to connect with God and Christ. He could not afford to stop studying the Bible, because by doing so he would lose touch with God and Christ. Tanaka Shōzō (1841-1913), a Japanese environmental activist, one day advised Uchimura to stop concentrating on Bible studies and to devote himself to the social movements that could improve people's lives (29:259).[4] But Uchimura did not accept Tanaka's advice, and said: "I'm not engaged in useless work like hitting the air. Even if there is a social reformer who tells me to give up the Bible, I will not abandon it. In fact, I believe I am engaged in the most powerful social reform. My social reform is fundamental reform. That is to say, it cuts the sin from its root. And the power which is capable of achieving this great work is in this old small book, the Bible" (10:110). The Bible is capable of cleansing individuals in all areas. In particular, it can enter their hearts where human power finds it difficult to enter such areas as affection. And it cleanses their hearts from the bottom, rooting out the evil of human nature. This is the great service that Christianity gives to the world, through its Holy Scripture, the Bible. Uchimura believed that only the Bible was capable of cleansing the world from its foundation. That is to say that by engaging in Bible studies he could contribute to the reforming of the world.

As we have seen, Uchimura studied at Sapporo Agricultural College

---

4. Masaike Megumu thinks that this event happened in or around 1902. See his *Uchimura Kanzō Den* (*The Life of Uchimura Kanzō*) (Tokyo: Kyōbunkan, 1977), 368.

and went on to study at Amherst College in Massachusetts. In Uchimura's time, these schools were located in rural areas or small towns that had easy access to nature. Such rural environments and living conditions, in the present writer's opinion, contributed to forming Uchimura's unique personality.[5] If he had chosen Tokyo instead of Sapporo, Boston or New York instead of Amherst, his subsequent life would have been very different from what it was.

Uchimura advocated *mukyōkai-shugi* (nonchurchism). This principle places emphasis on each individual's conscience and on the study of the Bible. Therefore, for *mukyōkai* Christians, Bible study is especially important.

The characteristic feature of Uchimura's teaching is that he placed great importance on the need for each individual to apply what he learned from the Bible in his actual life. This differs from Uemura Masahisa (1858-1925), a Japanese Presbyterian minister and Christian leader, nearly contemporary with Uchimura. Uemura placed great emphasis on the traditions of the church in his Bible studies.

Further, Uchimura placed great importance on labor. He said that those who do not work by themselves cannot understand the Bible correctly.

Thus, for Uchimura, to understand the Bible we must do more than merely study it. The study of nature, the study of history, individual work, and personal experience of what we learn from the Bible are things we must do to understand the Bible well.

---

5. Ohara Shin also points this out. See Ohara Shin, "Uchimura Kanzō niokeru tennen" ("Uchimura Kanzō and Nature"), *Uchimura Studies,* no. 18 (April 1982): 36.

Uchimura and His *Mukyōkai-Shugi*

SHIBUYA HIROSHI

A Foundation of Uchimura's Ecclesiology

Before addressing Uchimura's view of *ecclesia*, I'd like to offer a short remark or analogy to explain his view. The position of *ecclesia* in the history of salvation could be depicted with two glass disks, one "the kingdom of God," the other "the kingdom of earth." Put one partially on the other, and you will get the shape of a convex lens made by two partially overlapped disks. The *ecclesia* is in this convex-lens zone with everything of the same age and of the same area. How does Uchimura grasp this two-phased ecclesiology?

Uchimura wrote an English book, *Japan and Japanese* (1894), later renamed *Representative Men of Japan* (1908), which he published in German, *Japanische Charakterköpfe*, in 1908. He added a short postscript to the German translation. Though short, it has been read as his main statement of ecclesiological introduction or "the theory of grafting" (so named by Uchimura scholars). In this epilogue, he says,

> This book does not depict me at the present time. It shows the parent stock on which the present I as a Christian was grafted. . . . Before I was chosen as a servant of the Lord Jesus Christ, the work of election has continued for more than two thousand years among my people. . . . It is an error that "Bushidō," or the Japanese ethic, is enough [as the influence that formed Uchimura] and that it is higher and greater than Christianity. . . . It is however an error also to believe that it is possible to raise Abraham's Children from stones by Christianity alone (Matt.

3:9). . . . Even according to Christ's word, if it falls upon stony places, it withers soon. In order that it yields a crop, some one hundredfold, some sixtyfold, some thirtyfold, it must fall on good land. God's blessing must come not only from Heaven but also from the earth. Otherwise the good crop is impossible. The simple and sound common sense refuses a faith that ignores men's earthly part and thinks the heavenly gospel alone is enough for everyone equally. (3:295)

Uchimura's view that "the simple and sound common sense" can understand a multidimensional problem seems too simple; it is too colloquial to call it "sound" for those of us who have been accustomed to more sophisticated terms. Nevertheless, these layman-like and clumsy words do not show his inability to penetrate the riddle of a convex lens composed by God. Rather they suggest that Uchimura grasped the basic structure of ecclesiology.

His theory of grafting has a tendency to relate to nationalism. The earth on which seeds of the Word are sown is a mosaic of nations, all of which have some individuality. In political sociology, a nation is a community of practices. The axis of practices of an ancient nation is religion, while that of a modern nation is language; each nation, however, cannot be maintained by the axis-practice alone. However strong a force language may have, it is a system of practices (including, e.g., "Bushidō" or "the spirit of capitalism," etc.) that binds the clans and the families into a nation. The Uchimurian view of nation agrees, in rough outline, with that nation-practice theory.

Needless to say, however, his thought and logic are focused on that convex-lens-like area, so the practices he means sometimes take the shape of "forms," as in the following:

Here is then a form (form if it be called) of Christ-worship without forms, a wholly unintelligible idea to modern men, but indubitably the true Christian idea. Christ can be, — yea, must be — worshipped without forms, in spirit and truth. . . . For lack of a better name, I call this formless form of Christianity *Mukyōkai-shugi-no-Kirisutokyō*, Christianity of no-church principle. . . . Shintoism, the native religion (for I think it *is* a religion) of the Japanese, has mirrors and white paper as objects of worship. It is the simplest possible religion; and the true Japanese brought up under the influence, is naturally attracted by the religion which had its beginnings in worship of Jehovah who "had voice and no forms." Jehovism, Shintoism, Puritanism and No-Churchism, may be different manifestations of one and the same principle, that God is spirit, and they that worship Him must worship in spirit and truth. (30:193ff.E)[1]

A Way to *Mukyōkai*

We mentioned the spiritual environment in Japan during Uchimura's childhood. Now we discuss how one who grew up in that environment arrived at *mukyōkai-shugi*.

On January 8, 1891, Uchimura wrote a letter to a friend in Sapporo, in which he said, "It makes me *cry* to think that we have been brought to circumstances as we are [in] at present, when one of us must persist in his withdrawal from the church over which we wept and prayed so often. I do not like to give you my *reason* for doing so" (36:329E).

"The church" is the Sapporo Independent Church, which graduates of Sapporo Agricultural College and seniors at the college (Uchimura and his classmates) cooperated to set up; the story of the many hardships they suffered in the process is written in *How I Became a Christian*. In the quotation above, he said he was withdrawing from the church, but he refused to explain why. He may have sent a formal document explaining the reason to the church separately. It was supposed that he was afraid his presence at the First Higher School's ceremony of reception of the imperial rescript might cause, in the worst case, an incident that would hurt the honor of the Sapporo church. His course of action seemed not to have been understood by friends in Sapporo. With the event over, he withdrew from the Sapporo church, and seemed to try to enter the Hongō Congregational Church (named after one of the old wards in Tokyo), the minister of which was Yokoi Tokio, one of Uchimura's intimate friends. This plan, however, failed, because (according to Masaike Jin)[2] the trouble between Uchimura and the Congregational missionaries in Niigata three years earlier created

1. The official view of all the prewar cabinets of the Japanese government regarding Shintoism was that it was not a religion (but a good national practice). By taking this position, the governments could manage to avoid conflict with Article 28 of the former (Meiji) constitution. The article allowed for the freedom of religion.

2. Masaike Jin, *Uchimura Kanzō Den (A Life of Uchimura Kanzō)*, rev. ed. (Tokyo: Kyōbunkan, 1977), 193ff. Masaike's life of Uchimura has been considered the standard introduction to Uchimura studies.

a climate inhospitable to him. *Thus he became a Christian independent of any church, that is,* mukyōkai. "I became Mukyōkai," he wrote in chapter 6 ("When I Was Cast Off by the Christian Church") of his book *Kirisuto-shinto no Nagusame* (*Consolations of a Christian,* 1893). He claimed *Nagusame* was not an autobiography; it was undoubtedly a spiritual autobiography, at the least. In the sentence mentioned above, he used the word *mukyōkai* for the first time, the way that he believed God gave him to walk if he were a Japanese Christian.

Churchless Christians in the Western Countries

Uchimura's career was by no means smooth immediately after his return from America. He was hated both by his compatriots owing to his Christianity and by foreigners owing to his patriotism. Foreign missionaries controlled the Japanese churches; accordingly, he had no choice but to be *mukyōkai.* His occupations in those days were teacher, freelance writer, and journalist. He won national fame especially as an editorial writer for a national newspaper, *Yorozu Chōhō.* When he started evangelism later on, that fame as a journalist certainly contributed to his success.

Before addressing his *mukyōkai* evangelism, however, we must understand the difference between the Japanese *mukyōkai* Christianity and Western churchless Christianity. The Japanese *mu* (= non) *kyōkai* (= church) simply corresponds to an English word, "churchless," at least according to a Japanese-English dictionary. Wolfhart Pannenberg gives us a valuable hint as to the difference between the two, however. "From time to time Christians are shocked by reports in the secular press about the decline in church attendance. . . . Only 15 percent of West German Protestants regularly attend Sunday worship, and at present in the major cities only 25 percent of the Catholics go to church every Sunday."[3]

According to Pannenberg, churchless Christians whom we see everywhere today originated in the Western denominational quarrels of the sixteenth and seventeenth centuries. They are special products of the modern age. They have an ambivalent relationship to denominational Christianity.

---

3. Wolfhart Pannenberg, *The Church,* trans. Keith Crim (Philadelphia: Westminster, 1983), 9. If the theme of this chapter were *mukyōkai* itself, comparative research between *mukyōkai* and the British Fellowship movement (and perhaps the German *Gemeinschaft* movement) should be cited, since the latter two seem to carry the traditions of medieval and early modern European Christianity on their backs.

On the one hand, they "[are] unable to regard as believable the exclusive claims of the opposing denominations that each embodies the Church of Christ," but on the other hand, even Christians outside the church "still have their children baptized and confirmed, plan church weddings, and expect Christian burial, as well as bear the burden of paying their church taxes." In short, churchless Christians have converted from the traditional Christianity of communities to an individualistic Christianity that aims at the world community; yet, in spite of conversion, they still cannot sever their ties to traditional denominations. These are the Western churchless Christians' origins and problems according to Pannenberg. Has Uchimura's *mukyōkai* Christian the same origins and problems? I think the answer has been half given, but it must be fully explained.

Publishing *Seisho no Kenkyū*

The five years from 1891 to 1895 were perhaps the worst period in Uchimura's life. After coming out of the tunnel, Uchimura found himself famous as a popular editorial writer for a national newspaper. Soon he resigned from his full-time position to start his own organ of public opinion, *Tokyo Dokuritsu Zasshi (The Tokyo Independent Magazine)*. He edited this bimonthly (later on, trimonthly) review while overseeing about five full-time writers. It is very difficult to decide whether they could be called Christians or not, while it may safely be said that those rank-and-file writers were modern self-property individualists (who thought themselves their own private property that they could keep or kill of their own free will). A misunderstanding arose between them and the chief editor Uchimura, the root of which must have been their differing views of individualism. *Tokyo Dokuritsu Zasshi* was discontinued in July 1900, though the magazine was selling as well as usual.

At the end of September, Uchimura at last put into practice a plan he had dreamed up while studying at Amherst — a plan to publish a magazine, *Seisho no Kenkyū (The Biblical Study)*, by himself. On the opening page of the first issue of the magazine, he wrote the *Sengen* (declaration). "*Seisho no Kenkyū* is *Tokyo Dokuritsu Zasshi's* junior. The latter rose up to kill; the former was born to spare. That brandished his sword to wound; this is to give medicine to cure. To blame was the duty of that, and this wants comforting as vocation. Righteousness is to kill; Love is to keep alive. It is a proper order for propagation of Love to follow after that of righteousness. *Seisho no Kenkyū* just starts according to this or-der" (8:282).

The reverberations of *Tokyo Dokuritsu Zasshi* did not quickly fade. In spite of *Dokuritsu's* disappearance, the summer school *(Kaki Kōdankai)* scheduled for its readers took place from July 24 to August 3 at Tsunohazu, a village in the western suburbs of Tokyo. About eighty youths gathered; most of them came from the countryside, where they supported them-selves and their families with hard labor. Although a good number at-tended, their study under Uchimura typically would continue for only a few years. After the summer school, Uchimura pledged the publication of the first issue of *Seisho no Kenkyū*, which he fulfilled on September 30 in spite of many obstacles. One remaining problem was how to take care of the persons who followed him from the *Dokuritsu Zasshi* period onward. They were mostly serious and honest, but not Christian young men. If he was to teach his thought further, he had to preach to them the source of his thought, that is, the Christian gospel.

Once the publication of *Seisho no Kenkyū* began to run smoothly, he at last directed his attention to his followers, which took the form of issuing a new, small eight-page monthly, *Mukyōkai*, in March 1901. At the inaugura-tion of the short-lived magazine's publication (the last issue was in August 1902), Uchimura explained *Mukyōkai:*

> If they hear about *Mukyōkai*, they may think this is a tract of anarchists or of nihilists. This is, however, by no means such a thing. *Mukyōkai* is a church of churchless people, that is, as it were, a camp of homeless peo-ple, namely a spiritual foster care house or a spiritual orphanage. . . . What and where is our church in this world? It is the universe and na-ture that God has made. The fact is that *Mukyōkai* [churchlessness] is just *Yūkyōkai* [churchfullness]. Those who have no church indeed have the best church. (9:71)

Uchimura's paradoxical comprehension of *mukyōkai* (*"Mukyōkai* is just *Yūkyōkai"*) appeared at the same time that he first used the word *mukyōkai* in *Consolations of a Christian* (2:36), in 1893. These sketches of mental and natural beatitudes may recall a scene in the young Uchimura's life: his lonely, tearful prayer of praise for the discovery of an egg cell of ab-alone, at the top of Mount Akaiwa near the marine laboratory (1:15; 16:199). Especially for the young Uchimura, one of his firm convictions was that the tripod of God's revelation consisted of nature, history, and the

Bible (36:247E). The cause of deep gratitude was the thought that God opened for Uchimura one of the narrow ways to his mysterious Truth.

The thought of Christ and him alone surrounded by great nature creates a church set in his imagination not only by means of his poetry, but also with help from the new theological sense of those days. In other words, he had a room in his mind for realizing his responsibility to his followers, whom an evangelist would need to introduce to Christianity.

In the *Mukyōkai* issue of February 5, 1902, "A Notice" appeared under the name of "Tsunohazu Seisho Kenkyūkai." It stated that "the editing and accounting will be left to Tsunohazu Seisho Kenkyūkai (the members were remnants of the Kaki Kōdankai) from the next issue on." But the chief editor would remain Mr. Uchimura, the notice read. The important point here is that a *mukyōkai* fellowship was born among Uchimura's followers. He at last allowed the remnants to join his Sunday school, the name of which was changed to *Tsunohazu Seisho Kenkyūkai (The Biblical Study Society)*. He used "Bible class" as the translation of *Seisho Kenkyūkai*, for reasons that are not clear.

Church Problems

Uchimura could not but become *mukyōkai*, left out both by the Sapporo Independent Church and by the Japan Congregational Church. Things appeared to flow in that direction, but he interpreted it as divine providence that he should refrain from entering a church until the church proper for Japan would be given by God. This interpretation was, of course, in keeping with the theory of grafting mentioned above. The *Seisho no Kenkyū* March 1904 issue carried Uchimura's essay "Kyōkai Mondai" ("Church Problems"). He wrote,

> As you know, *churches on the earth, different from the ideal Church in Heaven, have historical qualities.* The Roman Catholic Church rose because of fitting into the surroundings of the European Middle Ages; and the Calvinistic Presbyterian Church stood constrained by the thoughts and social necessities of the 16th century. . . . Therefore, if there is a church in 20th century Japan, it should neither be the Catholic Church which arose in Europe 15 or 16 centuries ago, nor be the Methodist Church which did in England three hundred years ago. *It should be the church that rises naturally without foreign interference, as the result of today's Japanese be-*

lievers heartily receiving the Christian truth and deeply appreciating the grace of God's salvation. However eager we may be, we cannot have an Englishman's or an American's flesh make us: so however eager we may be, we cannot have the churches made by them make ours. (12:109)

A hypothetical debate follows:

Q. [A young church believer.] Then do you say that all today's churches are quite unnecessary?

A. [Uchimura.] Of course not. Anyone with common sense dare not say that today's churches built with good will, do nothing but evil things. It is, however, a historically well-known fact that a church out of its native country is not long successful. (12:109)

And on the "ceremonies," he said, "Any apostate priest or any priest with a magical way about him can take charge of even the solemnest ceremonies as an officiating priest. Nothing is more corruptible than religious ceremonies. And as sometimes it has been necessary to burn off houses contaminated by germs, so sometimes in the history of human progress it has been necessary to destroy church systems contaminated by corruption. And the prophets have been the destroyers of such systems" (12:108).

Then the questioner (again angrily?) asked Uchimura,

Q. If the church is such a bad thing, why does God allow it to be, when there has been no time in which there has been no church since Christianity was born?

A. You're right. God, however, allows the existence of a church (visible) on condition that *it should not be elevated to greatest importance by the believers' evaluation.* A church is not a source but a result. Not faith owing to church, but church owing to faith. God allows the existence of a church while it is a manifestation of faith. When it falls to a forger or pretender of faith, a church loses its reason for being and is destroyed by the prophets. (12:108)

The author then returns to the beginning of these questions and presents the theory of grafting, the last part of which (i.e., the theory of danger of transplantation of the church from its home country to a foreign country) wants more evidential demonstration. Near the end of the dialogue on this theme, we meet with these words:

Q. Then are you planning to remain a Mukyōkai believer permanently?

A. Yes, I am planning to remain as I am, until such a church as accepts my free faith appears. But as I said already, the faith will speak out itself sooner or later. Faith at last makes church while the latter does not make the former. If there is agreement of faith, there is no reason why a church of agreement will not come out at last. And I hope now that if an agreement of faith has already existed, the church of agreement will at last appear without fail. (12:121)

Uchimura's Evangelicalism

The *Tokyo Asahi Shimbun* (May 30, 1919),[4] a national newspaper popular then and now, reported an interview with Uchimura, in which he said,

At first I'd like to explain my standpoint, in order to make clear my principle. The gist of my religion is evangelical Christianity, which is quite contrary to the rational and critical belief of Mr. Ebina & Co. Indeed the rational point of view is popular among the Japanese, but belief is nothing but to believe and never to quibble. I don't hope for foreigners' help as churchmen do nowadays. I have never received it until today. They are pleased that I am an evangelicalist. But I am a patriot and think Christianity in Japan should be Christianity digested by the Japanese.[5]

---

4. Ishihara Hyōei, *Mijika-ni-Sesshita Uchimura Kanzō (My Memoirs of Uchimura Kanzō as His Secretary)*, vol. 2 (Tokyo: Yamamoto Shoten, 1972). See the photo album at the beginning of the volume.

5. Uchimura wrote in the letter to David C. Bell dated September 17, 1907, "I thank you very much for your good letter of Aug. 16, which reached two days ago. It was a veritable evangel to me, recalling to my spirit, not only your old friendship for me, but *my old evangelical Christian faith* also. . . . The best thing is in our old, old faith — faith in miracle and God's gracious providence" (37:188E, emphasis mine). The expression following "The best thing is . . ." is Uchimura's favorite way of reminiscing about his good old days. Both the *Asahi Shimbun* interview and the letter to Bell rather obviously indicate his evangelicalism. Because his lectures (he did not use the word "preaching") on the Bible appearing in *Seiken* were printed with the old prewar letters and in the old-fashioned style, his readers in the twenty-first century often get the impression that his lectures are not so easy to read through. But if you immerse yourself in the literature of the Meiji-Taishō era, you will see that his biblical explanations, using parables, examples, current affairs, and so on, are in-

Uchimura's talk quoted above seems well summarized, and though he must have read the newspaper routinely, he wrote no complaint about it. These words, then, have no small meaning, especially for historical theology, as he has applied a historical theological term, namely, "evangelicalism," to *mukyōkai*. Since the meaning of "evangelicalism" is, though, not quite the same as *mukyōkai*, understood internationally, the relation between this term and *mukyōkai* should be studied a little more. First of all, Uchimura mentioned only one word, "evangelicalism," to which he added almost no explanation. So we must look for a commentator of the word in place of Uchimura; an evangelical theologian, Alister McGrath, is most suitable for the role.

In his book *The Future of Christianity*,[6] McGrath borrowed the approach of D. Bebbington to evangelicalism, which, it is said, possesses four distinctive hallmarks:

1. *Conversionism:* the belief that lives need to be changed through the personal appropriation of faith.
2. *Activism:* the actualization of Christian faith in life, particularly in evangelism (the preaching of the gospel to others) and other forms of Christian activity.
3. *Biblicism:* a focus on the Bible as the most fundamental resource for Christian life and thought. Bible study is often at the heart of evangelical spiritual life, both individual and corporate.
4. *Crucicentrism:* a focus on the cross of Christ and the benefits this brings to humanity.

What impressions can we get if we consider these *hallmarks* with reference to Uchimura's life? These impressions may be a starting point for understanding *mukyōkai*.

Uchimura had a deep experience of conversion. He did not, however, demand conversion experience from his *deshi*. "Then, when you come to

---

tended to make you understand with ease, in one way or another. This method of lecturing, too, may be to some extent close to evangelicalism.

Mr. Ebina was Ebina Danjō (1856-1937), who was, in 1919, minister of the Hongō Congregational Church (a leading large church in Tokyo; Yokoi Tokio, an intimate friend of Uchimura, had once been minister there). Ebina attracted intellectuals and students with his new theology so he and Uchimura were sharply opposed to each other especially during the so-called Second Coming Movement.

6. Alister E. McGrath, *The Future of Christianity* (Oxford: Blackwell, 2002), 111.

us," he advised foreign missionaries, "come with strong common sense. Do not believe the words of those mission-circus men who tell you that a nation can be converted in a day" (3:159E). This advice suggests Uchimura's distrust of mass evangelism and mass conversion. Nevertheless, owing to his moving description of his own conversion, genuine experiences of conversion took place in *mukyōkai* fellowships.

As for activism, Uchimura held in high regard the actualization of Christian faith in life. But the life in which faith was to be actualized was just everyday life and not "particularly in evangelism." Uchimura was not necessarily very earnest in evangelism. He deplored the type of evangelism that aimed to develop the influence of the evangelist's own church or sect or denomination.

In one passage of "Church Problems," a fictitious young church believer asks, "Then what do you think the church of today must do?" Uchimura answers, "Preach Christ's salvation and not preach church. Leave church to God and believers; and don't recommend particular churches actively to a believer whose faith is yet shallow, saying 'enter such and such a church' or 'such and such a church is the best biblical church'" (12:112f.).

Uchimura's cherished opinion is "Be not more active to develop church's influence than to develop Christ's influence." Meanwhile, McGrath declares, "Evangelicalism refuses to allow any matter of church government to take precedence over the gospel itself; the term *evangelical,* by placing emphasis on this gospel, conveys both the focus and the substance of the movement. All else is deliberately subordinated, as a matter of principle, to this central theme."[7] Put more technically, "One of the most distinctive features of evangelicalism is thus that it is *nondenominational* (or better, *transdenominational* . . .)."[8] Thus, in "the most distinctive features," Uchimura's *mukyōkai* agrees with evangelicalism.

The final two of the four hallmarks of evangelicalism, namely, biblicism and crucicentrism, were also Uchimura's hallmarks, as explained elsewhere in this book. It is therefore our understanding that *mukyōkai* and evangelicalism have a strong relationship. I will return to this understanding later.

---

7. Alister E. McGrath, *Evangelicalism and the Future of Christianity* (Downers Grove, Ill.: InterVarsity, 1995), 23.

8. McGrath, *Evangelicalism,* 79.

Tsunohazu Seisho Kenkyūkai

By February 1902, Uchimura established Tsunohazu Seisho Kenkyūkai. A photo of society members taken after the lecture in front of his house survives, and shows forty-three members, including him and his wife (thirty-eight men; five women). Young men predominated, and among them are seventeen students with school caps or uniforms. There are likely more students there. If a person of samurai origin were to set up Seisho Kenkyūkai outside of a church, he probably could not help but select a *kangaku-juku* as a model. *Kangaku* is the study of Chinese classics (of Confucianism, mainly); *juku* means a small private school. Uchimura said,

> In East Asia, there was a person who was called *jusha* (who studied Confucianism and lived according to it). . . . He is a kind of samurai, a person who stands supported by morality. He is a teacher of people, so is free and independent. . . . We, as *sanctified Jusha*, should follow Jinsai and Tōju, bear poverty well in fortitude and independence, not visit the mansion of millionaires, not borrow the help of a person of power, not make believers by our own power but await people coming to us to learn our faith. In this way, we should show the glory of God, keeping dignity as samurai. (21:345)[9]

Indeed, Uchimura's formal model for Seisho Kenkyūkai was a revival of *kangaku-juku*, one of which he had attended while very young in Takasaki. Generally speaking, the discipline of *juku* was so rigorous that in one of the most famous *juku* (Yamazaki Ansai's *juku*), his disciples used to feel as if they had been revived when they came out of the master's house after one day's lesson ended. Of course, it is a gross exaggeration to say that the *deshi* (disciple or follower) felt frightened to death while Uchimura was relating the gospel of life in the classroom. He was aware that he was speaking not of cheap grace but of the costly grace of Christ's blood, and this awareness was accompanied by a grave seriousness that kept the *deshi* in awe. After the end of World War II, not a few of Uchimura's *deshi* continued in active evangelical service according to his way of teaching the Bi-

9. Jinsai, mentioned here, is Itō Jinsai (1627-1705). He tried to found his interpretation of Confucian classics not in the culture of the seventeenth century but in that of Confucius's own world, that is, on the principle "learn the Bible by the Bible." Tōju, mentioned in the quotation, is Nakae Tōju (1608-48). His short, critical biography is included in Uchimura's *Representative Men of Japan* (3:249E).

ble. I have been given some opportunities to see them in action, so I think I could guess why and how young *deshi* in Seisho Kenkyūkai felt in awe of him. The power of an evangelist's charisma is one reason for this. Another reason is more matter of fact: a teacher's own scholarship. In summation, Uchimura's Seisho Kenkyūkai had set up a *sensei-deshi* relationship as its visible or religio-sociological system. Uchimura explains a *sensei's* status toward the end of the Tokugawa era (during his boyhood) as follows: "No less weighty [than his lord] was to be the youth's consideration for his master (his intellectual and moral preceptor), who was to him no mere school-teacher or college professor or *quid pro quo* principal, but a veritable didaskalos, in whom he could and must completely confide the care of his body and soul" (3:10E). *Sensei* was the honorific title of such a master, and Uchimura brought such an ethical atmosphere (ethos) into his *kenkyūkai*.

Kashiwagi Seisho Kenkyūkai

Uchimura moved from Tsunohazu to Kashiwagi, a town not far away, in November 1907. A change of residence does not cause a change of ecclesiology, of course. With the passage of time, however, men's thoughts will fluctuate.

During this period (i.e., the last period in his life), Uchimura's ecclesiological essays can be roughly divided into two groups: one group is formed by the "absolutely" negative theory, which declares the failure of all existing churches as a historical necessity because of their basic misunderstanding of the Christian truths; the other group's common core is the "relatively" negative theory that asserts the failure of the American and European missionaries in Japan because of "the historically well-known fact that a church out of its native country has not long been successful as a church" (12:121). The latter theory leads to the theory of grafting and recalls the cherished view of his younger days (3:124E; see introduction above). "Japan's Best," which appeared in the first issue of the *Japan Christian Intelligencer* (29:422), belongs to the system of the latter theory, too. Further, it was an important essay owing to the worldly historical situation in which it was published. Until then, the "absolutely" negative theory seemed to "tighten a screw" on the *mukyōkai* spirit of the *deshi;* that is to say, relativism and absolutism had not been on the same ring. I'd like to highlight one more pair in Uchimura's ecclesiology at this time, according to a comparison of the social organizations of fellowships. The pair consists of *juku*-type and home-type (which has no articulated *sensei-deshi* relation, but has a system of division of labor among the members). In Uchimura's later years he showed a trend away from the *juku*-type. Nowadays, in the twenty-first century, it has become more and more difficult for us to find *juku*-type *mukyōkai* fellowship.

Conclusion

The theory of grafting has to be put at the forefront of Uchimura's ecclesiology. Since the seeds of the Word were sown on Japanese spiritual soil, the church that has grown on that soil "should be the church that rises naturally without foreign interference" (12:109). Nationalism also contributed to this view that spiritual and religious independence were necessary for Japan. His nationalism had been expressed in a short poem written on the title page of a worn Bible that might have been used during his stay in the United States: "I for Japan; / Japan for the World; / The World for Christ; / And All for God." (To these main lines, he attached an annotation, "To be Inscribed upon my Tomb" [40:3].) This epitaph (actually inscribed upon his tomb) might be a variation of Bunsen's aphorism, "The individual for the nation, the nation for Humanity, Humanity for God" (7:485E). Uchimura cleverly converted a free-theological short poem into orthodoxy. His epitaph has been well known as the core of his thought. In the *Japan Christian Intelligencer*, a prose poem, "Two J's" (30:53E), is rather better known for the same significance as the epitaph. The poem ends thus:

> O Jesus, thou art the Sun of my soul, the saviour dear;
> > I have given my all to thee!
> O Japan,
>
> > "Land of lands, for thee we give,
> > Our hearts, our pray'rs, our service free;
> > For thee thy sons shall nobly live.
> > And at thy need shall die for thee."
>
> > > > > > J. G. Whittier

At its end, the last part of Whittier's "Our Country" is quoted. Uchimura perhaps hoped that American readers would understand that his patriotism was the same as that of the best Americans. For him, every Christian should by fair means protect the prosperity of the nation that has been assigned to him or her by God. The pursuit of national prosperity by fair means was Uchimura's nationalism, and *he* believed it at the same time that it was an internationally common belief.

We conclude our chapter by revisiting a "theory" that forms the base of the theory of grafting, the theory of a convex-lens-shaped zone, the name of which was invented not by Uchimura but by me. The theory is not necessarily commonplace because it means that ecclesiology has two approaches at once in this age. On the one hand, the *ecclesia* has received from Jesus the order, "Go ye therefore, and teach all nations . . . : Teaching them to observe all things whatsoever I have commanded you" (Matt. 28:19-20). On the other hand, the *ecclesia* must be constructed with human beings who are called Christians (its material), who are as weak and as likely to stumble as any people in the world. In this sense, two studies are necessary to understand it; one concerns the Lord's order, namely, theology, and the other concerns human material, that is, anthropology, especially sociology of religion.

It is a further hypothesis for us to call *mukyōkai* a kind of evangelicalism. McGrath shows the homogeneity of evangelicalism by enumerating its common characteristics. If we follow Uchimura's way of believing, namely, his characteristic spiritualism that is not gnosticism but Pauline thought of the revelation of the Spirit (1 Cor. 2:10-12) (30:192), we set aside denominationalism. He says, however, that even if his denomination-free evangelicalism has national traits, its connection to the theory of grafting perhaps needs a carefully systematized review. But at least "Japanese evangelicalism," or *mukyōkai-shugi*, during Uchimura's lifetime, can be said to have some national aspect. *Mukyōkai's* national aspect is Christianity received in the Bushidō spirit. What is Bushidō? To this question, there have been many answers according to era, person, and happenstance. Uchimura's answer is that the Bushidō spirit means the drastic pursuit of righteousness. He finds this spirit in the life and death of Saigō Takamori, who appears in one of Uchimura's early works, *Representative Men of Japan* (31:253E). Uchimura certainly believes Saigō's motto of righteousness, "Loyalty to Heaven; Love to Humanity," in light of the phrase "I desired mercy, and not sacrifice" (Hos. 6:6). *Mukyōkai*, as Japanese evangelicalism, took form at Uchimura's pace, as he alone could be called a *mukyōkai* thinker, at least during his lifetime. After his death, especially after the end of World War II, *mukyōkai's* aspects began slowly changing; it has been a long time since *mukyōkai* lost its nationalistic color, and that was one important factor for *mukyōkai* to be *mukyōkai*. Some used to hold the view that *mukyōkai* should be a *mukyōkai* with social justice orientation; that said, some *mukyōkaiites* and their advocacy of social justice sometimes approached the level of socialist thought. Their voices have become smaller now than in the previous century, but the range of their social critique has grown ever wider. That they gain in breadth is perfectly acceptable as long as they do not lose insight into the theological truth in the depths beneath the visible surface.

Uchimura's View of the Atonement in *Kyūanroku*
(The Search for Peace)

LEE KYOUNGAE

The Background of *Kyūanroku* and Its Aim

Uchimura Kanzō wrote to Bell, an American friend, to inform him that he had finished writing his book in spring 1893. It was published with the title *Kyūanroku (The Search for Peace)* in August of the same year.[1] The book is the first-person record of Uchimura's search for peace. He had an extremely strong conviction of sin and made an effort to escape from it and thereby find inner peace.

Kyūanroku, however, had another aim. Uchimura wanted to make clear "what Christianity is." With the U.S.–Japan Treaty of Amity and Commerce signed in 1858, and the seclusion policy and the Christian persecution policy ended accordingly, Protestant missionaries went to Japan for the first time. Thus, the modern thoughts of Europe and America were introduced to Japan. This was especially true when *Kyūanroku* was published, for it was thirty-five years after the treaty was signed, and new theologies had gained power in Japanese Christianity. Uchimura wanted to make clear "what Christianity is" from an orthodox position.[2] First, I would like to survey the situation of Japanese Christianity in the days when *Kyūanroku* was published.

Missionary W. Spinner, belonging to the Allgemeiner Evangelisch Pro-

---

1. *Kyūanroku* was published by Keiseisha in Tokyo. It was reprinted in 1896, with a third edition in 1899; the fifteenth edition was issued in 1919.

2. Uchimura's orthodox position here means the Reformation orthodoxy, not the Greek or Russian Orthodoxy or Catholic orthodoxy.

testantischer Missions-verein, visited Japan in 1885. Because of his mission work, Fukyū Fukuin Kyōkai (Spread Evangelical Church) and Shinkyō Shingakkō (Protestant Theological Seminary)[3] were established in Tokyo, in 1887. Their stance was based on liberal theology and historicism, which was ascendant in Europe in the late nineteenth century. Minami Hajime and Maruyama Michikazu were baptized by W. Spinner, who also published the monthly paper *Shinri (Truth)*.[4]

In addition, in those days a large influence on the Japanese Christian world came from the teachings of missionaries dispatched by the Association of American Unitarianism. The politician and novelist Yano Fumio[5] submitted an essay, "The Point of the Unitarian Christian" (May 1887), to the *Yūbin Hōchi Shinbun (Post Report Newspaper)*. He often introduced Unitarianism in the newspaper, and suggested that the Japanese should adopt Unitarianism as the state religion, because it would be a very suitable religion for Japanese society. With the assistance of Yano and the Enlightenment thinker Fukuzawa Yukichi,[6] Unitarian missionary Arthur M. Knapp first visited Japan in 1887. Two years later, C. Maccauley came to Japan. He published the monthly paper *Unitarian* in 1890.[7] The next year he started Tokyo Liberal Theological College, at which the prominent philosopher Ōnishi Hajime taught.

The above-mentioned liberal theology and Unitarianism came to be called *Shin-shingaku* (the new theology) in Japan. *Shin-shingaku* caused quite a ripple in Japanese Christianity during 1890-91. This new theology was particularly well received by the Kumamoto Band, that is, the members of the Congregational Church from Dōshisha Ei-gakkō (Doshisha English School),[8] which was founded by Niijima Jō in 1875. Major exponents included Kanamori Michitomo and Yokoi Tokio. Kanamori was the first clergyman of the Congregational Church in Okayama Prefecture, and

3. Its German appellation is Protestantisch-Theologische Akademie.

4. *Shinri* was published from 1889 to 1900. Yamaji Aizan said that "*Shinri* is a terrible revolutionary spark which will shake the basis of the orthodox faith." Sumida Mikio, *Tokutomi Sohō, Yamaji Aizan* (Tokyo: Chūōkōronsha, 1984), 403.

5. Unitarianism was first introduced in Japan by Yano Fumio.

6. Fukuzawa Yukichi established Keiō Gijuku University, also founded *Jijishinpō (The Current Newspaper)* in 1882, and wrote numerous books.

7. *Unitarian* was published by Yūichisha (Unitarian Association of Japan), and it was reissued under the new title of *Shūkyō (Religion)* in 1891.

8. They became Christians at Kumamoto Yō-gakkō (Kumamoto English School) in Kumamoto in 1876, and then were transferred to Dōshisha Ei-gakkō (Doshisha English School) in Kyoto in the same year.

he served as principal of Doshisha. He was at the vanguard of the new theology and published a book, *Nihon Genkon no Kirisuto-kyō narabini Shōrai no Kirisuto-kyō (Present and Future Christianity in Japan)* in 1891, which had a great influence on the world of Japanese Christianity.[9] Yokoi was a clergyman of the Hongō Church, which was a Congregational church in Tokyo. He was also an editor of *Rikugō Zasshi (Cosmos Magazine)*[10] and published many articles in the magazine from the position of this new theology, including "A Confession of My Faith" in 1891.[11]

Uchimura read Yokoi's article and immediately contributed an identically titled article, "A Confession of My Faith," to the same magazine. He wrote, "Yokoi, who was a friend of mine, announced 'A Confession of My Faith.' . . . I would like to write 'A Confession of My Faith' like him" (1:209). Uchimura defended the divinity of Jesus Christ, the Trinity, original sin, and the atonement of Christ. Yokoi had denied all these doctrines and clarified his own claims to legitimate faith. *Shūkyō (Religion)*, which was a bulletin of the Japan Unitarian Church, "[struck] a defamatory blow" against Uchimura's confession of faith (1:233). And Uchimura immediately submitted a paper, "Reading *Shūkyō's* Criticism on the Confession of Faith," to *Kirisuto-kyō Shinbun (Christianity Newspaper)*,[12] responding to the criticism.

Uemura Masahisa had an orthodox faith like Uchimura's. He published a magazine, *Nihon Hyōron (Japan Critique)*, and a weekly periodical, *Fukuin Shūhō (Weekly Gospel)*. In these magazines Uemura tried to defend his Christianity and also opposed the new theology.[13]

9. *Nihon Genkon no Kirisuto-kyō narabini Shōrai no Kirisuto-kyō* (Tokyo: Shūeisha, 1891). The following year, Kanamori resigned his position with the Congregational Church, and entered a political party.

10. *Rikugō Zasshi* was founded in 1880 as the Christian general magazine.

11. This article was published in no. 130 of the magazine. Cf. Yokoi Tokio, "Nihon Shōrai no Kirisuto-kyō" ("The Future of Japanese Christianity"), *Rikugō Zasshi*, no. 114 (June 1890). See also, in the same magazine, "Genkon Honpō niokeru Kirisuto-kyō no Jōtai 1, 2" ("The Recent State of Christianity in Our Country 1, 2"), nos. 134, 135 (February, March 1892); "Kirisuto-kyō no Sōgōteki Tokusei" ("The Synthetic Characteristic of Christianity"), no. 146 (February 1893); "Kirisuto-kyō towa Hatashite Nanzoya?" ("What Is Christianity?"), no. 153 (September 1893); "Shin-shingaku no Kensetsu" ("The Construction of a New Theology"), no. 163 (July 1894); *Wagahō no Kirisuto-kyō Mondai (The Christian Problem in Our Country)* (Tokyo: Keiseisha, 1894).

12. The article ran in *Kirisuto-kyō Shinbun*, no. 438 (December 1891).

13. Cf. Uemura Masahisa, "Shingaku-jō no Haran" ("Theological Trouble"), *Fukuin Shūhō*, nos. 8, 9, 11 (May 1890); "Shingaku-jō no Funsō" ("Theological Dispute"), *Fukuin Shūhō*, no. 18 (July 1891); "Nihon Genkon no Kirisuto-kyō narabini Shōrai no Kirisuto-kyō" ("Present and Future Christianity in Japan"), *Nihon Hyōron*, nos. 33, 34 (July, August 1891).

These controversies between the orthodox theology and the *Shin-shingaku* were called "the new theology problem" in the 1890s. Japanese essayist Yamaji Aizan pointed out that Uemura and Uchimura possessed orthodox faith, but they did not argue with the *Shin-shingaku* directly.[14] I think Aizan's criticism is faulty. *Kyūanroku* was written and published as an argument against those who claimed the new theology, namely, *Shin-shingaku*. Uchimura tried to clarify the atonement of Christ, which they denied, while citing the faith of Luther and Cromwell to effectively develop his theory of atonement. *Kyūanroku* was the first book in Japan written against the new theology that predominated in the 1890s.[15] This book is one of Uchimura's essential works, along with *Kirisutoshinto no Nagusame (Consolations of a Christian)* (February 1893) and *How I Became a Christian* (May 1895).[16] These books have had a great impact on modern Japan.

Uchimura's Experience of the Atonement

The background of *Kyūanroku* contains Uchimura's experience of the atonement of Christ at Amherst College. Therefore, before discussing the contents of *Kyūanroku*, we will look back on that experience through his autobiography, *How I Became a Christian*.

Uchimura suffered from a conviction of sin from his early days, even before his conversion to Christianity. This conviction of sin influenced him more and more once he converted to Christianity. He wrote of it as follows: "I described in myself an empty space which neither activity in religious works, nor success in scientific experiments, could fill. What the exact nature of that emptiness was, I was not able to discern. . . . At all events, a vacuum there was, and it must be filled *somehow* with *something*. I thought *something* there was in this vague universe which could make me feel happy and contented; but I had no idea whatever of what that something was" (3:67E). He also confessed the following in a diary entry (April

---

14. Sumida, *Tokutomi Sohō, Yamaji Aizan*, 404-5.

15. Uemura Masahisa published *Shinri Ippan (A Fragment of Truth)* in 1884, *Fukuin Michi Shirube (The Way for the Gospel)* in 1885. In his books, he tried to defend Christianity against the theory of evolution and the social evolutionary theory of Herbert Spencer that were prevalent among many Japanese intellectuals, and greatly influenced Japanese society at the time. When these books were published, however, "the new theology problem" was not yet an issue in Japan.

16. *How I Became a Christian* was written in November 1893 (36:385).

22, 1883): "Repented my past sins deeply, and felt my total inability to save myself by my own efforts" (3:68E).

Uchimura went to the United States with the sense of vacuum *(shinkū)* in his heart open to repentance of sins.[17] He worked as an attendant at the Pennsylvania Training School for Feeble-Minded Children[18] at Elwyn, in order to study a charitable undertaking. During that period, he recorded the following state of mind in his diary:

> Conception of God is perfectly clear till we come to Christ. Here all stumble. I often think how clear a view must I have with regard to my God had there been no Christ.
>
> Christ a stumbling block, not only to the heathen Greeks of old, but to the heathen Japanese, Chinese, and all other heathens of this very day. The Unitarian explanation of him is too simple for the mystic Oriental, but the Trinitarian "theory" is no less unbelievable. Who shall roll away the stone for me? (3:106E)

It is clear that Uchimura was openly perplexed as to how he should interpret Christ. Along the way, Uchimura entered Amherst College and met Dr. Julius H. Seelye, who was the president of the college. Uchimura wrote about him as follows:

> But none influenced and changed me more than the worthy President himself. . . . That God is our Father, who is more zealous of His love over us than we of Him; . . . that our real mistakes lay in our very efforts to be pure when none but God Himself could make us pure; that selfishness is really hatred of self, for he that really loves himself should first hate himself and give himself for others; etc., etc.; — these and other precious lessons the good President taught me by his words and deeds. (3:113-14E)

The teachings of Seelye led Uchimura in this way, and he wrote of a decisive experience in his diary entry of March 8, 1886: "[This is a] very important day in my life. Never was the atoning power of Christ more clearly revealed to me than it is to-day. In the crucifixion of the Son of God lies

17. Uchimura wrote, "But the search after personal satisfaction was not the only motive that impelled me to take this bold step. . . . *To be a* MAN *first, and then a* PATRIOT, *was my aim in going abroad*" (3:77E).

18. The superintendent of the school and his wife were faithful Unitarians (3:96E).

the solution of all the difficulties that buffeted my mind thus far. Christ paying all my debts, can bring me back to the purity and innocence of the first man before the Fall. Now I am God's child, and my duty is to believe Jesus" (3:117E).

This description evokes a famous sentence from the core of Paul's epistle to the Romans: "Whom God hath set forth *to be* a propitiation through faith in his blood, to declare his righteousness for the remission of sins that are past, through the forbearance of God" (3:25).

The experience of March 8 was an experience of the vicarious atonement; Uchimura wrote that "Christ paid all my debts." Uchimura continued:

> You say that "it stands against reason" that faith in a dead Saviour should give a man life. I do not argue with you then. Perhaps a thing like "the responsible soul before the Almighty God" has never troubled you much. Your ambition may not extend beyond this short span of existence called Life, and *your* Almighty Judge may be that conventional thing called Society, whose "good enough" may give you all the peace you need. Yes, the crucified Saviour is necessary only to him or her who has eternity to hope for, and the Spirit of the Universe to judge his or her inmost heart. To such the religion of Luther and Cromwell and Bunyan is *not* a tradition, but the verity of all verities. (3:118E)

Since studying at Sapporo Agricultural College, Uchimura had possessed the idea of "God Almighty," the idea that God created the world and rules over it through natural law. God also gave laws to human beings, and punishes those who break them. Under this concept of God, Uchimura suffered a sense of guilt. After the experience of atonement, Uchimura represented himself and God as "the responsible soul before the Almighty God" or "the Spirit of the Universe to judge the inmost heart." Here it seems that Uchimura's sense of guilt grew even deeper.

The Principle of Sin and Atonement Faith — Paradise Exile and Paradise Recovery

The Sin of Adam and Eve: Exile from Paradise

Kyūanroku consists of part 1 and part 2, and the subject is the basic issue of "sin and liberation from sin." Part 1 mentions Uchimura's own trials attempting to escape from sins. The core parts of *Kyūanroku*, however, are the chapters "The Principle of Sin," "Paradise Regained," and "Philosophical Principles of the Atonement" in part 2. These chapters will now be considered in detail.

From the first, Uchimura distinguished "the outcome of sin" from "sin itself," a belief that did not change during his lifetime. Uchimura thought that "the Good itself is God, and the Bad (Sin) is that we are going to stand apart from God, alone" (2:189). Therefore, murder, stealing, and adultery are the result of our leaving God, but those acts are not sin itself. According to Uchimura, the act of Adam and Eve to eat the fruit of the tree of knowledge is a result of the sin. The act is not sin itself by any means. Then what is the sin that the human ancestors committed? Sin is a human being separated from God, standing by himself alone.

Uchimura quoted Gottfried Wilhelm Leibniz, the philosopher, as saying that "the article of the corruption of the founder of the human race in Genesis is the explanation that is the most reliable when I consider the history of humanity" (2:190). Uchimura had a similar opinion. Adam and Eve ate the forbidden fruit, and their story of expulsion from the paradise of Eden shows what a human being was and what kind of path he has walked up to the present. "The human possessing intellect" and "the human being separated from God" contradict each other, but this is the real essence of the human way. Uchimura described the circumstances as follows:

> After the human left the Creator, his soul and body lost equilibrium. The soul cannot influence the body, and the body cannot follow the soul. The body desires what the soul is not allowed, and the soul desires the outside influence of the body. The historian Neander says "the Internal Schism" begins here. (2:191)

> Those who do not self-rule can never keep the rights and freedoms of their neighbors. Emptiness has been produced in the human being since he lost sight of God and he cannot fill this emptiness by himself. (2:192)

> If there were a microphone picking up the voices of the trouble of the human heart and we could hear the voices, the sound of the pains would tear the sky and move the ground. (2:196-97)

Our ancestors (Adam and Eve) left God, who is the source of the water of life (paradise exile). Humans, who were the descendants of Adam and

Eve, depended on their own "broken puddle" (2:191) and walked through history these six thousand years in suffering. "The Principle of Sin" chapter ends with the following questions:

> Will not there be someone to save me?
> Will not the Messiah yet fall?
> Will not there be God?
> Will the human have been discarded? (2:197)

Atonement Faith: Paradise Regained

The chapter "Paradise Regained" is Uchimura's answer to the previous questions, and in it he says that God has already shown a way of returning to him, namely, a way of "paradise regained" through the atonement of Jesus Christ. Uchimura quotes the words of Dr. M. Dott: "Don't think about this world as the place to which Christ does not descend" (2:209), and explains it as follows: "Our relief is connected to God in Christ, the life and death of Christ are conditions of our relief; we human beings could not be united with God if it did not depend on Christ" (2:210).

Uchimura prayed to God as follows: "I do not have 'good deeds' to give to you now and do not have one good characteristic to assume my justice either. I can only give my broken heart to you" (2:214). Uchimura quoted Psalm 51 to explain this "broken heart" (2:214-16): "O LORD, open thou my lips; and my mouth shall shew forth thy praise. For thou desirest not sacrifice; else would I give it: thou delightest not in burnt offering. The sacrifices of God are a broken spirit: a broken and a contrite heart, O God, thou wilt not despise" (Ps. 51:15-17).

Another aim of *Kyūanroku* was to clarify the meaning of Christ from the position of the orthodox faith in contrast to the new theology mentioned above. Uchimura introduces the interpretation of Christ rendered by the new theology as follows: "God has given us the Law, and commanded us to obey it in following Christ. That is why our duty is to carry out the Law with our own effort" (2:218). According to Uchimura's view, everyone has sinned and is far away from God's saving presence. By the free gift of God's grace, all are made right with him through Christ Jesus, who sets them free. We are made right with God only through faith in Christ. Uchimura quoted Christ's saying, "Be of good cheer; I have overcome the world" (John 16:33), and continued: "In other words there is relief for the Christ-believer and a source of courage in the victory that Christ already accomplished, no matter what a moralist or Unitarian says. Christ has already accomplished what we should do. Therefore, as for our justice, we have already acquired it in Christ. In consequence, this is the reason why true Christ-believers always spend their lives with great composure" (2:221).

The Philosophy of Atonement

The Theory of Atonement: "Justice Is the Foundation of the Gospel"

Uchimura wanted to defend the doctrine of atonement against the new theology from the position of the orthodox faith. In the chapter "The Philosophy of Atonement," he does so in a unique way.

Firstly, Uchimura says that "religion is fact and experience." Subsequently, he distinguishes "the interpretation" from "the fact itself" and says: "The fact is fact, the interpretation is interpretation, the fact is testified by the experience of all men, but the interpretation changes according to the times and the situations" (2:228). Therefore, many interpretations of the atonement have been provided until now. For instance (2:228-29):

1. Harmony was lost between human beings and God, and Christ, having the quality of both God and humanity, restored intermediation.
2. Because humans forgot affection for God, God helped our faith in Christ and showed the way to return to God.
3. The justice of God does not stand without a criminal being punished. Therefore, God let his Son, Christ, descend and perform the expiation of sins in place of humanity through the penalty of death on the cross.

According to Uchimura, none of these three interpretations is independently sufficient. Each, however, includes some kind of truth. Uchimura thinks that (3) is the best, and the theory of atonement does not hold without it. Paul emphasizes this interpretation in the epistle to the Romans, and Uchimura follows it in interpreting Christ.

Yokoi, who believes in the new theology, accepts (1) and (2) but rejects (3). His reason is that (3) represents "a theory about the justice of extremely barbarous times," namely, the view of "An eye for an eye, a tooth for a tooth." The difference in opinion between Uchimura and Yokoi about the atonement is fundamental; it is also a basic difference for understanding Christianity. Yokoi says:

> The main idea of Christianity is Jesus Christ, the purpose of Christianity is to realize what Christ is to me, and perform the teaching of Christ to the world.[19]

> Jesus Christ, for human beings, represents God in justice and love, for God, represents human beings in piety and obedience.[20]

> The universe is a phenomenon, it has a deep psyche. Law, truth, justice, and love have been actively realized; they are the true body of the universe. I learned that in Christ, the true body of the universe is the living God and Father in heaven.[21]

Yokoi thinks the whole creation is "the body of God," "representing the Spirit of God," but the creation could never realize the Spirit of God completely. Only in Christ was God's love fully manifest. In short, Christ is the embodiment of love, representing the heart of God by himself. Therefore, the cross of Christ is a natural event resulting from the position and the conflict in his life. Holding to these concepts, Yokoi did not accept (3).

Additionally, Yokoi wrote a book review of *Kyūanroku* for *Rikugō Zasshi* in 1893. He said "The Philosophy of Atonement" was the most important and yet the most obscure chapter in *Kyūanroku*. He summarized Uchimura's atonement faith as follows: "Our salvation is possible by connecting with God in Christ. The life and death of Christ is necessary for the salvation of souls. It is truth that humans can become one with God and the sin against God will be forgiven through Christ only."[22]

Yokoi accepted this also. However, as noted above, Yokoi rejected (3); therefore he grasped the act of Christ only as an act of sacrificial love. According to Yokoi, Uchimura did not explain (3), which was the core of his atonement faith, in "The Philosophy of Atonement" chapter, the most important chapter of *Kyūanroku*. Instead, he emphasized only the sacrificial

---

19. Yokoi Tokio, *Kirisuto-kyō Shin-ron (An Essay on Christianity)* (Tokyo: Keiseisha Shoten, 1891), 11-12.

20. Yokoi, *Kirisuto-kyō Shin-ron*, 14.

21. Yokoi, *Kirisuto-kyō Shin-ron*, 96.

22. Yokoi Tokio, "Kyūanroku," *Rikugō Zasshi*, no. 153 (September 1893): 49.

act of love of Jesus and good people in history. Yokoi criticized this chapter as being most ambiguous.[23]

Uchimura immediately submitted an essay, "Reply to an Editor of *Rikugō Zasshi*," in response to Yokoi's criticism.[24] Firstly, Uchimura said that the most important chapter of *Kyūanroku* was not "The Philosophy of Atonement," but the chapter written about "the atonement itself," namely, "Paradise Regained." Secondly, as to the life and death of Jesus being sacrificial love, Yokoi agreed. But he did not agree that the salvation of humans is possible only though redemption by Jesus Christ's life (2:254-55).

Let us consider Uchimura's insistence in the chapter "The Philosophy of Atonement" of *Kyūanroku*, that even people who deny the divinity of Jesus can accept his noble character absolutely. This means that the noble character of Christ has redeeming power and influence, and that wanting to become like Jesus is the main purpose of the Christian. On the other hand, Uchimura said that "I can never become like Jesus, because there is sin in me; even with the strong influence and power of morality, the sins will not disappear" (2:234). Further, Uchimura presented the structure of the atonement thus: "The work of salvation in Jesus Christ has two aspects. The first was to teach a complete life for mankind. The second was to bear the sins of humanity in order to eliminate its sins. The former is the ultimate goal of salvation, the latter is the means to the former" (2:234).

Uchimura also asked (a) "Why do the sins of Christians disappear with the death and suffering of Jesus?" and (b) "What is the philosophy of the atonement?" He answered these questions in the chapter "The Philosophy of Atonement" as follows:

> It is a universal principle that if an innocent person does not bear the sin of a person having committed a crime, the sin does not become extinct.
>
> It is clear to me that joint responsibility is most necessary for the human being. Humanity is formed by virtue of virtuous persons.
>
> All good people possess a property of the atonement. Human beings are joined together by joint liability. That is why humanity develops by the act of a good deed and the atonement of good people like Abraham Lincoln and George Brown. (2:234-36)

---

23. Yokoi, "Kyūanroku," 49-50.
24. *Rikugō Zasshi*, no. 154 (October 1893).

Uchimura emphasized joint responsibility, good deeds, and the vicarious suffering and atonement of good people. Uchimura's description is the only answer to question (b), "What is the philosophy of the atonement?" Yokoi's previous criticism was aimed at this description. Uchimura clearly distinguished (a) and (b). Also, he believed the atonement of Christ to be a onetime event, but the atonement of good people in history is not so. The main difference between Uchimura and Yokoi is in the matter of sin. Yokoi interpreted the life of Jesus without the concept of sin, but for Uchimura, the greatest concern was for the problem of sin and the most serious issue was a release from sin.[25]

Very interestingly, twenty-three years later, in 1916, Fujii Takeshi,[26] a follower of Uchimura, wrote an article entitled "The Simple Gospel" (March 1916), and rejected interpretation (3) as Yokoi had done. Uchimura promptly wrote an article, "The Wrath of God and the Atonement" (April 1916), and argued against it. The assertion of "The Wrath of God and the Atonement" has been the core of Uchimura's Christianity. In fact, it was already explained in *Kyūanroku*, and some years later it would be further expanded in *Romasho no Kenkyū (The Study of Romans)*, Uchimura's masterpiece.

Uchimura explained the wrath of God and the necessity for the atonement as follows (22:237-45): God gets angry because the essence of God is justice. The death of Jesus on the cross is necessary not only to promote repentance to people and to recall the love of God to them, but also to show that God himself is righteous. The cross of Jesus is a place where the holy God and sinner meet, and where love and justice are combined. The essence of the Buddha in Buddhism is "mercy." In contrast, the essence of the Yahweh Christian God is "justice and love." Uchimura asserted that "love" is different from "mercy," because "love" includes "justice." Uchimura stressed this point in many places. In the epistle to the Romans, Paul says: "For all have sinned, and come short of the glory of God; being justified freely by his grace through the redemption that is in Christ Jesus: whom God hath set forth to be a propitiation through faith in his blood, to declare his righteousness for the remission of sins that are past, through the forbearance of

---

25. Stated quite simply, Yokoi adopted a moral influence theory, while Uchimura took up a penal substitution theory.

26. After graduating from Tokyo Imperial University, Fujii Takeshi became a public official of Yamagata Prefecture, but he resigned from the position and became an assistant of Uchimura. In 1922 he wrote an article, "Daishoku wo Shinjiru made" ("Until I Believed in Substitution"). That is, he finally accepted Uchimura's atonement theory. Later, on the model of Uchimura, he worked as an independent evangelist until his death.

God; to declare, I say, at this time his righteousness: that he might be just, and the justifier of him which believeth in Jesus" (Rom. 3:23-26).

Uchimura names the short last chapter of *Kyūanroku* "The Last Problem" and speaks to it as follows. I will quote every sentence, as this is the essence of his Christian faith.

> I discovered a way by which I can find peace. However, to know the way is not necessarily to enter it. Faith in Christ is the way to save me from sin. However, faith is also the gift of God (Ephesians 2:8). . . . It is true that I am saved by faith; but at the same time I am the one who is saved by letting me believe. Hereby I understand that I have no power to save myself. Then what shall I do? Simply I am seeking even my faith from God. The Christian must pray incessantly. Her life is prayer. If she is imperfect, she should pray. If he lacks faith, he should pray. If he cannot pray enough, he should pray. Even if he is filled with grace, he should pray. Even if he is cursed, he should pray. Even if I am raised to the height of the heaven, or even if I am put down to the lowliness of the Erebus, I will pray. What a powerless man I am! What I can do is nothing but to pray. (2:249)

Uchimura also quotes the following phrases from A. Tennyson's *In Memoriam:*

> But what am I?
> An infant crying in the night:
> An infant crying for the light:
> And no language but a cry. (2:249E)

As stated earlier, Uchimura had an extremely strong sense of sin and made an effort to escape from it and find peace. Under the guidance of President Seelye, he came to believe in the atonement of Christ and found that peace. *Kyūanroku* is Uchimura's record of that search for peace and his faith in the atonement, that is, the vicarious atonement of Jesus Christ (penal substitution). He introduced the following words of Seelye: "Uchimura, you look at only your own mind. Stop reflecting on yourself. Why do you not look up to Jesus who expiated your sin on the cross?" (29:343). As shown in these words, for Uchimura, Jesus Christ is not the subject but the object to look up to; he is the one who redeems our sins. That understanding is shown also in the last chapter of *Kyūanroku*, "The Last Problem," especially in the following words: "Faith in Christ is the way to save me from sin. However, faith is also the gift of God."

In 1921, the seventeenth edition of *Kyūanroku* came out. In its preface, Uchimura wrote that many new theories had come out into the world, but for him the gospel of Christ is the old one and the new one also. "So now, I continue to repeat the old gospel which was asserted in *Kyūanroku* twenty-eight years ago" (33:384).

The Principle of Atonement and the
Progressive Civilization View of History

Uchimura's view of atonement is in line with a legitimate traditional theology, as similar views are adopted in M. Luther, J. Calvin, J. Milton, and J. Bunyan. Another intellectual current, however, is included in his "Philosophy of Atonement": Uchimura had believed in the theory of evolution ever since attending Sapporo Agricultural College (SAC). At Amherst College, he attended the lectures of Anson D. Morse, a professor of history, and came to believe in the progressive view of history. Six months later, Uchimura experienced the atonement of Christ, and he told Miyabe Kingo, a classmate from SAC: "I rejoice to know that Nature, History, and the Bible are the tripod of God's revelation to mankind. They can be studied side by side with devout interest. Christ is the key to open the secrets of not only the Bible, but of the other two" (36:247E).

How, then, does Uchimura unfold and understand history and nature by "the key of Christ"? According to Uchimura, history is a record of human progress. The history of a nation is only one small portion of human progress. A nation gains power and makes a contribution to all of human history, and then it declines. Then another nation gains power and inherits the foundation of the old nation, adds a new element to the old civilization, and cedes the way to the nation next rising to power. The world is one organism and moves toward its destiny through the rise and fall of various nations.

In Uchimura's view, civilization came into existence from West Asia and passed from infancy to youth on its way through Europe and then grew up in the United States by moving farther westward. This time, civilization will grow up by moving to Japan from the United States. "We" the Japanese must improve it and contribute to human progress then. Here is the "true vocation of Japan" (1:284-94). "If civilization advances westward in the Northern Hemisphere and goes around the world and Japan definitely accomplishes its true vocation, this time, it advances in the Southern Hemisphere and covers there. Truth, Good and Beauty came to cover the whole earth and as for the purpose of the creation, it is completed" (2:479).

Uchimura combined this view of history and Japan's vocation with his atonement faith. It was evident in "The Philosophy of Atonement" chapter of *Kyūanroku* and in the article "In What Sense Is Christ the Creator of All Things?" (July 1909). As already indicated, Uchimura emphasized the joint responsibility of human beings and atonement by the sacrificial life of good people, and he thought the history of humanity had progressed by their sacrificial lives. Further, Uchimura said:

> A principle of the atonement is a law of the natural world. In the mineral kingdom, it is Equilibration of Forces, and in the world of creatures, it is the act of healing and in the spirit world, it is expiation.
>
> Therefore if the tree loses one branch, each branch and leaf discharges nourishment, and tries to cure it. (2:240)

Uchimura applied this principle of atonement to history and nature, and he named it "christocentric cosmology" (16:419). First, Uchimura quotes, "All things were created by him, and for him" (Col. 1:16). He explains that there are two interpretations: First, that Christ is the head of all things and the end of creation, because he is the Son of God and the head of human beings, and Christ is the purpose and ideal of all things, because he is the end of creation. Second, "by him [Christ]" is also used in the sense of means, that is, "Christ" is not the historical Jesus, but the Logos, the principle of creation, recently called the law of nature (16:413-16). Uchimura describes the latter thus: "The purpose of the universe is love, the way of the formation of the universe is love, the principle or spirit of the universe is love too. . . . Christ is the origin and the principle of the universe. . . . In the beginning of the world, already the origin of the universe was love, its principle was a sacrificial lamb" (16:417-18).

Hence, Uchimura interpreted the overall history of mankind and the universe through Christ on the cross, and this understanding would lead him to the second coming of Christ, but only after much time and more painful experiences.

The Sino-Japanese War began in July 1894 over the domination of Korea. Uchimura wrote an article entitled "Justification for the Corean War"

(August 1894),[27] in order to justify the war to those inside as well as outside of Japan. Among his arguments were the progressive-civilization view of history, Japan's vocation, and the "christocentric cosmology." Uchimura said Japan should punish China for its savageness in refusing new civilization, should advance Korean independence from Chinese oppression, and should keep Oriental peace. That was why this fight was necessary even if the war sacrifices much human life. At that time most Japanese Christians, as well as most media, agreed with the Sino-Japanese War. There existed then a near consensus in Japan that the Sino-Japanese War was "a war between civilization and barbarism," with Japan symbolizing civilization and China symbolizing barbarism. For this reason most Japanese did not doubt the justification of the war. This general view was very similar to Uchimura's.[28]

After the Sino-Japanese War, however, Uchimura began to take a different view. He watched the policy of Japanese imperialism over Korea come into effect after the war and knew that he had been wrong, so he wrote a letter to D. C. Bell (May 22, 1895). "The war developed all the goodness and boldness in our national temper, and the kind Providence gave us a check for the latter aspect of our nature. A 'righteous war' has changed into a *piratic* war, somewhat, and a prophet who wrote its 'justification' is now in shame" (36:414E).

Uchimura also explained the situation after the Sino-Japanese War as follows: "What did the Japanese get from the war? Japan spent a great deal of money (about two billion yen) for the war and one million Japanese people were sacrificed. . . . The independence of Korea, a goal of the war, weakened more and more and China's division began. The Japanese burden increased greatly. Japanese morality took a serious turn, too. For this reason, the whole East fell into a crisis" (11:296-97).

27. It was published in the *Japan Weekly Mail* (August 11, 1894). In the same year, it was published in *Kokumin no Tomo* and titled "Justification of the Corean War" (no. 233, August 23, 1894), and "Nisshin Sensō no Gi" ("Justification of the Sino-Japanese War") (no. 234, September 3, 1894).

28. Cf. Uchimura Kanzō, "Japan's Future as Conceived by a Japanese [Japan: Its Mission]," *Japan Daily Mail*, February 5, 1892; "Sekai Rekishi ni chōshite Nisshin no Kankei wo Ronzu" ("A Discussion of the Relationship between Japan and China in World History"), *Kokumin Shinbun*, July 27, 1894; "Nisshin Sensō no Mokuteki Ikan?" ("What Is the Purpose of the Sino-Japanese War?"), *Kokumin no Tomo*, no. 237 (October 3, 1894); *Japan and the Japanese* (Tokyo: Minūsha, 1894); Fukuzawa Yukichi, "Nisshin no Sensō wa Bunya no Sensō nari" ("The Sino-Japanese War Is a War of Civilization and Barbarism"), *Jijishinpō*, July 29, 1894; Uemura Masahisa, "Tōzai no Bunmei, Nihon no Kōsei" ("The Civilization of the East and the West, the Rehabilitation of Japan"), *Fukuin Shinpō*, August 24, 1894.

As a result, on the occasion of the Russo-Japanese War a decade later, Uchimura objected to the opinion of the Japanese majority and came to insist on strict pacifism.

The Change of Uchimura's "Christocentric Cosmology"

As mentioned, Uchimura's philosophy of atonement includes two elements. One is a theory about the atonement of Christ, in keeping with what Paul says in Romans 3. The other is the progressive-civilization view of history that applied the principle of the atonement to human history and nature, namely, "christocentric cosmology." Uchimura did not change his views about the former during his entire life. The latter, however, is a different matter.

In 1914, World War I began. This war was an enormous shock to Westerners. Uchimura was also shocked, but he believed that America would intervene between the warring states to stop the war. Much to Uchimura's surprise, American President Wilson, far from trying to intervene, subscribed to a declaration of war against Germany in April 1917. Uchimura came to an impasse (24:60). It became difficult for him to maintain still further the progressive-civilization view of history.

The decline of the progressive view of history is a major cause of his new apocalyptic faith in the second coming of Christ. Further, the death of his beloved daughter, Rutsuko, was another factor leading Uchimura to the second advent. She suffered from an unidentified intractable disease at the age of nineteen and, in spite of the family's devoted nursing, died six months later in 1914. This event provided an occasion for him to think about the problem of resurrection more deeply.

In this situation, Uchimura wrote to Bell: "I now see that *'Parousia'* is the key to the Holy Scriptures; that without it the Bible is a great enigma from the beginning to the end. It is certain that the writers of the New Testament were thoroughly *surcharged* with the faith and idea of the Second Coming, so that without it, we cannot understand their writings. Much of the voluminous commentaries in my library may go to the rubbish once I begin to reread the N.T. in the light of this idea" (38:209-10E).[29]

---

29. Bell sent Uchimura C. G. Trumbull's article, "Is the Truth of Our Lord's Return a Practical Matter for Today?" which was published in the *Sunday School Times* in 1916. Uchimura read it and replied to Bell in his letter. Uchimura also wrote as follows: "I felt so

Here we can divide Uchimura's Christian thought into three periods. His early thought comes before the atonement experience at Amherst College. His middle thought comes before he reached a belief in the second coming in 1916. The core of this middle thought is shown in his book *Kyūanroku*. His later thought comes after he embraced the second coming. Here, his progressive view of history retreats. His late thought consists of the theory of Christ's propitiation and the second coming of Christ.

In the previous section, we were introduced to Uchimura's idea that "Christ is the key to open the secrets of the Bible, history and nature." Here, he said that "*Parousia* is the key to the Holy Scriptures"; that is, he came to understand all things by Christ on the cross and the second coming.

Uchimura's view of the atonement of Christ and the second coming was developed in an original way; he thought Greek thought and Confucianism were doctrines of secularism, and that Buddhism and Hinduism were doctrines of a purely spiritual life. And he insisted that both doctrines were wrong. The horizontal bar of the cross expresses secularism, and the vertical bar expresses thoughts about God and the soul. The significance of the cross of Christ involves the intersection of the bar of secularism with the bar of God and the soul. It is spiritualization of the flesh endowed with a soul.

For Uchimura, however, the cross of Christ was not only a symbol, but also a historical and personal event. He put the event at the hub of the universe and interpreted the universe through the event. He also explained that the body should not be defeated, but glorified by the Spirit. The significance of the cross of Christ is that the vertical bar of the Spirit lifted the horizontal bar of the secularism of the earth up to heaven. Christ was killed in the intersection. Uchimura also wrote: "The Second Coming, which I insist on, is not a thought of pure substance; it is that Christ, who was crucified, revived and ascended, returns with the Resurrection body (with a body made spiritual). . . . The Second Coming is not an idea of pure spirit, that only spirit will ascend from the flesh, but a spiritualization of the flesh such as transfigured Jesus, the glory of the world; all things in the universe changed to Heaven by the glory of Christ" (24:289-90).

---

impressed with the importance of the subject that I at once subscribed for the S.S. Times [*Sunday School Times*] through my book agency in this city. I am thankful to know that such a paper still flourishes in America. It is an evidence that all America has *not* gone into the new theology and 'ethical evangelism' of its chief seminaries. I ought to make distinctions between American Christians and Christians *in* America" (38:210E).

As described so far, Uchimura interpreted all things of the world through Christ on the cross, from the experience of the atonement of Christ in the middle period. At that stage, however, there was no second coming of Christ; therefore, he could assert "a principle of the atonement" at work in history and nature in *Kyūanroku*. In contrast, in the later period, there is a unification of the atonement and the second coming, and all creatures are interpreted through the lenses of both the atonement and the second coming. The unification of the atonement and the second coming is illustrated in the following words of Uchimura:

> The Cross of Christ is not only for sinners, but also for all creatures. (24:390)

> The purposes of the Second Coming and the first Coming of Christ are the same. (24:458)

> The hope of the Second Coming is built on the foundation of the Faith of Atonement. (26:19)

> The Cross is the premise of the Second Coming. . . . The Cross is where love and faith touch; the Second Coming is the realization of hope. (32:327-28)

For Uchimura, Christ on the cross and the second coming are matters concerning both human beings and the universe. The atonement of Christ is "the central truth," and the second coming is "the final truth," of Christianity (32:327).[30] The hope of the second coming is built on the atonement of Christ. This is the path of Uchimura's faith from his middle period to his later period.

---

30. Uchimura also wrote, "God created the universe with His unlimited power, and He will complete the first purpose of the creation surely" (26:312). "God's salvation in Christ on the Cross is the new creation, while God's salvation in the Second Coming is the completion of the new creation" (26:503). That is, God has forgiven our sins, has justified us, and will glorify us in Christ. So we who are living now should live between the atonement and the second coming, and look up to Christ who died on the cross, is helping us now, and will come again someday.

Uchimura Kanzō on
Justification by Faith in His *Study of Romans:*
A Semantic Analysis of Romans 3:19-31

1. Introduction

From January 1920 to October 1921, in the center of Tokyo, Uchimura
Kanzō gave a sixty-part Sunday lecture series on the apostle Paul's epistle to
the Romans. His lectures were held in a German-style building called
Ōtemachi Eiseikai Hall, which was located east of the Imperial Palace.[1] This
regular meeting was organized as the Tokyo Bible Study Meeting, and was
described as the "Central Lecture Meeting" in Uchimura's journal. Atten-
dees were required to read Uchimura's monthly journal, *Seisho no Kenkyū*
(The Biblical Study), for at least a year; to pay a regular fee (the amount was
left to the individual's discretion); and to dress appropriately. Average attendance, half of which were students, was between 600 and 700. The largest number that attended one lecture was about 800 people. Before
Uchimura's lectures, assistants such as Kurosaki Kōkichi, Fujii Takeshi, and

---

1. J. Howes describes Uchimura at that time as follows: "Uchimura considered his four
years there [Ōtemachi] between the ages of fifty-nine and sixty-three the 'high tide' of his
career. [Having previously lectured on the book of Daniel and Job, he] began an even bigger
project [lecturing on Romans], the one that many would consider his greatest work." J. F.
Howes, *Japan's Modern Prophet: Uchimura Kanzō, 1861-1930* (Vancouver, Canada: UBC Press,
2005), 280-88.

This is an improved and expanded version of a paper similarly entitled, published in *Journal
of Graduate School of Letters* 7 (Hokkaido University, 2012). I thank Professor Shibuya
Hiroshi, Professor Shin Chiba, Professor Michelle La Fay, and Dr. Jack McKelvey for their
helpful comments. I thank Professor David Charles, who commented on this paper on a
warm autumn day 2011 on the west coast of Wales at a place called New Quay.

Azegami Kenzō gave lectures on different passages from the Scripture. These men, together with other assistants like Tsukamoto Toraji and Yanaihara Tadao, later became independent preachers and trained their own disciples. They were said to be "the second generation" of *mukyōkai* (followers of nonchurchism).

At each of the Sunday programs in this series, Uchimura's lecture lasted for over an hour. One anecdote has it that it was so quiet that a small pin falling on the floor made an echo in the hall. One day, Uchimura wrote in his journal, "It looks like the audience was impressed so strongly that the silence overwhelmed the hall for a while. Sobbing was heard here and there. All of the audience felt thankfulness for the Cross. The hall was filled by the atmosphere of evangelism. It was indeed a joyous holy day (1921.12.11)." However, Uchimura sometimes reflected that he could not satisfactorily deliver the lecture.

> My lecture was not one that satisfied the ardent audience. My effort to explain the central truth of Romans 8:1-8 was partly a failure. I have realized that Paul's thick words cannot but be tasted by harmonizing each drop with water. However, when my lecture was unsatisfactory, my prayer for God's assistance and blessing became more eager. Sometimes, it may be best to transmit God's truth by supplementing the lack of preaching with prayer. Anyway, there sometimes occurred the undeniable fact that my cry "God, have mercy on this useless servant!" was uttered from the bottom of my heart (1922.1.15).

Uchimura dictated each lecture to his assistant, Azegami, who edited the text. The lectures were then serialized in *Seisho no Kenkyū*, volumes 247 (February 1921) to 268 (November 1922). At that time, the journal's subscription list numbered over 3,000, coming from throughout Japan and overseas.

Later these lectures were published as a book called *A Study of Romans* (September 1924). In his introduction to this book, Uchimura reflected:

> The audiences [for the lectures] comprised all classes, among which there were believers of various sects of Christianity, believers who did not belong to a church, people who did not regard themselves to be believers, and even Buddhist monks. Indeed, ever since Christianity spread to Japan, it seemed that this country never saw such [large] audiences [for this type of lecture]. The keen enthusiasm of the audience was evi-

dent from the fact that each time some [of the audience] traveled from Utsunomiya or even Nagoya [260 kilometers away]. And as for me, it was the culmination of my own life between the ages of fifty-nine and sixty-three. I cannot be more thankful that I engaged in this enjoyable enterprise. . . . The Epistle to the Romans that was dictated through the Apostle Paul is the one that summarizes the essence of Christianity. Without an understanding of this epistle, one cannot understand Christianity. For forty-seven years, over the course of my life of faith, this epistle is the one I have studied with the most care. In lecturing on Romans, I have been speaking of my own faith. Therefore, giving sixty lectures on the Epistle to the Romans was a continuing pleasure for me. I would not have gotten tired of this lecture, even if I delivered it 100 times or 200 times. This [epistle] tells us of the Gospel of God's grace. This is information about the Love of the Heavenly Father. There cannot be any more enjoyable thing than this. I could not help but weep a little when I finished the sixtieth and final lecture. (*Works*, 27:356)

This book is the most consistent and comprehensive of all of Uchimura's works, which are composed mostly of collections of short essays. His works amount to forty volumes in their most recent edition. One of Uchimura's disciples, the philosopher Mitani Takamasa, wrote an article called "Truth and the Short Essay," in which he discussed Uchimura's characteristic style of writing.[2] According to Mitani, there are two types of talents: the "frontier" type and the "systematic" type. These are exemplified, respectively, by Heraclitus and Plato, Augustine and Aquinas, and Lessing and Goethe. Mitani describes Uchimura's talent as follows:

Our teacher, Uchimura Kanzō, does not belong to the same type as Thomas, but rather to the type of Augustine. His Mukyōkaiism is, in other words, non-systematism. I do not mean that a lack of system itself should be respected. Truth, however, often springs up while neglecting a system. Life cannot be enclosed within a closed system. It is like a big net drawn up to the seashore. Innumerable fishes, small and large, jump up flashing their scales. Fishermen grab them randomly, throw them down, and grab them again. There is not such a thing as a closed system. Fish are lively, and man is lively too. There is not anything but liveliness. Fishers of men are also like this. "The word of the Lord is in mine heart

2. Mitani Takamasa, *Complete Works* (Tokyo: Iwanami, 1965), 4:158 (1934).

as it were a burning fire shut up in my bones and I am weary with for-
bearing and I cannot contain [it within me]" (Jeremiah 20.9). There is
no leisure time for such a man to consider a system. Thus, it was a necessary part of teacher Uchimura's being that forced him to choose the
short essay form.[3]

I have quoted Mitani's impressive remarks on Uchimura to remind
readers of the liveliness of his writings. His study of Romans, though more
than 400 pages long altogether, is no exception to this. In this chapter, I
shall focus on Uchimura's understanding of faith and justification by faith
as a central doctrine of Paul, within the context of a general application of
his methods and thoughts. Although this chapter is an introduction to his
thoughts on Romans, I shall also point out the germ of the Second Reformation (Re-Reformation) in his interpretation of faith, which he was keen
to develop throughout his life. Since Paul himself, as I understand him,
reached out a hand of reconciliation to Catholicism and Protestantism
well before the Reformation in the sixteenth century, I shall demonstrate
that Uchimura was compelled by the text itself to this kind of encompassing interpretation. In parallel with introducing Uchimura's thoughts, I
shall carry out a semantic analysis of the text of Romans at a more basic
level than his theological interpretations so that Uchimura's thought can
be made more clear with some constraints.

2. Uchimura's Lectures

2.1. Lively Descriptions of Paul's Character and Thought

One characteristic, which anyone who reads these lectures of Uchimura's
cannot fail to notice, is his joy in Jesus Christ's atonement, as well as his joy
in talking about Paul and his mission. Uchimura expressed his strong affinity with Paul and his work, describing Paul's character as follows:

He [Paul] was a man who held his own against everyone. This was
proved by his whole life and by his letters. He was extremely powerful
against anyone who tried to hold him back. This unyielding tempera-
ment poured out in whatever he said and whatever he did anytime, any-

3. Mitani, *Complete Works*, 4:158.

165

where. However, this man, Paul, had chosen the way of absolute obedience to Christ alone. Indeed, for Paul the greatest shame was to be the slave of man, a shame that could not be mitigated even by death. It was Paul's usual wish that "it were good for me rather to die, than that any man should make my boast void" (1 Cor. 9:15). But being a slave of Christ was the greatest glory for him, one that Paul would not exchange for anything. He did not take the road of shame but [rather] the road of glory. We should follow him. We should not become a slave of man in any situation, even if we are threatened by death, but we should stand in the place of a servant towards God's only son, the savior of mankind, our lord Jesus Christ. This must be the resolution at the time of our repentance and of our whole life. (26:34)

Uchimura always found joy in speaking of Paul and understood Paul's dedication to Christ as somewhat similar to his own. Only Christ can make proud men such as Paul and Uchimura become obedient slaves. Just as Paul was persecuted by his fellow Jews and his fellow Christians, Uchimura was also persecuted by his fellow Japanese and his fellow Christians; and he was driven from the established church. Just as Paul was sent to the Greeks as a pioneer missionary to the heathen, Uchimura was sent to preach to people who were outside the established churches. This led to Uchimura's founding of the *mukyōkai* (nonchurch movement) — a movement that pays no attention to ritual ceremonies or to formal organization. Rather, *mukyōkai* avoided sacramental activity and concentrated on living a life in Jesus Christ, through Bible studies and the practice of the central message of the Bible, that is, love through faith. Just as Paul claimed the dynamism of faith against traditional moral laws (the Jewish Torah), Uchimura emphasized faith as *the easy path* in contrast to *the difficult path* of self-salvation (depending on one's own good deeds for salvation). This terminology was transferred from eleventh-century Buddhist tradition, as first expressed by Honen.[4]

If I must select one single characteristic of Uchimura's lectures on Paul's epistle to the Romans, I would choose Uchimura's effort to contrast *faith* with *work* as the central core of Pauline doctrine. Uchimura came back to this issue many times in the course of his lectures, discussing it in different contexts and from different perspectives. Uchimura emphasizes, as his peculiar characteristic in understanding faith, that having faith on

4. Howes, *Japan's Modern Prophet*, 231.

our part regardless of its intensity or content is in itself complete before God with respect to receiving God's righteousness at any moment through the faith of Jesus Christ.

There is no doubt that Paul rationally argued for the gospel on the basis of what had happened through Jesus Christ (the Christ event), nor any doubt that Paul simultaneously refuted his opponents (primarily the Judaizers, who emphasized the law of works, that is, Mosaic law, which is also God's true revelation of his will). In reference to Romans 1:15, Uchimura described Paul's situation as he informed the Romans of his readiness to preach the gospel as follows:

> It should be noted that when he [Paul] wrote this epistle, more than twenty years had passed since he came to this [Christian] faith. He had spent most of this period in missionary work. Thus, Paul's controversies with his opponents were great in number. When we ponder his solitude and his struggles, while surrounded by inflexible Jews and intellectual Greeks, we can imagine the intensity of these controversies. Many of his epistles were written amid the clouds of smoke from battlefields. Therefore, the smell and the sound of gunfire naturally remained in the documents. When Paul wrote to his allies, too, he appeared to argue as if he were about to face enemies who might appear suddenly; and he developed cautious arguments to prevent his enemies from being able to take advantage of his unguarded side. Since his epistles were written under this sort of tension, they contain inexhaustible truth. (26:77)

Uchimura's biblical study of Romans was a rational process in which, alongside the apostle Paul, he discovered peace and joy in Jesus Christ. In fact, Uchimura denied that his lectures on Romans were biblical commentaries: "Leaving the detailed verse-by-verse explanation of Romans to the commentators, let us be satisfied with an explanation of the overall spirit, the main area, the marrow of the thoughts: unfortunately for us, that is all that time will allow" (26:28).[5] In other words, Uchimura's rational scrutiny of the relevant passages ceased when he understood the vividness and liveliness of the Scripture, and its connection with events around him in the secular world. Uchimura's lectures contained something solid that struck a

---

5. Cf. M. La Fay, "'Love' and 'Righteousness' in Uchimura Kanzō's *A Study of Romans*," *Journal of the Graduate School of Letters,* Hokkaido University, p. 100, available at http://hdl.handle.net/2115/42868.

chord in the heart of his audience, because he could not deliver his message without himself being moved by his thoughts on the relevant passages themselves and by his awareness of the relevant contemporary issues. Just as living things cannot live without nourishment, Uchimura never tired of studying the Bible as the source of life. In what follows, through an analysis of Uchimura's lectures, I shall try to make clear the solid basis for his thought.

2.2. Uchimura's Central Concept:
Finding Salvation through the Epistle to the Romans

In his first lecture, Uchimura described how this epistle brought him his own salvation, by explaining the relevant events of his predecessors, such as Augustine, Luther, and John Wesley, all of whom found salvation in this epistle.

> I myself am also a person saved by this epistle. We, who are born and brought up in a Confucian country, are inclined to think of Christianity as a way of becoming a saint and a gentleman of noble character, and [we might think] that reaching perfect moral status is the goal of the Christian faith. Under such a presumption, the fact that our real state does not match our ideal status causes agony and distress. In my case, weeping and struggling with this sin, I could not find the solution in Japan, so I went to America to drive away this anguish. A kind teacher [J. H. Seelye, the president of Amherst College] at one time instructed me saying "You do not have to make efforts to be righteous by yourself, as if a child were examining whether a potted plant was rooted and growing by pulling it up every day. There is no chance [to be righteous] in this way. You should not try to be sanctified, but should gaze up at Jesus on the Cross and then peace will fall upon you." I have been convinced by this teaching, and I finally achieved peace through a careful reading of Paul's Epistle to the Romans. Gaze up and be saved: this is the way of gaining peace that is shown in Romans. It is the opposite way and against evangelism, to try to be a righteous person so as to reach peace in this way. The gospel is only one thing, that is, being made righteous by God based on one's faith so as to reach peace. Romans, which is the objective of our study, is the book which teaches this way [that is, gaze up and be saved]. (26:24)

This is a reason why Uchimura wrote the following in the preface of *A Study of Romans:* "By lecturing on Romans, I spoke of my own faith." He experienced his conversion to Christianity on the basis of a new understanding of faith, which he experienced as a young man at Amherst College, under the guidance of J. H. Seelye. Uchimura's careful study of Romans confirms that Paul's work was important to his spiritual development, through his analysis of the power of faith. As explained by J. F. Howes, "The Epistle to the Romans is perhaps his [Uchimura's] favorite or rather most influential book among the sixty-six books of the Bible in the thirty-seven years of his career as a biblical scholar."[6] Apart from this series of sixty lectures, Uchimura also wrote on such issues as Paul's soteriology, atonement, and resurrection in more than twenty articles in his monthly journals of over twenty-five years.

In the *Supplement* to the last lecture of Romans, Uchimura said:

> Therefore, in reading Romans, although Paul's figure appears prominently [in this epistle], what appears far more (more than seventy times) are the figures of God and Christ. Indeed, God's love and Christ's salvation stand out prominently in this epistle, pushing aside the individual writer, Paul. Yes, God and Christ clearly stand out, for they receive brilliance from the whole of heaven. . . . Man becomes keenly interested in the study of what this God is, what this Christ is; the love and salvation which Paul tried to reveal [in his epistle], hiding himself as much as possible [in the writing]. In this sense, Romans is an epistle of a great missionary. We do not need to look beyond Romans to find the greatest work in the world. There are not few books that are called great works or masterpieces. Although Goethe's *Faust* is sometimes called "the bible of modern man," it cannot be compared with Romans. Other books, such as Dante's *Divine Comedy,* or Shakespeare's *Hamlet,* cannot possibly compete with Romans. Who can be consoled on his death bed by the so-called great works of this world? However, in any situation of life or death, the greatest companion is always Romans. There is no book in the world superior to this epistle. (27:574)

6. Howes wrote, "Uchimura had conceived of Bible study as a vocation while a student in the United States and started it with his comments on Ruth in his first six months as a writer. During the succeeding thirty-seven years, he analyzed almost all sixty-six books of the Bible. The exceptions were all in the Old Testament: Nehemiah, Song of Solomon, Lamentations and five of the minor prophets, Joel, Micah, Nahum, Haggai and Malachi. Uchimura's studies of the Bible still form the largest single corpus of commentaries on the Bible in the Japanese language." Howes, *Japan's Modern Prophet,* 283.

2.3. Adherence to Romans 3:21-31

As he was dying in early spring 1930, Uchimura said, "The problem of life has been already solved by Romans, chapter 3:21-31," and he asked for this passage to be read at his funeral. Earlier, in 1914, he had written, "The key to the Bible is the following: One should understand the Old Testament through the New Testament and understand the New Testament through Romans and also understand Romans through chapter 3 verses 21 to 31. I believe that a person who could understand verses 21 to 31 under God's aegis is the person who is bestowed with the precious key which enables him or her to understand the whole Bible" (21:113). In the first lecture on Romans, Uchimura claimed that 3:21-26 was "the heart" of this epistle (26:22). Throughout his life, he remained attached to Romans, especially chapter 3 verses 21 to 31. In the last of his sixty consecutive lectures on Romans, Uchimura's concluding words were as follows:

> Modern men would say, "We do not worry about this sort of thing [the agony of sin and conscience experienced by John Bunyan]. We are worried about money matters, passionate love, and about life [in general]. But there aren't such difficulties for us as wounded conscience, yearning for a living God, or how to deal with this dead body [of ours]. Therefore, even if we do not deny that we are moved a bit by reading this epistle and the author's ardent sincerity in his lectures, it does not create in us such an ardent faith as the faith which gripped Luther and Wesley. Then don't we gain any benefit through standing in the row of the study of this epistle?" Indeed, aren't these things that modern men lack the most, [such things] as yearning for the love of God and the anguish of sin? Thus, modern men do not study Romans and Galatians as the people of former times did with irresistible enthusiasm. But modern men are also men. Insofar as they are men, they will somewhere, sometime experience such things as the agony of conscience. It may happen that, when they fail in their businesses and their reputations are destroyed, they eventually sense that they have nothing to rely on. Or when they face death or are judged in the next world for all the things which they have done, although they do not feel any need of reconciliation with God in this world, their dormant conscience may suddenly awake and be unable to bear their own filth. Yes, I believe that insofar as a man is a man, such an awakening takes place at least one time [in each life]. On such an occasion, Romans will become useful. Indeed, it is useful in an

emergency. On such an occasion, the title of Doctor or a huge fortune and knowledge of this world do not help. Paul's old Romans, however, becomes a reliable guide for our salvation. Then chapter 3 verses 23-28 surround me as the rock of a thousand years and enable me to avoid the burning fire of judgment. On that occasion, our year-and-a-half study of Romans will bring actual profit. A proverb says that it is worthwhile to spend one's whole life to be prepared for the last three minutes. Likewise, it is worthwhile to study Romans with one's whole effort to prepare for the judgment day. For all have sinned, and all fall short of the glory of God, being justified freely by his grace through the redemption that is in Christ Jesus, whom God set forth to be a propitiation, through faith, by his blood, to show his righteousness, because of the passing over of the sins done formerly, in the forbearance of God; for the showing of his righteousness at this present season, that he might himself be just, and the justifier of him that hath faith in Jesus. Where then is the glory? It is excluded. By what manner of Law? Of works [the law of works]? Nay, but by a law of faith. We reckon therefore that a man is justified by faith apart from the works of the law (Romans 3:23-28). (27:111)

2.4. *Epistle to the Romans and the Gospels ("The Road of Galilee")*

After his sixty-lecture series, Uchimura wrote an impressive short essay entitled "The Epistle to the Romans and the Gospels." In this essay about the life of Jesus in the Gospels ("The Road of Galilee"), Uchimura commented:

Leaving Romans, and entering the Gospels, I feel as if I am leaving a great artificial public garden and entering into a great natural forest. Although Paul is a great [man], he is a man of strenuous endeavor. Jesus is the son of God and is a saint in nature. I feel I am drinking distilled water when reading Romans; but I feel I am ladling water from a spring that splashes among rocks when studying the Gospel. There is no argument in Jesus; there is only a fragrance. There is no theology, but [only] irresistible inspiration. I do not know why, but I am aware that I am naturally unified to Jesus by studying his words and deeds in the Gospels. He is a wonderful man and it is a wonderful book. I cannot describe it as anything but inspiration. First of all, it would be futile to examine the articles of faith. Why is it so? It is so because it is so. I shall become like Jesus by touching him in the Gospels. Arriving at this point, church, ritual, theology, and articles of faith are useless, but I am aware that just as eagles mount up with stretched wings towards heaven, I am drawn to pure heaven through forgetting earth and self. (27:252)

This short essay conveys Uchimura's relief after such hard work on Romans that we can even, as it were, detect his sigh of relief. It is necessary for me to quote this passage, to make his soul's character known and to produce a balance or complementariness between Uchimura's attitude to Romans and his attitude to the Gospels, between his intellectual hard work and his infant-like devotion to Jesus. This should lead us to treat his lectures on Romans as initially appealing to our intelligence, rather than as inspiration, although nothing hinders us from ladling the water of the spring of life through hard intellectual analysis of the Epistle to the Romans.

3. Uchimura on Redemption in Romans 3:21-26

3.1. Uchimura's Understanding of the Relation between the Righteousness of God and Man's Faith

The relevant passages in Paul's epistle to the Romans that we will examine closely are, first, 1:16-17, and second, 3:21-26. The English translation of the texts Uchimura used (King James Authorized [Revised] Version, 1881) is as follows:

> 1:16For I am not ashamed of the gospel: for it is the power of God unto salvation, to every one that believeth; to the Jews first, and also to the Greeks. 17For therein is revealed a righteousness of God by faith unto faith: as it is written, But the righteous shall live by faith.

> 3:21But now apart from the law a righteousness of God hath been manifested, being witnessed by the law and the prophets; 22even the righteousness of God through faith in Jesus Christ unto all them that believe; for there is no distinction; 23for all have sinned, and fall short of the glory of God; being justified freely by his grace through the redemption that is in Christ Jesus: 24whom God set forth to be propitiation, through faith, by his blood, to shew his righteousness, because of the passing over of the sins done aforetime, in the forbearance of God; 25for

the shewing, *I say,* of his righteousness at this present season: [26]that he might himself be just, and the justifier of him that hath faith in Jesus.

Uchimura paid attention to the two occurrences of the word "faith" in 1:17 ("by faith unto faith"), and he offered several scholarly interpretations of the phrase. He justifiably rejected the ordinary understanding of this phrase as the "mere progress of faith," because this reading would separate its close connection with "the righteousness of God," by focusing merely on man's mental state as having faith to a degree. Instead, Uchimura introduced the following interpretation of the phrase as a plausible one: "from God's faith in man towards man's faith in God" (26:94). That is, the flow of faith is not confined in man's mental state but is derived from God's faith in man toward man's faith in God. Uchimura understood the fact that the word "faith" appeared twice in connection with God's righteousness, as showing a close connection between God's righteousness and God's faithfulness. "God's faith *(pistin theou)*" (3:3) toward man must be understood as the main theme of the epistle in relation to God's righteousness. Although he did not explicitly state this, Uchimura properly considers God's faithfulness as his own independent state of mind in a general context by stating that "God is absolutely faithful and the idea of God is never compatible with such a thought as unfaithful or untrue" (26:141). It is unfortunate that Uchimura did not explicitly pursue this interpretation of the passage as "based on God's faithfulness to man's faith." This sentence, "For therein [in the gospel] is revealed a righteousness of God by faith unto faith," corresponds to 3:22: "through the faithfulness of [in] Jesus Christ unto all them that believe." God's faithful attitude and act are distinct from and also basic for man's faith toward God as being the faithful revealer and as being the faithful receiver, both of whom are mediated by the faithfulness of Jesus Christ. If Uchimura had gone further in this line of thought in his analysis, this thought would have constituted a dimension in which God's character such as righteousness and faithfulness is revealed as independent of man's mental state toward God. This would have opened the possibility of a semantic analysis of these passages as a preliminary step to and a prestage of any theological interpretation. Without referring to God's faithfulness, what Uchimura really meant to convey cannot be properly understood.

In fact, Uchimura commented as follows:

It is evident in the text that the phrase "by [based on] faith unto faith" is closely linked to the manifestation of "the righteousness of God." Also from the context, it is inappropriate to take the view of "the progress of faith." I do think here that Paul meant by this phrase that the righteousness of God is something to be received based on faith, to be retained in faith, and being complete based on faith. As I have said before, God's righteousness is the righteousness which God gives and reveals to man and is not based on the product of man's effort. Man is justified only on the basis of faith, not by his own deeds and merits. That is, man receives God's righteousness based on faith. This is a great grace that is bestowed on man and the privileges which man embraces. No matter who he is, if he returns and believes in his Father, God and in Jesus Christ, he is forgiven by faith alone and justified and he basks in grace. If so, is it required for its continuation of grace to make one's effort? No, it is sufficient with faith which gazes up at Christ alone. That is, the way of continuing in righteousness and the way of being sanctified consist in merely to keep holding faith. In other words, the life after having been made righteous by faith is the one sanctified by faith. That is, to keep retaining God's righteousness by faith. Then, how is this righteousness completed? By man's effort? No, it is bestowed as the result of faith which gazes up at Jesus alone. In other words, the life which is justified by faith and sanctified by faith results in being glorified by faith at the end. The glorification is the completeness of righteousness. That is, God's righteousness is made complete by faith.

God's righteousness is the one which is received by faith, retained in faith and completed by faith. This is the meaning of the sentence that "a righteousness of God is revealed by faith unto faith." One begins with faith, proceeds with faith and ends with faith. In its inception and in its intermediate road and in its end, i.e. throughout everything the faith is center. The maximum beatitude being possibly added in this universe is bestowed on man standing on the mere one line which is constituted by coming to believe and holding its faith in duration. To convey this is the gospel. Therefore this is good tidings. That is why there are many people who hesitate to believe this. God's grace is however filled in this universe, isn't it? God's love is overflowing over everything, isn't it? God, who moistens grass and tree by dipping dew from heaven and makes birds sing high the joy of life, is always prepared to bestow infinite grace on mankind. Man who is supposed to receive this, however, does not come to think the unique qualification of receiving this by wandering around in the dark valley of vacuous effort or rejecting it due to his stubbornness. Insofar as man does not hold the faith which is the unique qualification, God who waits for bestowing does not find a way to bestow it. (26:95)

In this passage, we can find how Uchimura argues the completeness of righteousness with respect to the completeness of faith. While Uchimura presupposes as the meaning of "by faith unto faith" the diachronic situation of "duration" in which "One begins with faith, proceeds with faith and ends with faith," he refuses to see any progress in faith at any stage of its diachronic situation. Instead, Uchimura emphasizes such an understanding of faith that the faith is retained and is itself being complete as something corresponding to God's faithfulness with respect to the reception of God's righteousness. Unless faith is in itself complete, it will not be sufficient to receive the completeness of God's righteousness. In any stage of having faith in the diachronic situation, anyone, no matter who he is, who receives God's righteousness and keeps holding it is being completed in terms of his faith. This is what Uchimura grasped in the allegedly central message of the whole Bible in Romans 3:21-26.

The concept of "[God's righteousness] being complete based on faith" as well as the idea of faith as a "great grace" in this passage are comprehensible only by considering God's faithful act through the faithfulness of Jesus Christ, regardless of the mental act of faith in humankind that is inevitably varied in degree and depth. There are some unique characteristics of faith in this argument. First, one's faith does not depend in any degree on one's mental state, but is complete in itself. Anyone who receives God's righteousness must be regarded to be himself complete with respect to his faith. Second, faith is simply a passive act of receiving God's righteousness. Third, this passive act itself is a grace. These characteristics come from Uchimura's understanding of human faith as not being severed from God's faithful act. Uchimura expressed his unqualified faith in man's part in this process. This is because Uchimura did not want to sever the faith that man holds from God's faithful act and from his righteousness. This is the gist of Protestantism. Martin Luther simply connected it to *fides Christi* (faith of Christ), which is emphasized in the introduction of his *Lectures on Galatians* (1535).

Along the same interpretive vein, Uchimura, who took Romans 3:22 as a passage in which "necessary and explanatory verbs are omitted," supplied them as follows: "The righteousness of God [the righteousness being revealed]/through faith in Jesus Christ [the righteousness being received]/unto all people [the righteousness being issued]/all them that believe [the righteousness being retained]/for there is no distinction" (26:171). That is,

God's righteousness is the one that is being revealed, issued, and received, and furthermore retained by all people who believe. As for the phrase "through faith in Jesus Christ" (although I read "of," which is adopted in the marginal note of KJV instead of "in" [as I shall discuss in due course]), we may wonder why man's mental state can become a medium of God's revelation. This is because, as was generally understood by figures like Martin Luther, man's faith is itself God's initiative and is an act of grace through which God causes man to believe in Jesus Christ (*Preface to Romans,* 1545). One is supposed to understand God's initiative in man's having faith in Jesus Christ. This is a pious or theological reading of the text.

God's initiative act is emphasized in receiving, retaining, and being complete by one's faith. *Faith* should be understood as not severing one's mental state but as having faith *from* God's faithfulness toward man. The characteristics of faith as receiving, retaining, and being complete are something that can and should be carried out *in front of God* without paying attention to the degrees and varieties of faith. In other words, these characteristics of faith must be factual about human faith in front of God, that is, God's cognition of man's faith on the basis of the revelation of faith of Jesus Christ, regardless of how we think of our own faith. What is revealed through the faithfulness of Jesus Christ is that anyone who is regarded by God as being "the person based on the faith of Jesus" *(ton ek pisteōs Iēsou)* is justified (3:26; cf. "the person based on the faith of Abraham" [*tōi ek pisteōs Abraam*], 4:16).

This language belongs to a different grammar from the language of our own flesh, in which there are progress and variation among people who have faith. In the sight of God, faith is understood as something that is received, is retained, and is complete with respect to God's righteousness through the faith of Jesus Christ.

3.2. *Uchimura's Distinction between "before God" and "before Man"*

Uchimura distinguished between "before God" (in the sight of God) and "before man" (in the sight of man) as follows:

> What Paul dealt with is not "before man" but "before God." He [Paul] did not care how he appeared to be before man. Some may be saints or men of noble character. Further, some may be sanctified or may be men of great faith. There may be found in them nobility of character and

depth of intellect. But each of these [qualities] is something "before man" and thus is reflected through the eye of man, but is not [a quality that exists] "before God." It is looking at earthly phenomena from the same point of view as that same earth rather than looking down from the viewpoint of heaven. When "the Lord looks down from heaven, all men are sinners" (Ps. 14:2). In front of God, all men are sinners. (26:157)

Although Uchimura did not distinguish these two perspectives according to a semantic analysis of the text, nor always keep this clear distinction in his interpretations of Romans, I believe that the distinction was essential for him, when he thought of Christ as a new revelation of a righteous man before God. In this view, insofar as one is confined to one's own kind, that is, insofar as one lives only in front of other fellow human beings, one is led astray and remains in darkness. I construe this as based on Uchimura's theological soundness of judgment in not severing our mental states from God's initiative acts.

In Uchimura's way of thinking, it is not enough for one merely to be rid of any matter before man, but of any matter thought under the law of works. Thus he can concentrate on the Christ event — an event that represents the overcoming of the bondage of the Mosaic law of works. "But now apart from the law the righteousness of God has been manifested, being witnessed by the law and the prophets" (3:21). Uchimura said:

> The sudden change of the situation is indicated by "but now." The fact that there is an entirely different world is suddenly revealed to a man who hitherto had been kept roaming in the darkness under the bondage of the law [of works]. The border of change from the world of darkness to the world of lightness is marked by the short but important phrase "but now." While the previous stage is one of a disordered world, the censure of sin, and destruction by the law, the latter [stage] is one of the forgiveness of sin, the manifestation of righteousness, and salvation by the Gospel. . . . The "but now" indeed is the ringing bell that announces the dawn of the new world. The emergence of the new world is based on the advent of Christ. Due to this advent, the bondage of the old law disappeared and the salvation of freedom became reality among us. (26:166)

Although he did not make a semantic analysis of the text, Uchimura intuitively knew that 3:21-26 is the language of revelation of a righteous man. It is the language before God in which God's faithful act and under-

standing of man through Jesus Christ are dictated and reported by Paul.
Uchimura said:

> In the last part of the twenty-second verse, there occurs a phrase, "for
> there is no distinction." Because of this concise expression, it is not cer-
> tain what kind of distinction is denied in this sentence. . . . Since the
> verse says that there is no distinction in the degree of God's righteous-
> ness bestowed to people who believe, it must mean that there is no dis-
> tinction among people. This is what everyone can immediately agree
> upon. That is, Paul claimed that anyone, whoever he is, is justified by his
> faith . . . [that is] there is no distinction in nationality. Man, however
> good or bad he may be as an individual, is justified by his faith alone.
> There is also no distinction between old and young, man and woman,
> wise and stupid, rich and poor, righteous and unrighteous, or good and
> bad men. It is the ordinary view that only righteous and good men are
> saved, and sinners and bad men perish. However, the Gospel does not
> draw the distinction between a good and a bad man, a righteous and an
> unrighteous man. A man is justified only if he believes. On this vital
> point, any man *who comes to belong to God* and *who is obedient to Christ*
> through his own repentance, is given God's righteousness. (26:173)

In his explanation of justification by faith alone, Uchimura stated, as
an objective fact, that the person who is justified is "any man who belongs
to God and is obedient to Christ." This is a fact *before God,* in the sense that
God's understanding of man's belonging to him is the reality of the human
being before God. Uchimura developed the language of "before God" by
describing the objective fact of man's situation without its clear conceptual
grasp.

Uchimura commented on this phrase as follows: "The phrase 'there is
no distinction' is indeed great. In an era [when men were] seeking for distinction in anything, how great Paul was, standing his ground through
conviction! Anyone, whoever he is, is justified by faith. Therefore, on this
one point of salvation, any difference that exists among human beings
ceases to be any difference at all. Therefore, even a sinful man is saved if he
believes. By this reasoning, we are at peace for the first time" (26:174). Before man, there are many distinctions among people. But before God,
through the redemption through the blood of Jesus Christ, any distinction
has disappeared. Uchimura grasped the difference of situations between
what is present before man and what is present before God.

Uchimura's own commitment to this paragraph comes from its clear statement of redemption through Jesus Christ. He said:

> The last phrase of verse 3:24 is "through the redemption that is in Christ Jesus." The question is why a man is justified freely only by grace. This extreme grace is beyond our comprehension because it is so good, and it is hard to believe why this extreme privilege has been bestowed on man. This phrase [3:24] answers the question of what is the foundation for this grace. Paul says "through the redemption that is in Christ Jesus." This is the explanation of the fact that a man who is not righteous is [nevertheless] made righteous. That is, man is continuously made righteous by faith alone because of the redemption of Christ. To see Christ's cross as the redemption of all humanity's sin is the indispensable basis of evangelism. Although new theology today excludes this [concept] as an old thought, the precious nature of the redemption itself represents a spiritual medicine that cures the wounds of the soul. The precious blood of God's only son is shed for all people, and thus Christ's death is the death of redemption in which Christ himself bears the sin of all people. Thus, we who are sinful and unrighteous are regarded as not sinful and as righteous. Therefore, the redemption of Christ is indeed the foundation of the Gospel. . . . As heaven is high and the earth is wide, this one thing is very sure. (26:185)

The foundation of the gospel is thus laid down in the faithful act of Jesus of Nazareth, whose life is seen by God as the medium for conveying his own faithfulness and righteousness. Uchimura reports, through Paul, God's cognition of Christ's death as "the death of redemption in which Christ himself bears the sin of all people." This is what is revealed in the life of Jesus of Nazareth in front of God.

4. Semantic Analysis of Romans 3:19-31

4.1. Ergon and Logos as Paul's Basic Way of Thought: Complexity of Works and Its Articulated Demonstrations

The above passage explains the marrow of the gospel as Uchimura understood it through the study of Romans. In this section, I shall look further into what Uchimura intended to say from the perspective of my semantic analysis of the relevant text. I shall endorse the direction and intention of Uchimura's interpretation so as to confirm that he intuitively grasped the argument in 3:21-26 as the language before God.

Paul's basic attitude in proclaiming the gospel in Romans consists in the complexity of his *ergon* (deed, work) and its articulation by *logos* (account). He says, "I will not dare to speak of any things save those which Christ wrought through me, for the obedience of the Gentiles, by word *(logos)* and deed *(ergon)*, in the power of signs and wonders, in the power of the Holy Spirit" (15:18). According to his own cognition, his *ergon* expressed in this epistle consists of the complexity of God's act, man's (Paul's) act, and the intercession of the Holy Spirit. On the basis of this *ergon*, Paul writes in such an articulated way that anyone can understand what he means without appealing to the interceding Holy Spirit in one's soul. In one passage, he says that "we write none other things unto you, than what you read and you understand" (2 Cor. 1:13). Paul understands his mission of proclaiming the gospel for Gentiles as being a "debtor both to Greeks and to Barbarians, both to the wise and to the foolish" (Rom. 1:14). I construe this to mean that to persuade both wise and foolish people among the Gentiles, Paul adopted two methods in this epistle.

God's cognition of righteous man is dictated and delivered by Paul in such a general way that anyone who knows Greek grammar and the current language can understand what God conceived and revealed about these matters. This kind of argument should be taken as "persuasion of wisdom" that is contrasted with "demonstration of the Spirit and of power" in his "argument and [his] preaching" (1 Cor. 2:4). In fact, I deduce that while he delivers an argument of persuasion of wisdom, for instance, in Romans 1:18–4:25 and chapters 9–11, Paul argues chapters 5–8 as a whole according to the demonstration of the Spirit and of power, although nothing restricts his every word from being spirited, insofar as we can detect the dimension of rational persuasive argument in it. The distinguishing mark between these two ways of argument consists in whether Paul directly mentions the Spirit in his argument or not. Paul persuades wise people through the articulation of complexity of *erga* (works) by constituting three mutually independent and coherent language networks: (A) (3:21-26), (B) (3:19-20), and (C) (3:27-31). These three dimensions are articulated without referring to the Holy Spirit. On the other hand, Paul also adopted the demonstration of Spirit and power without conceding the weakness of flesh in connecting (A) + (C) (e.g., chapters 5, 6 [except 6:12-20], and 8) together with (B) + (C) (e.g., chapter 7), where + stands for the mediation by the Holy Spirit.

4.2. Language of Revelation: A Semantic Theory

In general, any theory of meaning is concerned with the relation among language, soul/mind as the agent of the language, and reality. When we make a semantic analysis of Romans according to the persuasion of wisdom, we find that Paul articulated at least three types of human beings. Paul is a realist in his linguistic behavior, just as his notion of "revelation" *(apokalypsis)* implies (1:17, 18; 8:18). This word in its verbal form appears in three crucial passages, thus opening new dimensions in 1:17 and in 1:18. The last appearance informs us of the revelation of the last day to open the new heaven and earth (8:18).

In the realist semantic theory, the meaning of a term or what a term signifies is supposed to correspond to the way in which the relevant thing in the world consists. The significance of a term is fixed by objects in the world.[7] In our context, what God thinks and reveals establishes the reality before him. Paul believes a current human language such as Greek, however limited it is, can capture God's initiative act as the revelation, including his will, cognition, and judgment on mankind. I am simply concerned with Paul's language networks without considering his biblical, historical, and theological backgrounds so that we can establish the basic constraints within which biblical and theological interpretations should be carried out.

God makes known his righteousness based on his faithfulness through the faithfulness of Jesus Christ (3:21-26). This revelation is reported in its introductory and parallel passage: "God's righteousness is revealed in him (Jesus Christ) on the basis of [God's] faithfulness to [man's] faithfulness. As it is written, 'But the righteous shall live on the basis of faithfulness'" (1:17). God was faithful and thus righteous, when his promise was realized in the faithfulness of Jesus Christ. When Paul looks at "the faithfulness of Jesus Christ," which is not separated from God's righteousness, and spins the words, it constitutes an independent language network on righteous man before God. God's cognition of man through the faithfulness of Jesus Christ can be called type (A), "a report of the revelation of righteous man in the gospel."

Likewise, God makes known his righteousness based on his work through the letters on the tables of stone to Moses and his people. He re-

---

7. Cf. K. Chiba, "Aristotle on Essence and Defining-Phrase in His Dialectic," in *Definition in Greek Philosophy,* ed. D. Charles (Oxford: Oxford University Press, 2010), 203-51.

veals his righteousness based on his work by applying the Mosaic law to human deeds (1:18–3:20). Paul reports that "The wrath of God is revealed from Heaven against all ungodliness and unrighteousness of men, who hold down the truth in unrighteousness" (1:18). God is righteous when he carries out his works by punishing the ungodliness and evilness according to distributive justice. When Paul looks at "the law of works" and spins the words, it constitutes an independent language network on sinners before God. It is constituted by putting "the law of works" in its center, which is accompanied by such words as "work," "sin," "unrighteousness," and "wrath." God's cognition of man through the law can be labeled type (B), "a report of the revelation of sinners under the law."

When Paul, in turn, sees mankind as being independent of God's initiative, he describes the reality from the man-centric perspective. The third group, type (C), comprises autonomous beings who live in responsible freedom. Paul describes this third type by saying, "I speak after the manner of man *(anthrōpinon)* because of the weakness of your flesh" (6:19). "Flesh" means the principle of life for a natural entity having a body made of earth. The weakness of the flesh consists of its propensity or tendency to consider the limit of body as the limit of self by being unable to think of the spiritual realm as his own constituent. This phrase "the manner of man" suggests that the autonomous being (type C) understands man from a human-centric standpoint, in which, for instance, the word "slave" is applied in the neutral way either to "the slave of sin" or to "the slave of righteousness" (6:17-20). Paul understands such a man to be one who could become either a righteous being (type A) or a sinful being (type B). Groups (A) and (B) constitute the languages of "before God," and group (C) constitutes the language of "before man." Paul spares no pains to articulate these dimensions because of his love for weak people.

On the basis of this semantic analysis, what I intend to convey in the name of "philosophy of faithfulness" should be located as a prestage of biblical and theological interpretations so that anyone, whether a believer or a nonbeliever, can agree with my analysis, insofar as the text is concerned. I am simply concerned with the language networks Paul spins by taking God's revelation just as it is. Any human language that is no doubt created from the man-centric perspective within a given society and environment is inevitably limited and insufficient to capture God's initiative act and state. Nonetheless, Paul assumes that it is possible for him to report God's cognition, judgment, and act on human beings, as far as our understanding is concerned.

My translation of the relevant passage (3:19-31) in which we find these three language networks, (B), (A), and (C), in order, is as follows:

(B) ¹⁹Now we know that whatever things the law says, it speaks to those who are under the law, that every mouth may be closed, and all the world may be brought under the judgment of God. ²⁰Because on the basis of the law of works, no flesh will be justified before God. For there is [God's] knowledge of sin through the law.

(A) ²¹But now apart from the law, God's righteousness, which is witnessed by the law and the prophets, has been manifested, ²²God's righteousness manifested to all those who believe through the faithfulness of Jesus Christ. For there is no separation [between the righteousness of God and the faithfulness of Jesus Christ]. ²³For all have sinned and fallen short of the glory of God, ²⁴being now justified freely by his grace through the redemption in Christ Jesus, ²⁵whom God set forth as a propitiation [i.e., a compensation from God] through the faithfulness in his blood resulting in the indication of his righteousness because he passes over sins committed beforehand ²⁶in God's forbearance, toward a vindication of his righteousness in this present opportunity in which he might himself be righteous as well [as in the law], in justifying anyone at all on the basis of Jesus' faithfulness.

(C) ²⁷Therefore, where is the boasting? It is excluded. By what manner of law? Of works? No, but by a law of faithfulness. ²⁸For we recognize that a man is justified by faithfulness apart from the law of works. ²⁹Or is God the God of Jews only? Is he not the God of Gentiles also? Yes, of Gentiles also, ³⁰since indeed there is one God who will justify the circumcised [not on the basis of the law of works but] on the basis of faithfulness, and the uncircumcised through *the* faithfulness [of Jesus Christ]. ³¹Do we then nullify the law through faithfulness? May it never be! No, we confirm the law [of works].

In these passages, Paul distinguishes these three language layers by articulating the initiative of act that may either belong to God (A, B) or man (C). A basic characteristic of the language before God consists in that insofar as the agent of revelation is God, the relevant words and sentences that report God's cognition and act must be understood, first of all, by God himself as they are. Thus, what Paul does in the language before God is, as it were, translating into Greek what God has revealed through Jesus of Nazareth and through the law of works.

According to our understanding of the distributive justice that is seen in the precept, for instance, "an eye for an eye," if man is made righteous through the obedient act of law, he is entitled to claim being righteous as a due wage of his own merit and to claim that he knows God's righteousness through his own virtuousness. But this is denied by (B) (3:19-20). It is already revealed in (B) that any flesh on the basis of the law of works has no chance to be righteous through works of the law, because there is God's knowledge of sin through the law. This passage must be understood from God's perspective such that "knowledge of sin through the law" does not primarily belong to man's mental state as "awareness" of sin as it is usually understood, but belongs to God's knowledge of sin through the law.

The traditional translations of (A) must be corrected according to the perspective of God's revelation through the faithful event as well. First of all, there is an extremely important linguistic fact (which has escaped the notice of commentators). The proper name "Jesus Christ" was never used in Romans to designate an agent of an action. While "Jesus" was viewed as an agent, as a responsible human being (see 3:26; 4:24; 8:11; 10:9; 14:14), "Christ" was viewed as a heavenly resurrected agent who makes intercession for man at the right hand of God (e.g., 8:34; 15:7, 18). But Paul could not ascribe any action to a person who is constitutive of two types of agents, *both* man *and* God. Jesus Christ is the entity who has incorporated both the being Jesus (wholly a man), and the being Son of God (thus opening a new reality for human beings in the [D] perspective). Since Jesus Christ is such a unique entity, Paul employed locutions such as the prepositions "in" and "through" before the proper name "Jesus Christ," so that the being, Jesus Christ, could be understood as the medium *in* whom and *through* whom God reveals his judgment and his intention toward human beings (see 2:16; 3:24; 5:1; 6:3; and 8:1).

Therefore, the reading of "[*pisteōs*] *Iesou Xristou*" (3:22) as the subjective genitive by taking it as Jesus Christ himself having faith as an agent should be rejected, because this proper name is never taken to signify an agent. On the other hand, reading it as the objective genitive, according to which it designates one's mental state of having faith in Jesus Christ, should be rejected as well, because it cannot be a medium of God's revelation. Instead, it should be read as the genitive of belonging, in which it conveys that the faithfulness belongs to Jesus Christ, who is the mediator.

This might be resisted by people such as Luther and Uchimura, as we saw in 3.1, who take that having faith on our part itself is God's act in such a way that to believe in God is to be made to believe by God. Thus, they would claim that our mental act of having faith can be taken to be the mediation of the revelation of God's righteousness. This is the reading not to sever (A) horizon from (C) horizon by demanding the intercession of the Holy Spirit to unite them as (A) + (C) = (D). Paul, however, writes this paragraph so that it can be understood without appealing to the intercession of the Holy Spirit, although nothing hinders the Holy Spirit's working simultaneously in any human faithful act. I shall discuss this issue again when we develop (C) language.

4.3. Asymmetry in the Meanings of the Term

We should grasp the meaning of the term according to the differences of God's act and man's act. It is evident that when the same word is applied both to God and to man, there are asymmetries in the meaning of the term. Paul is, no doubt, aware of this asymmetry. The following fact shows his awareness that when he ascribes *pistis* to God and man, while he employs its noun case only for God (3:3, 22), he employs its verb too in man's case (e.g., 4:3; 15:13).

In (A), Paul reports what God understood in terms of *pistis*, that is, "faithfulness." In the language of (A), "the faithfulness of Jesus Christ" is placed at the center of the language network. The word *pistis*, which is ascribed to both God and man, contains cognitive and ethical aspects, as the ordinary Greek as well as other languages imply. In terms of the cognitive virtue *(dianoētikē aretē)* and the moral virtue *(ēthikē aretē)*, while God does not lack anything by being himself sufficient in these respects, man is insufficient at least in cognition with respect to his relationship with God (cf. Aristotle, *Nicomachean Ethics* 1.13.1103a5). Insofar as God is concerned, given that the cognitive aspect is not considered in him in showing his *pistis* toward man, we cannot render its translation as "faith." The "faith" inevitably involves man's insufficient cognitive state in which one believes God without fully knowing it. When God is faithful toward man through the faithfulness of Jesus Christ, man's ethical aspect is at stake whether man is faithful so as to correspond to "God's faithfulness" (3:3; cf. Mark 1:11). God's righteousness based on his faithfulness is realized in Jesus of Nazareth to the effect that God has kept his promise to Abraham in the Christ event and not told a lie. Keeping a promise and not telling a lie are reported to characterize an aspect of God's faithfulness as "truth" (Rom. 3:4). Any faithful relationship is realized by overcoming any cognitive insufficiency, just as it is confirmed in a story of Jesus that a man in crisis cried out and said, "I believe; help thou mine unbelief" (Mark 9:24). In such a situation, the faithful relationship between God and man alone is what matters.

Where God's initiative act is concerned, the words and sentences must be understood from the perspective of what God understands by the relevant words. In (A), God's faithfulness is revealed through the faithfulness of Jesus Christ to all who believe. Here the word *pistis* refers primarily to what God understands by the word. Thus this word in "all those who believe" (3:22 [A]) as well as anyone at all on the basis of Jesus' faithfulness (3:26) is not directly describing anyone's mental state, except Jesus'. Insofar as God regards anyone to be the one whose faith is based on the faithfulness of Jesus, he justifies him/her. It becomes the proper vehicle for the revelation of his righteousness so as to bestow it to the people who believe. This explains that his righteousness based on his faithfulness is not separated from that of Jesus Christ. Thus this (A) dimension is focally constituted by the faithfulness of Jesus Christ so that any constituent of this horizon should be construed by locating itself with respect to the relation to the faithfulness of Jesus Christ. We cannot get out of this gravitation.

Thus, when man is taking initiative in his having *pistis*, it should be translated into "faith," which is supposed to correspond to God's initiative faithfulness. On the other hand, when God's *pistis* is at issue, we have to pick up God's ethical or character aspect alone so that it should be translated into "faithfulness."

4.4. Redemption Based on the Faithfulness

Insofar as we stick to God's initiative in (A), we can see why the traditional interpretations have been so controversial and thus unsettled. The second part of verse 22 has been, insofar as I know, unanimously translated "For there is no distinction [among all people who believe]." This is supposed to explain why the addressee of the revelation is "all those who believe." This reading explains at most "all" by appealing to the negative reason as being lack of distinction due to the fact that all have sinned. It is unlikely that God does not see any distinction between the faith of, say, Mother Teresa, and my faith or Hitler's faith (cf. 5:14). I believe verse 22 should be translated from the perspective of God's self-cognition: "For there is no separation *(ou gar estin diastolē)* [between God's righteousness and the faithfulness of Jesus Christ]."[8] This sentence must describe God's state, cognition, and act based on his faithfulness rather than man's mental state, provided that the perspective of (A) is focally constituted by God's initiative act through the faithfulness of Jesus Christ. Thus this sentence is supposed to give a reason why God's righteousness is revealed to "all those who believe" rather than to all people who keep the law of works. God was and is faithful in Jesus Christ, by having kept his promise to his people.

If we appeal to more basic relations among the words "righteousness," "faithfulness," "to all those who believe," and "reveal," we must know at the formal level of this analysis what these words mean. The addressee of God's revelation must be referred to as "all those who believe" due to a formal constraint at the level of language and epistemology, which are basic ingredients of any theological language, for the relevant people to know God's righteousness. Insofar as the theological language can be understood at all, it must presuppose a current use of language and a cognitive structure that are basically shared by God as well. These are the most basic elements, so that any theological interpretation must be constrained by these analyses ultimately based on the principle of noncontradiction. As is evident to anyone, it is impossible to believe that someone is "faithful" if one also is "doubtful" about that person. Just as one cannot swim without presupposing water and thus one cannot grasp the meaning of "swimming" without grasping the meaning of "water," it is necessary for anyone who "knows" God's righteousness to have "faith" on his part. On this point, Paul does not consider how much faith one must have in order to be regarded by God as a man having faith

Then verses 23-26, which are in fact one long sentence with the explanatory particle *gar* (for), explain why there is no separation between the relevant righteousness and the faithfulness. Paul reports God's self-cognition of the inseparability. His righteousness is now severed from his law but is bound with the faithfulness of Jesus Christ. We now understand why Paul employs three similar phrases to emphasize the indication of God's righteousness in one sentence as "the faithfulness resulting in the indication of

---

8. W. Bauer offers only one translation of *diastolē* as *Unterschied.* I suspect that New Testament scholars have been and will be influenced by his dictionary. *Wörterbuch zum Neuen Testament* (Berlin, 1971). Liddell and Scott offer "drawing asunder," "separation," then "distinction." *Oxford Greek-English Dictionary,* 8th ed. (Oxford, 1996).

his righteousness," "toward the indication of his righteousness," and "himself to be righteous." All these are connected with the faithfulness of Jesus Christ. From God's perspective, it is indeed a good opportunity for God to take the faithfulness of Jesus Christ so as to indicate his righteousness. Paul reports their nonseparateness by mentioning "through [Jesus'] faithfulness," "resulting in the indication of his righteousness" and "justifying anyone at all on the basis of Jesus' faithfulness."

Now God's righteousness is separated from the law because Jesus of Nazareth carried out his faithful obedience on the cross. God is well pleased with his faithful life as the one that corresponds to his righteousness based on his faithfulness. Therefore God could reveal it not to the people who keep the Mosaic law, but to all those who believe. God took this chance to make it possible to redeem all sinners freely without any cost on man's part. All men are now to be justified freely by his grace through the redemption in Christ Jesus. Paul reports the reason why God set forth Jesus Christ as an atonement in his blood as compensation on his own part "*because* he passes over sins committed beforehand in God's forbearance." That is, Paul reports that God had his own cognition of not having shown his righteousness enough thus far. God regards the faithful obedience of Jesus as a good opportunity to compensate for the lack of his showing righteousness due to his forbearance in abstinence of applying the Mosaic law to the sins previously committed. On this occasion, God has compensated it not by his righteousness based on the law of works, but based on his faithfulness. He can now justify anyone at all who is based on the faithfulness of Jesus. The righteousness based on the faithfulness is now shown to be more basic for God himself than the righteousness based on the law of works.

In comparison with biblical and theological studies thus far, we can tell this much as the necessary and minimum extraction of the relevant passage, insofar as we only stick to God's initiative act. It has been debated whether this passage conveys the substituted punishment against Jesus or whether the death of Jesus as the ransom is paid to the devil, and so on. Paul does not report in (A) that God punished Jesus nor anyone else. God compensated his lack of showing righteousness to the people who believe by setting forth Jesus Christ as their atonement. It is true that God put him as a substitute by his death for sinners to redeem sinners. But God revealed in this event that the righteousness based on the faithfulness made it possible for God to redeem sinners without any cost on the part of people.

One may be able to say from Jesus' perspective that he is determined to be a sacrificial offering for the sake of sinful men's atonement. In this substitution, however, God did not regard Jesus as the sinner. When Paul says in 2 Corinthians 5:21 that "him who knew no sin he made to be sin on our behalf; that we might become the righteousness of God in him," God's cognition of "him who knew no sin" was kept throughout in the act of redemption (cf. Matt. 26:39). Sinless Jesus died for their redemption, as the substitute for sinners. The expression "him . . . he made to be sin" means merely the substitution for sinners from God's perspective. Consider also the sentence "Concerning sin, God has punished the sin in the flesh [of Jesus]" (Rom. 8:3). God did not punish Jesus but the sin, by offering him as a substitution for sinners on the cross. In this semantic analysis, however, I offer this minimal, and most confirmable, reading of "the atonement" by confining the matter to God's initiative act.

4.5. Justification by Faith on Man's Part: An Outcome of the Language of Revelation

Given that God's revelation is generally stated, God's cognition and will are not so much clearly revealed to each particular individual as revealed in Jesus Christ. We should say that God's cognition of and will to human beings are revealed most evidently in Jesus of Nazareth. Therefore the language of revelation should be differently treated from the human-centric (C) language network. In (C), 3:27-31, which is introduced by "therefore" *(oun)*, Paul's own conviction is stated. Paul states a result deduced from the language of revelation, that is, (B) and (A) thus far developed. First, Paul deduces that any boast on one's own part (such as regarding oneself as righteous and virtuous) is excluded (3:27). Through the faithfulness of Jesus, no boast is permitted anymore; that is, Paul is convinced that God is well pleased with the faith of a person who is like a child or a repentant sinner. Then Paul deduces in 3:28, which later became the locus for "justification by faith": "For *we recognize* that a man is justified by faithfulness apart from the law of works." Paul, as a representative of humanity indicated by the subject "we," understands the significance of God's revelation in the faithfulness of Jesus Christ as the justification by faith on "man's" part from perspective (C). But we should keep in mind that unless God is well pleased by man's faith, man will not be justified. In this sense man's faith is always treated as a response to God's faithfulness. This sentence is delivered by Paul, who considers God's initiative within the framework of his conviction indicated by the main clause that "we recognize."

Now that the righteousness based on the faithfulness is more basic than the one based on works for both God and man, man has the possibility of encompassing the law of works by "the law of faithfulness" (3:27). We can understand this basic state in God's soul analogically with man's soul. We can keep a precept superficially in terms of what we do without having a faithful attitude. On the other hand, when we are faithful, we sincerely try to keep a precept. Thus, having faith itself contains the possibility of fulfilling a precept. In this sense, the faithfulness is more basic than work in both God and man.

Passage (C) sheds light on the solution of the tension between the gospel and the law. Jesus of Nazareth fulfilled the law of works "summed up" by love of neighbor by his faithfulness (13:9-10). Paul concludes that "indeed there is one God who will justify the circumcised [not on the basis of the law of works but] on the basis of faithfulness, and the uncircumcised through *the* faithfulness [of Jesus Christ]. Do we then nullify the law through faithfulness? May it never be! No, we confirm the law [of works]" (3:30-31). Anyone who has infant-like faith at the bottom of his soul corresponding to the faithfulness of Jesus is able to confirm the law as God's will and tries to be faithful by fulfilling the law. The righteousness based on faithfulness can certainly do this, insofar as man's soul carries faithfulness at its bottom as well. God sees the bottom of one's soul rather than one's works. This is the conclusion Paul deduced from the (B) and (A) passages.

In this way, Paul secures the (C) perspective. It is necessary to hold this dimension based on one's own responsible freedom, because God's will is not revealed more clearly to anyone than in Jesus of Nazareth. Paul, who is cognitively limited in terms of his own salvation, says, "I buffet my body, and bring it into bondage: lest by any means, after that I have preached to others, I myself should be rejected" (1 Cor. 9:27). He does not know sufficiently enough about his future, although he well knows himself to be righteous insofar as he takes himself to be in Jesus Christ, who is revealed by God as faithful and righteous. Man's faith is not sufficient for the perfect cognition of God, insofar as he is in flesh. "O the depth of the riches both of the wisdom and the knowledge of God! How unsearchable are his judgments, and his ways past tracing out!" (Rom. 11:33). That is why man needs to have faith in what was revealed in Jesus Christ. Paul's orders to the people of Rome are as follows: "The faith [C] which you have according to yourself *(kata seauton)*, have you [A] before God" (14:22). This order is addressed to the person in group (C) so as not to sever his faith, which is held according to his own free responsibility *from* the faithfulness revealed in Jesus Christ as constituting the faith of people in group (A).

When Paul observed the different states of human beings, and addressed the people of Rome in the imperative mood, this dimension of his language was different from the language of the revelation "before God" for groups (A) and (B). When Paul spoke to the Romans, he ordered, "Even so, reckon you also yourselves to be dead unto sin, but alive unto God in Christ Jesus" (6:11), and he presupposed that the people of Rome might or might not obey the order. For if Paul did not presuppose the possible disobedience of the Romans, he would not have delivered his statement in the imperative mood. The persons Paul addressed in the imperative mood were capable of being either righteous or sinful. The conditional clause "if Christ dwells in you" (8:10) presupposes a similar situation. In this clause, Paul considers the possibility of Christ's not dwelling in believers. The possibility is that the person addressed by an imperative is one who lives, not in front of God, but in front of man. It is not clearly revealed to each person who is righteous and who is not. That is why having faith is always substantial for every man. In this way, Paul develops these three language networks, (A), (B), and (C), which are mutually independent.

4.6. Uchimura's "Only Qualification" on Man's Part

Uchimura, however, explains Romans 3:21-31 at the theological level by saying, "God is always prepared to bestow his unfathomable grace to man. But man who is supposed to receive this grace does not come to think of only one qualification so as for it to be received either by being unprepared or by rejecting it with his obstinate heart or by wandering around in a dark valley of vacuous endeavor. When one does not hold faith, which is the only qualification of receiving grace, there is eventually no way of bestowing grace for the Heavenly Father who is waiting and willing to bestow it" (26:96). Uchimura, who did not semantically distinguish between the dimensions of man's reality before God and before man, is here obliged to put one's mental state of having faith as "the only qualification" of justification and thus as an exception of "no distinction." While my translation of verse 22, "there is no separation," is different from the usual translation, I can agree with Uchimura that there is no distinction among all men, insofar as we stick to God's cognition that "all have sinned." But, as we have seen, this sentence constitutes only a part of one long sentence that explains why there is no separation. Paul primarily reports the revelatory activity by God to the effect that God's righteousness is not separated from its mediative faithfulness of Jesus Christ.

In his attractive short commentary on Romans, W. Barclay says something similar: "God gave man free-will, and God respects that free-will. In the last analysis not even God can interfere with that free-will. . . . Before man there stands an open choice. It has to be so. Without choice there can be no goodness, and without choice there can be no love. . . . If men deliberately choose to turn their backs on God, then, after God has sent His Son Jesus Christ into the world, not even He can do anything about it."[9] Barclay delivers theological language on the basis of (C) language. Barclay, in what follows, guesses God's mental state by the analogy of the father whose son turned his back, in the comprehensible language network of "free-will."

If our having faith as a mental state is the qualification for and the condition of being justified, it is contradicted by the statement "since all have sinned and fallen short of the glory of God, being now justified freely by his grace through the redemption in Christ Jesus" (3:23-24). I think that "free grace" cannot be reconciled with any human condition. Anyone who believes in God's sight knows that God is righteous through the faithfulness of Jesus Christ and receives righteousness through it.

Before God all people receive righteousness freely by his grace through the redemption that is in Christ Jesus. God justifies "the ungodly" "freely by God's grace" (3:24; 4:5). God's free grace rejects any involvement of the human condition, insofar as we stick to the meaning of the term. We should not call having faith "a qualification" of receiving grace. This is merely a formal constraint of the linguistic and epistemological level in order to understand God's revelation of justification, insofar as God's revelation can be understood by us at all and we stick to the perspective (A) in which any human condition is not considered. If God's righteousness were not separated from the law of works, there would be no room for faith coming in (Gal. 3:25). Only the doer of the law of works may know God's righteousness and receive righteousness as due reward. Since this faithfulness is a mediator of God's righteousness, Paul could say "all" people who believe know that God is righteous and receive it.

---

9. W. Barclay, *The Letter to the Romans* (Edinburgh, 1963), 21.

4.7. The Gospel and the Law

When Uchimura said, "Christians are not under the law," he was aware of the contrast in terms of reality before God between (A) and (B). He wrote:

> Paul says, "For sin shall not have dominion over you: for you are not under the law, but under grace (6:14)." One thing that should be noted is that Christians are not under the law. It is required for us to be insulated from the law [of works] either by abolishing the law completely, or by ourselves being sanctified to such a degree that we do not violate any law. In a word, morality is unnecessary. Therefore, this is very revolutionary. Indeed, it is quite dangerous if we misunderstand it. However, we cannot keep away this important truth by being frightened of misunderstanding. Unless man reaches the mental state in which morality is unnecessary, one cannot know the delight and preciousness of faith. Indeed, sanctification is the border which shows the needlessness of morality. Thus, abolishing morality is a necessary element if man is to come to authentic faith and sanctification. When one is [living] under morality, one only realizes one's own sin and [one] is never able to reach the delight of faith, and of being blessed of sanctification. (26:259)

When we carry out a semantic analysis of the text, which results in at least three perspectives on the reality of human beings, we no longer find any alleged contradiction in Paul himself. However, commentators are puzzled by the following, apparently contradictory (or at least conflicting) sentences between types (A) and (B). While Paul says in one passage about group (B): "God will recompense every man according to his works" (2:6), in another passage he says about group (A): "Now if a man does have works to his credit, his wages are not reckoned as a matter of grace but as a debt; but to the man who has no work to his credit but believes in him who justifies the ungodly, his faith is reckoned for righteousness" (4:4-5). Some commentators take the (B) claim as "a warning."[10] These two passages are

---

10. E. Jüngel, *Paulus und Iesus* (Tübingen: J. C. B. Mohr, 1962), 70. Similarly E. Käsemann construed the doctrine of justification as superior to the doctrine of judgment according to the work by presupposing both doctrines as being comparable at the same level. In his commentary on Rom. 2:11, Käsemann wrote: "One cannot simply establish the contradiction and demand that it be upheld. Otherwise Paul becomes schizophrenic. Christ as the fulfillment of the law is not yet treated in this passage, so that the problem also cannot be blunted in this way. The decisive thing is that the doctrine of judgment according to works

not contradictory, however, because 1:18–3:20 points to the language network of (B), that is, to the Mosaic law of work. This should not be understood as "the work of the law," as it usually is. While "the law of works" is written as *ex ergōn nomou* (3:20, 28) and *dia poiou nomou; tōn ergōn* (3:27), "the work of the law" is written as *to ergon tou nomou* (2:15). He makes it specific in the latter meaning by putting the definite articles before each word. God's will (B) as the law must be distinguished from man's deed (C) of law. Anyone who lives under the law must fulfill the law of works in every respect, because on the final day God will deliver judgment on the person who is regarded by God to have lived under the law according to his works. The person who lives under the law of works must satisfy all applicable laws or precepts. Paul said, "As many as have sinned under law shall be judged by law; for not the hearers of a law are righteous before God, but the doers of a law shall be justified" (2:12-13; cf. Gal. 5:3). It has been revealed in (B), however, that such a man would be condemned by God through his cognition of sin according to the law of works *(dia gar nomou epignōsis hamartias)* (Rom. 3:20).

5. Intercession of the Holy Spirit

Each of these realities (A, B, and C) has its own consistent or coherent language network. Besides these language networks (or rather, as the basis for these articulations), Paul captured the reality of Jesus Christ, who is both the Son of God and a man. In this, Paul offered a language network that is not concessive but authentic. This language is based on the connection between (A) and (C) through the Holy Spirit. The Holy Spirit is the glue (+) that makes the realities (A) and (C) as the reality (D), that is, realities (A) + (C). Also, it is the glue that makes the realities (B) and (C) as the reality (E), that is, realities (B) + (C). I shall call these realities the "theological entity." In this analysis, (D), which integrates (A) and (C) through the Holy Spirit as (D = A + C), and the corresponding language network (that is, the "theological language," or the "language of Jesus Christ" [D]), contains reference to the Holy Spirit.

---

not be ranked above justification but conversely be understood in the light of it, although this perspective is not yet apparent here." E. Käsemann, *Commentary on Romans,* trans. G. W. Bromiley (Grand Rapids: Eerdmans, 1980), 58. Besides, I read *telos nomou* (10:4) not as "(Christ as) the fulfillment of the law," but "(Christ as) the goal of law [of works]."

In Romans 7, Paul develops a language network (E) by introducing an imaginary agent with the first-person pronoun "I." Paul reports that anyone under the law is supposed to agonize over his own sin, when he is interceded for by the Holy Spirit (7:14). The imaginary agent "I," who is set as the respondent to God's precept "*Thou* shall not covet" (7:7), cries, "O wretched, I, man *(talaipōros egō anthrōpos)!* Who shall deliver me out of the body of this death?" (7:24). Here, "I" represents "man," whoever he is under the law of works. When the person under the law says that "For I know that in me, that is, in my flesh, dwells no good thing" (7:18), the man before God is supposed to cry an agony of sin interceded by the Holy Spirit. Paul says he has a fleshy part, which is contrasted with his "intellect" part, which grasps "God's will" "in accordance with the Spirit" (7:25; 8:4; cf. 12:1-2). Man is constituted by these two apparently conflicting parts. Although this is developed in an imaginary situation, nothing hinders one from having this agony of sin in one's mental state.

In Romans 8, Paul develops a (D) language. Paul says that "You are not in the flesh but in the Spirit, if so be that the Spirit of God dwells in you. But if any man hath not the Spirit of Christ, he is none of his. And if Christ is in you, the body is dead because of sin; but the Spirit is life because of righteousness. But if the Spirit of him that raised up Jesus from the dead dwells in you, he that raised up Christ Jesus from the dead shall quicken also your mortal bodies through his Spirit that dwells in you" (8:9-11). If one is spirited, he is not any more "in the flesh," that is, in (C) dimension. Because, somehow through the mediation of Holy Spirit, he is in the reality (A) + (C) = (D), which is not anymore in (C) only.

If Paul had not conceded that the flesh is weak, he would have only used the language of (D), in other words, that of Jesus Christ as a theological entity. Talking about Jesus Christ would be the same linguistic act as talking about each of us. Paul would have claimed that everything is clear in front of God, because God created all creatures in front of him. The human being is a relatively autonomous creature of God, insofar as he is free and responsible (cf. Ps. 8:5). Uchimura, as well as Luther, is committed to the theological language of reality (D), for Uchimura did not sever the concept "before God" (A) from the concept "before man" (C) in his consideration of Jesus Christ, the being who is located in both dimensions in full. Calvin also claimed that "this [severing] would be, as it were, to rend Christ asunder."[11] This adherence to the language of reality (D) is adhering

11. J. Calvin, *In Epistolam Pauli ad Romanos Commentarii,* chapter 8, verse 9.

to the complexity of *ergon* in any man of faith. This is the gist of Protestantism. Uchimura's remark (that "any man who belongs to God and is obedient to Christ is righteous") was delivered as (D) language, although in my view this is actually (A)-type language, insofar as we stick to the *logos* (account) level rather than the Holy Spirit's *ergon* (work) level. We can understand the meaning of this sentence at the formal level at least by articulating three realities without appealing to the Holy Spirit. Although the language of (A) can be understood without appealing to the Holy Spirit, the language channel that was opened up by Jesus of Nazareth was (D)-type language. Insofar as we are obedient to Christ (in front of God), we may be able to claim that our own language belongs to the (D) category. Furthermore, one may add one further claim such that we are at work *(ergon)* of D category as the Holy Spirit's being poured in us in which one will not describe reality (D) as (A) + (C), which presupposes the articulation in order to state the Holy Spirit (+) but will simply deliver (*ergon* [D]) language, without severing the reality before God from the one before man. But Paul concedes to talk (A in C) as a (C) language instead of (D) due to the weakness of the flesh.

6. Conclusion

Romans 3:21-26 is in the language of the (A) group, that is, the "before God" language, through which God's understanding, judgment, and action concerning human beings are all reported. In other words, God is the agent of this paragraph, and the meaning of the terms in dimension (A) is not the same as in the dimension Paul used in his understanding of man as an agent because of the weakness of his flesh. Paul distinguished according to the different dimensions of language the "faithfulness of Jesus Christ" (3:22), which I will term "f1," from "faith" (f2), which is the mental disposition or state of all human beings. When Paul gazes at our flesh and utters "faith," it refers to a mental state emerged in our soul. This (f2) type of our own flesh varies from person to person, and it also varies from time to time within one person. Paul described this type of faith by associating it, as well as the believer, with the ideas of "weak," "progress," "lack," and "growth" (see 14:1; Phil. 1:25; 1 Thess. 3:10; 2 Cor. 10:15). This pronouncement came from Paul's human manner of speaking, due to the infirmity of flesh. The criteria, by means of which Paul distinguishes a person's varied faith, belong to his understanding of the phenomena that can be observed in the human dimension. That is, this worldly dimension is man's responsibility, although this dimension itself is ultimately under the control of God, existing with his permission (cf. 2 Cor. 10:13).

Paul described (f1), "the faithfulness of Jesus Christ," as the language of revelation from God's side (that is, he used [A]-type language and concepts). Paul stated that "the faithfulness of Jesus Christ" is the medium for the revelation of God's righteousness. Because of this mediation, God can see man's faith in (f2) as the faithfulness of Jesus Christ (f1). God regards the faith of Jesus of Nazareth as sufficient to convey his faithfulness and thus his righteousness toward mankind. In general, for any entity to become *a medium* of two entities of different genera, it must embody (at least potentially and preferably actually) characteristics of both original genera.

Uchimura has grasped man's faith in terms of (f1), the faithfulness of Jesus Christ, as complete with respect to receiving God's complete righteousness. Without carrying out the semantic analysis of the text, Uchimura has intuitively grasped the main theme of Romans 3:21-26. God's righteousness is revealed through his faithfulness to all men who believe. People who believe (so understood by God) know that God is righteous through the faithfulness of Jesus Christ the mediator. Uchimura cleaved to *fides Christi* as his own complete faith.

Catholicism developed its theological view on the basis of Paul's concession that the flesh is weak, and by employing Aristotelian language (that is, [C]-type language). When Thomas Aquinas said that "Christ did not have faith, because he had a clear vision *(apertam visionem)* of God,"[12] Aquinas understood "faith" only in the (C) dimension, and only as a mental state (that is, as [f2]). Aquinas did not consider the existence of *fides Christi* based on 3:22, the passage to which Luther cleaved. Paul already offered a means of reconciliation between Catholicism and Protestantism by distinguishing three dimensions of mutually independent languages — that is, by ascribing the "faithfulness of Jesus Christ" to the language of (A) group, and by ascribing our mental state of having faith to the language of group (C). If Uchimura had been clear on this point, he would have shown more fully the persuasiveness of the Christ event to which he dedicated his whole life.

---

12. Aquinas, *Summa Theologica* II-1.q65ad(3).

Uchimura Kanzō and His Atonement Eschatology: On "Crucifixianity"

CHIBA SHIN

The Bible is a book of God's promises concerning His comings. In the Old Testament, He promised through His prophets that He would come among men and save them. And He did come in His Son; but men rejected Him and crucified Him. Then God in His infinite patience promised in the New Testament through His apostles and evangelists that He would come again. And so the promise stands now. And as sure as He did come the first time, He will come the second time. His First Coming was a surety for His Second Coming; and as the prophecies concerning the First Coming were all and literally fulfilled, so those concerning the Second will be likewise fulfilled.

"The Book of Comings" (24:354E/November 1918)

The aim of His Second Coming cannot be different from that of His First Coming. As in His First Coming, He came not to judge the world, but to save it, so it cannot be otherwise in His Second Coming. "As in Adam all die, so in Christ all be made alive." But each in his own order: the Christian to his resurrection-life, the Jew to his Messianic blessings; and the Gentile to the brightness of His glory. And all will be saved that God may be all in all. Judgement necessarily accompanies salvation; but judgement is an accompaniment, and not the aim. The Second Coming of Christ is a cosmic affair; all are interested in it, and all will be blessed by it.

"The Aim of the Second Coming" (24:451E/January 1919)

Uchimura Kanzō was a man of many interests and commitments who played an important role in the public life of early modern Japan. He was a well-known pioneer and preacher of the gospel of Christ, a founder of the *mukyōkai* (nonchurch) type of Christianity. He was a social critic and a prophetic patriot during the Meiji and Taishō eras. He was also a seminal introducer of Western science, literature, history, and thought. Moreover, he was a prolific biblical scholar and commentator. He did not become a professional, academic or sophisticated type of Christian theologian. He never wrote his own Christian theology or *Dogmatik* full of theological abstractions and refinement. Rather, he addressed himself to the common people and to lay Christians of Japan in easily accessible, plain, and eloquent Japanese language. Having played many diverse roles, Uchimura exerted a considerable influence on the people and society of early modern Japan.

Uchimura wrote and lectured during Japan's early modern period when the country was faced with unceasing domestic and international problems. Some of the robust ideas and perspectives he developed were comparable to the great trends of twentieth-century Christian theology in the world. Especially significant were Uchimura's later ideas on the need for a second Reformation, on the second coming of Christ, and on the eschatological redemption of humanity and the universe. In his later years Uchimura called his own Christianity *jūjikakyō* (Crucifixianity — or, literally, "cross-religion"), an expression he first used in 1921. I believe that Uchimura's position on "Crucifixianity" and what I will call "atonement eschatology" had some basic features in common with the evangelical and prophetic strain of the late-nineteenth- and twentieth-century Protestantism with its reformative theological lineage of Europe in particular. Here I have in mind such Christian theologians and preachers as Johann Christoph Blumhardt and Christoph Friedrich Blumhardt (father and son), Hermann Kutter, Leonhard Ragaz, Karl Barth, and Emil Brunner.[1] When Uchimura was writing about such eschatological themes in 1910-19, he was scarcely aware of these theological developments in the West. In historical hindsight, furthermore, Uchimura's ideas on atonement eschatology and his theological attitude toward culture and society resembled

---

1. Uchimura had sympathetic correspondence with Leonhard Ragaz over the futility of a world war and the need for a new Christianity. And Uchimura's European and Japanese friends intimated to him the emergence of the young theologians of eschatological crisis, Karl Barth, Eduard Thurneysen, Emil Brunner, and others. In his diary Uchimura favorably referred to Barth a few times. Cf. 34:441, 452, 551.

some of the theological ideas expounded much later by Dietrich Bonhoeffer, John Yoder, Jürgen Moltmann, and Stanley Hauerwas.

This atonement eschatology is correctly seen at the center of Uchimura's soteriology. This is a perspective of eschatological redemption where the three *presences* or *arrivals* (παρουσίαι) of Christ — the cross, the resurrection, and the second coming — are indissolubly connected and intertwined with one another. Before he began to advocate his atonement eschatology in later years, Uchimura had already expounded his important social and political ideas such as the "two J's" (his double commitment to Jesus and Japan), small-country-ism, an organic and ecological view of nature, prophetic patriotism, internationalism, pacifism, and world peace. It is regrettable that he had no occasion to reformulate these fascinating and creative ideas in the light of atonement eschatology. Critics like Ienaga Saburō observed a certain retreat on the part of Uchimura from his earlier progressive and reformative social and political attitudes. Ienaga was right about this. This retreat of the later Uchimura from the social and political issues of the age can be partly ascribed to the loss of a lively sense of history he experienced in these later years. I assume, however, that this later eschatological development in his thought *could potentially* deepen and strengthen his earlier invigorating and reformative politics suggested above.[2] But it is regrettable that he left little trace that suggests that he had attempted to develop *his own eschatological political thought and practice* in those later years.

In the following my task will be to elucidate the theological logic underlying Uchimura's atonement eschatology. In addition, I will deal with one

2. Due to the limited space allocated to this chapter, I will not be able to deal squarely with this issue here. Perhaps, because of his preoccupation with atonement eschatology as well as his increasing pessimism about humanity's historical activities on earth, Uchimura somewhat deviated in later years from his well-trodden path of reformative politics. For instance, Uchimura wrote rather hesitantly or negatively about the possibility and role of the League of Nations and of Taishō democracy in those years. Suffice it to say that he could elaborate more consistent and convincing arguments for his reformative politics from this newly gained eschatological standpoint. For instance, the later Barth could more effectively speak of his own transformative politics in the post–World War II years in terms of the possibility of the analogy *(Gleichnisfähigkeit)* of the kingdom of God and the analogy of faith *(analogia fidei)* as well. E.g., Karl Barth, "Christengemeinde und Bürgergemeinde," *Theologische Studien* 104 (1970): 65-76. Cf. Tanaka Osamu, "Taishō demokurashī to Uchimura Kanzō" ("Taishō Democracy and Uchimura Kanzō"), *Uchimura Kanzō Kenkyū (Uchimura Kanzō Studies)*, no. 33 (December 1998): 1-45; Chiba Shin, *Gendai protesutantizumu no seiji shisō (The Political Thought of Contemporary Protestantism)* (Tokyo: Shinkyō Shuppansha Publishers, 1988), 413-17.

characteristic element of his atonement eschatology, that is, his advocacy of universal salvation. He insisted on the possibility that not only the believers but also all humankind shall be saved under the reign of Christ. Besides this, he maintained that the whole of the universe and the entire creation shall be saved in their completion at the end of history. This was a unique and characteristic insistence in Uchimura's eschatological advocacy. It unmistakably showed an apocalyptic element of his atonement eschatology. I would like to take up briefly this latter theme at the end of this chapter.

I. The Ideas and Logic of Atonement Eschatology

1. Synopsis

Looking back over his own journey of faith, Uchimura divided his life into three periods. He stated that, first, in 1877 at Sapporo he had experienced his first encounter with the only God of the universe. When he entered Sapporo Agricultural College in 1877, he was pressured to become a Christian convert through the strong solicitation of senior students. Those students arrived at Sapporo one year earlier and became Christians under the inspiring guidance and care of William S. Clark, the first president of the college. At that time Clark was the president of Massachusetts Agricultural College at Amherst. He had been asked to come to Japan by the Meiji government, and stayed in Sapporo for eight months to teach new students both agricultural science and the Bible at the newly established college.[3] As he related later, Uchimura had been "half-forced" to sign the Covenant of Believers in Jesus prepared by Clark. The second moment was in 1886 at Amherst, Massachusetts, when Uchimura came to believe in the redemptive power of the crucified Jesus. Uchimura received this atonement faith under the spiritual guidance of Julius H. Seelye, then the fifth president of Amherst College. The third period of Uchimura's spiritual journey started in 1918 at Kashiwagi in Tokyo, when Uchimura came to believe firmly in the second coming of Christ as the basic core of his Christian faith.[4] He insisted as follows:

3. Cf. Raymond P. Jennings, *Jesus, Japan, and Kanzō Uchimura* (Tokyo: Kyō bun Kwan Publishers, 1958), 14-15; Hiroshi Miura, *The Life and Thought of Kanzo Uchimura* (Grand Rapids: Eerdmans, 1996), 17-21; John F. Howes, *Japan's Modern Prophet: Uchimura Kanzō, 1861-1930* (Vancouver, Canada: UBC Press, 2005), 28-38.

4. E.g., "Shinkō no sandai jiki" ("Three Great Moments of Faith"), *Zenshū* 24 (February 1918): 43-44; "Kirisuto sairin o shinzuru yori kitarishi yo no shisōjyo no henka" ("Changes of

The Second Coming of Christ, the words are very simple. Its meanings are, however, profound and its principle fundamental. Aspects of the Second Coming of Christ include the restoration of all things, the re-modeling of the universe, and the resurrection of the saints. Other aspects are the victory of justice, the last judgement, and the realization of theocracy. What sums up all hopes of humankind, that is the Second Coming of Christ. Therefore, one understands all when one understands this event. Conversely, unless one understands this event, everything is unclear. . . . For this event constitutes what all things shall return to and what is ultimate of all things. (24:385)

As this passage shows, this is a fairly orthodox and traditional view of the second coming of Christ. Uchimura maintained that when he came to believe in the Lord's return, he felt as if he had left the old world and entered a new one. He maintained that with this newly gained faith in the second coming of Christ, his universe was enlarged, his future was opened wide, new power was given to him, his eyes could see things clearly, and his entire life changed (24:384-85). Uchimura proclaimed that this newly given faith in the second coming of Christ made the entire message of the Bible intelligible to him. Not only that, but this faith allowed him to understand more deeply the meaning of human life, including the pain of death. He also mentioned that once he understood the second coming, he could clearly understand the meaning and destiny of the whole of nature itself and especially the depth of Romans 8:18-25.

Several reasons or moments led Uchimura in 1918 to believe in the second coming of Christ. Among the most crucial reasons was that his progressive view of history and his biblical tenets and methodology came to a deadlock. This impasse was brought about by the outbreak of world war in 1914 and the sudden death of his beloved daughter Rutsuko in 1915. Beginning in January 1918, Uchimura — along with Nakata Jūji of the Holiness Church, Kimura Seimatsu of the Salvation Army, and others — launched the so-called second coming movement, and traveled around some regions of Japan. During 1918 Uchimura delivered fifty-eight lectures on the second coming of Christ in Tokyo and elsewhere. Each lecture attracted an audience of between one hundred and six hundred people.

However, Uchimura carefully guarded himself against dubious efforts

---

Ideas Deriving from My Faith in the Second Coming of Christ"), *Zenshū* 24 (December 1918): 384-85.

like that of some second-coming advocates to specify the precise date of Christ's return, the superstition that faith in the second coming could impart to the believer the supernatural gift of divine healing, and so forth. Especially he warned against the appearance of "second-coming maniacs." His eschatology basically belonged to the premillennialist view rather than the postmillennialist one, but he showed no interest whatsoever in either too literal or too schematic an understanding of millennialism.[5]

Furthermore, in Uchimura's eschatological proclamation the issue of the so-called "prolongation of the second coming" was not fully addressed. This is surprising, especially when we think about the discussions of eschatology in Europe and North America in the late nineteenth and early twentieth century. In the theological milieu of Europe the delay of Christ's return was one of the key and troublesome issues. The very issue was persistently taken up and discussed by such diverse theologians as Albert Schweitzer and Johannes Weiss, who belonged to the so-called school of religious history, and Karl Barth, Emil Brunner, and Rudolf Bultmann, who belonged to the lineage of the theology of crisis.

Most of the prominent church leaders in Japan of the day, such as Ebina Danjō, criticized not merely Uchimura's advocacy but also the entire second-coming movement as antiscientific, as a Jewish delusion, and as an excessively literal understanding of certain biblical passages. But the movement attracted lay Christians as well as many non-Christian Japanese people. And major Japanese newspapers and magazines reported on the movement rather favorably. The second-coming movement lasted about a year and a half until around the summer of 1919.

2. A Unified Understanding of Christ's Cross, Resurrection, and Second Coming

Uchimura emphasized that the cross, the resurrection, and the second coming of Christ have to be understood as the unified whole of the event of salvation. Christ's second coming is the result of his atoning death on the cross; the former completes the redemptive process inaugurated by the

---

5. E.g., "Yo ga Kirisuto sairin nitsuite shinzezaru koto" ("What I Do Not Believe regarding the Second Coming of Christ"), *Zenshū* 24 (February 1918): 49; cf. Kurokawa Tomobumi, *Uchimura Kanzō to sairin undō (Uchimura Kanzō and the Second Coming Movement)* (Tokyo: Kyōbunkan Publishers, 2012), 145-51.

latter. Therefore, the believer's righteousness, holiness, and redemption unmistakably reside solely in Christ. Thus, the believer is saved when he or she comes to repent and to believe in Christ and looks up to him on the cross (24:116-17).

The atoning death of Christ on the cross and his second coming are thus indissolubly united in the thought of Uchimura. At the same time, the resurrection of Christ is considered to be inseparable from, and integrated with, his death, since the former is the proof of the forgiveness of sin and the justification of repentant sinners. The resurrection is also closely united with the second coming, since the former constitutes the premise and foundation of the latter. Furthermore, for Uchimura the continuity of the resurrection and the second coming has become the basis for underscoring the unity of the spiritual and the physical, the spirit and the flesh, and the discussion of "spiritual body" as the resurrected body of the believer. According to Uchimura, the resurrected body is nothing else than the "glorious body," "new body corresponding to new spirit," and "spiritualization of the flesh."[6]

3. The Principle of Uplifting the Flesh by the Spirit

Uchimura wrote an interesting essay in August 1918 under the title "Tsurubetsukoi kō no jūjika kan" ("Prince Trubetskoi's View of the Cross"). Prince Trubetskoi (1862-1905) was a profound mystic, philosopher, and theologian in Russia. Uchimura explained Prince Trubetskoi's view of the cross as follows. The cross symbolized the crossing of the vertical rod and the horizontal rod. The vertical rod symbolized "heaven," whereas the horizontal rod represented "earth." The vertical rod was there to lift up the horizontal rod — earthly things — toward "heaven."

Uchimura valued Prince Trubetskoi's image of the cross very highly. And he understood that there should be no dualistic chasm between the things belonging to "heaven," which is to say, God, the afterlife, eternity, faith, aspiration, the spiritual, on the one hand, and the things belonging

---

6. E.g., "Kirisuto no fukkatsu to sairin" ("Christ's Resurrection and Second Coming"), *Zenshū* 24 (May 1918): 183; "Karada no sukui" ("Salvation of the Body"), *Zenshū* 24 (August 1918): 268; "Tsurubetsukoi kō no jūjika kan" ("Prince Trubetskoi's View of the Cross"), *Zenshū* 24 (August 1918): 289-90; cf. Lee Kyoungae, *Uchimura Kanzō no kirisutokyō shisō (The Christian Thought of Uchimura Kanzō)* (Fukuoka: Kyūshū University Press, 2003), 122-30.

to "earth," that is, society, economics, politics, civilization, industry, technology, the material, on the other hand. The creation of "earth" did not mean the emergence of something deficient or inferior. It rather meant that "earth" has its own inestimable value and that it is in its own inherent nature to be transformed to "heaven." Therefore, the flesh should be understood not as something to confront always the spirit but rather as something that has potential to be transfigured by the spirit. Here Uchimura found significance in the symbol of the cross as envisaged by Prince Trubetskoi (24:288).

To be sure, the imagery of the cross suggested by Prince Trubetskoi was not entirely novel. In the fourth century A.D., Tyconius was already writing about two kingdoms, that is, the kingdom of God and the kingdom of the earth. And it is well known that Augustine made these contrasting notions into his methodological concepts to narrate universal history in his magnum opus, *De Civitate Dei* (413-426). When it comes to the theological context of the twentieth century, one might also be reminded of Reinhold Niebuhr's language of the dialectic between eternity and history, between love and justice. One might also think of the Japanese philosopher Hatano Seiichi's dialectic between *toki* (time) and *eien* (eternity).

Moreover, Prince Trubetskoi's argument for lifting up the flesh by the spirit shows an intriguing resemblance to H. Richard Niebuhr's distinctive type of "Christ transforming culture" as developed in his 1951 classic, *Christ and Culture*. As in the "Christ transforming culture" model, Prince Trubetskoi's language, as interpreted by Uchimura, was conspicuous for its strong emphasis on the motif of the powerful pull that heaven exerts on earth and that the spirit has for the flesh. By reinterpreting Prince Trubetskoi's view of the symbol of the cross, Uchimura could see the significance of the cross of Christ both in the upward lifting of the bar of earth to heaven and in the sanctification of the flesh by the spirit. Thus, Uchimura maintained that the cardinal principle of the redemptive ideas in the New Testament consisted in the spiritualization of the flesh and in the sanctification of this world. He argued that it also resided in that the universe becomes heavenly, inasmuch as the universe comes to embody the glory of Christ. All the fundamental ideas of Christianity such as the cross, the resurrection, and the second coming of Christ stood on the ground of this truth (24:290). He maintained as follows in his characteristic manner: "The nature of the Gospel resides in moving up to heaven with the horizontal rod penetrated by the vertical rod. . . . Herein one can find the cross being realized for certainty" (24:290).

II. The Basic Logic and Features of Atonement Eschatology

1. The Advocacy of "Crucifixianity"

In January 1921, in a short piece entitled "Crucifixianity," Uchimura proposed that the cardinal tenet of Christianity is to proclaim Christ crucified and that Christianity should be better called "Crucifixianity" (26:3E). It might be correct to interpret this proposal of Crucifixianity as expressing his aforementioned unified understanding of the cross, the resurrection, and the second coming of Christ. We must be cautious here, however, since he seldom used the expression "Crucifixianity." At any rate, by 1921 Uchimura's understanding of the cross came to be situated more solidly through his faith in the second coming in the perspective of the history of salvation *(Heilsgeschichte)*. This meant that his theology of the cross began to acquire richer and deeper meanings by then. Perhaps "Crucifixianity" can be understood as an appropriate expression of Uchimura's Christianity, like other expressions such as *mukyōkai* (nonchurch) or *mukyōkai-shugi* (nonchurchism). The former might be said to be a more positive expression of his own view of Christianity than the latter two.

Izumi Harunori also presupposed that Uchimura's Crucifixianity was an eschatological concept. Izumi argued that in Uchimura's thought Christ's second coming was the final truth that provided the cross with an unchanging and solid meaning, since all would meet Christ through the cross and every creation would aim at the *persona* of Christ at the end of time.[7]

Allow us to summarize here the core of Uchimura's understanding of the history of salvation. First, the cross of Christ (his atoning death) is considered to be nothing else than the central truth of Christianity. Second, the event of the cross ceases to be simply an event of the past. Instead, at the end of time, the event of the cross moves to the historical present to enter into the event of the second coming of Christ in order to accomplish the redemption of humankind and the restoration of all things. Thus, the truth and power of the cross now begin to unfold themselves in the midst of world history. As a result, the secret truth that basically belongs to the

---

7. Izumi Harunori, "Shokuzai to sairin" ("Atonement and Second Coming"), *Uchimura Kanzō Kenkyū (Uchimura Kanzō Studies)*, no. 1 (December 1973): 88. Uchimura maintained in his last years that the second coming was the final truth of Christianity rather than its central truth. This was his last word for his understanding of the history of salvation. Cf. "Sairin teishō no hitsuyō" ("The Need for Proposing the Second Coming"), April 1930, in *Zenshū*, 32:327.

history of salvation and hence has been invisible in the ordinary sequences of world history will suddenly begin to appear and become manifest. That is to say, the truth and power of God's salvation of humanity and the whole of the universe will now become visible, audible, and receptive by the bodily organs and sentiments of every creature. All in all, the central truth of the Scripture, namely, the cross of Christ, is thus organically unified with the second coming of Christ. Which is to say, the second coming of Christ as the final moment and final truth of salvation history will accomplish the work of redemption completely and perfectly.[8]

2. Some Aspects of Uchimura's Theory of Atonement Eschatology

Uchimura's notion of Crucifixianity harbors within itself a theory of atonement eschatology that consists of several important notions. These are no less than the components that make up his theory of atonement eschatology. They are, for instance, (1) the Christology of gaze-up *(gyōsen)*, (2) substitutive punishment and atonement *(daikei daishoku)*, (3) the simultaneous realization of love and righteousness, (4) eschatological life and spirituality, and (5) the redemption of nature. In what follows I examine them one by one as concisely as possible.

(1) **The Christology of Gaze-Up** *(gyōsen)* Uchimura came to obtain a certain conviction of the atoning power for his sin deriving from Christ on the cross while he was a student at Amherst College, struggling with the problem of sin and forgiveness. This advice from President Seelye became the initial occasion in which he came to believe in and experience the redemptive power of Christ: "Why do you not cease to examine within yourself and instead gaze up at Jesus who atoned your sin on the cross?" (29:343). Perhaps the following entry in his diary was made on the same day he received this precious advice from President Seelye:

> March 8 [1886]. — Very important day in my life. Never was the atoning
> power of Christ more clearly revealed to me than it is to-day. In the cru-

---

8. Uchimura seldom used the expression "salvation history." But it is apparent that he believed it and took it for granted. Cf. Harashima Tadashi, "'Kyūsaishi' to 'sekaishi' no setten: Uchimura Kanzō no shingaku" ("The Point of Contact between 'Salvation History' and 'World History': Uchimura Kanzō's Theology"), *Uchimura Kanzō Kenkyū (Uchimura Kanzō Studies)*, no. 14 (April 1980): 60-96.

cifixion of the Son of God lies the solution of all the difficulties that buffeted my mind thus far. Christ paying all my debts, can bring me back to the purity and innocence of the first man before the Fall. Now I am God's child, and my duty is to believe Jesus. For *His* sake, God will give me all I want. He will use me for His glory, and will save me in Heaven at last. (3:117-18)

One may correctly call Uchimura's Christology one of gaze-up, since he repeatedly said he did not have any recourse except that of gazing up at Jesus on the cross, at the one who atoned for his own and humanity's sins.[9] The following is a typical short quotation that expresses Uchimura's Christology of looking up: "My peace and joy are not in the success of my works: are not in the ever-new attainment of knowledge; are not in the satisfaction of my conscience. My peace and joy are in Christ and His Cross. By looking at the Cross and waiting upon Him, there are in me peace and joy that pass all understanding. They who think I am a man of thought, and they who treat me as a moralist — they are they who know not the Redeemer who is at the foundation of my very being" (21:111E).

(2) Substitutive Punishment and Atonement *(daikei daishoku)*

Uchimura used to call the gospel in which he believed "an old, simple Gospel of Christ and His Cross" (e.g., 21:138-39). And his theology of the cross consisted of some themes that traditionally go back to the "new Protestantism" of the Puritans and pietism, to the "old Protestantism" of the Reformation (especially Martin Luther and John Calvin), and the New Testament itself. However, Uchimura did make a significant revision of the Reformation soteriology. He rejected the Calvinist theory of double predestination of the saved and the damned, and came to support the possibility of universal salvation. At any event, what comprised his theology of the cross included repentance ($\mu\varepsilon\tau\dot{\alpha}\nu\omicron\iota\alpha$) of sin, conversion, forgiveness of sin, substitutive punishment and atonement, and reconciliation.[10] Uchi-

---

9. Cf. Nakazawa Kōki, "Gyōsen no kirisutoron" ("The Christology of Gaze-Up"), *Uchimura Kanzō Kenkyū (Uchimura Kanzō Studies)*, no. 7 (December 1976): 1-13; Tomioka Kōichiro, *Uchimura Kanzō* (Tokyo: Libroport, 1988), 25-26; Lee Kyoungae, "Kindai nihon no kirisutokyō shinkō no ichi tenkei" ("A Turning Point of Modern Japan's Christian Faith"), *Uchimura Kanzō Kenkyū (Uchimura Kanzō Studies)*, no. 37 (March 2004): 52-55; Nemoto Izumi, "Uchimura Kanzō to Julius H. Seelye" ("Uchimura Kanzō and Julius H. Seelye"), *Uchimura Kanzō Kenkyū (Uchimura Kanzō Studies)*, no. 37 (March 2004): 59-79.

10. Uchimura made numerous references to the components that constitute his theol-

mura used to explain typologically the event of the cross in the light of the doctrinal history of atonement: (1) the release from sin (ἀπολύτρωσις), (2) the reconciliation between God and human beings (καταλλαγή), (3) substitutive punishment and atonement by Christ (propitiation; ἱλασμός), and (4) the sinner's return to God as the consummation of (1) through (3) (redemption; σωτηρία or ἀπόλυσις).[11]

One may correctly say that Uchimura's view of the atonement is fairly traditional and conservative especially in his emphasis on the substitutive punishment of, and atonement by, Christ. And his understanding of substitutive punishment and atonement can rightly be called an evangelical atonement. For Uchimura, whoever repents his or her own sin is visited with God's salvation and grace. Every repentant sinner receives the cloth of righteousness of Christ (justification by faith alone) and is granted the forgiveness of sin. This is clearly an evangelical view of the atonement. But Uchimura further makes a quite bold and universalistic redefinition — or a further reformulation — of this view. Since Christ will have a chance to encounter everyone as a repentant sinner *either on earth or in heaven after earthly death, there will be nobody who is unsaved.* Only in this way, Uchimura argues, will God's plan for salvation become complete. Here is presupposed the *universal* effect of the forgiving and atoning power derived from Christ's sacrificial death.

But one caution here. Uchimura showed a tendency to regard the realization of the principle of atonement and sacrifice as taking place not merely in the atoning event of Christ but also in our mundane and social life and in natural phenomena as well. To be sure, I do not hesitate to acknowledge Uchimura's deep insight into the occurrences of history, society, and nature. But his application of this Christ-centered atonement to the sphere of mundane and natural phenomena seems to harbor within itself some problems.

---

ogy of the cross. The following are merely a few selected examples of these references: *Kyūanroku (The Document of Search for Peace)*, 1893, 2:134-249; "Shokuzai no shingi to sono jijitsu" ("The True Meaning of Atonement and Its Facts"), March 1909, 16:260-65; "Kuiaratame no igi" ("The Meaning of Repentance"), July 1914, 21:11-14; "Daitan naru shinkō" ("Bold Faith"), October 1917, 23:373-74; "Tsumi no yurushi" ("Forgiveness of Sin"), December 1917, 23:430-35; "Reconstruction and Conversion," February 1920, 25:242-43E; *Romasho no Kenkyū (The Study of Paul's Epistle to the Romans)*, February 1921 through November 1922, 26:16-448; "Konborusyon no jikken" ("The Experiment of Conversion"), March 1930, 32:312-16.

11. E.g., "Waga shinkō no hyōhaku" ("The Confession of My Faith"), November 1891, 1:212-18; *Kyūanroku*, 2:228-49; "Shokuzai no shingi to sono jijitsu," 16:260-65.

One of the problems is its tendency to obscure the "infinite qualitative difference," using Søren Kierkegaard's and Karl Barth's expression, between what occurs at the level of the Being of God and what happens in the human world and in nature. Certainly, there are things that are worthy and respectable, sacrificial acts and phenomena observable in the human world and in the world of nature. One might argue, however, that there remains an infinite depth of difference in the soteriological logic of the New Testament between what is happening within the Trinitarian Being of God in terms of God the Son's suffering unto death and his crucified death, on the one hand, and what one can observe of the atoning and sacrificial acts and phenomena on the plane of humanity and nature, on the other.

Thus, there remain some theological difficulties to speak of human sacrifice and atoning acts in the same breath as God the Son's self-sacrifice on the cross. In the light of the theology of the atonement, the crucified death of innocent and sinless Christ generally means that Christ received substitutive punishment by paying the penalty himself for the sins of humankind in its lieu (or instead of it). And it implies that the very sacrificial and atoning death of God the Son could rescue humankind and the whole universe from the bondage of sin and evil.

When the Japanese state began to inaugurate war against Russia in 1904, Uchimura took a firm pacifist stand against the war and strongly criticized the war efforts of either state up until the war declaration. But after the actual war started, Uchimura suddenly became silent about the war and admonished pacifists to go to war to attain courageous sacrificial deaths. For, he argued, the precious lives sacrificed by the pacifist soldiers of both nations and the precious blood poured out on the battlefield would help the world realize the criminality and futility of wars; and that would help wars become obsolete. As Takahashi Tetsuya pointed out in a recent public lecture at the memorial symposium celebrating the sesquicentennial of Uchimura's birth, this logic of sacrifice and atonement on the part of the pacifist soldiers not only romanticized their deaths but also condoned the criminality and problematic of the states that engaged in the war. Takahashi was right in showing the unexpected resemblance between Uchimura's logic of beautifying the sacrificial death of the pacifist soldiers and the Japanese state's *kenshō* (public honoring) of Japanese war victims at Yasukuni (State-Shintō) Shrine.[12]

---

12. Cf. Takahashi Tetsuya, "Uchimura Kanzō to gisei" ("Uchimura Kanzō and Sacrifice"), a lecture delivered at Uchimura Kanzō Symposium held on March 20, 2011.

(3) The Simultaneous Realization of Love and Righteousness

Uchimura's understanding of substitutive punishment and atonement expresses the utter tension between God's love and his righteousness as revealed in the event of the cross. As Jürgen Moltmann superbly portrayed it in his masterpiece, *The Crucified God* (1974), this severe conflict and tension between God's love and righteousness was played out within the very triune Being of God.[13] Which is to say, God the Father and God the Son simultaneously and identically experienced the utter death of God on the cross. The death expressed the unbearable, utterly painful, and despairing separation between the two. Hence, Jesus' despairing utterance: "*Eli, Eli, lama sabachthani?* that is to say, my God, my God, why hast Thou forsaken me?"

Uchimura oftentimes explained this godly despair within the triune Being of God in terms of the utter tension between God's love and God's righteousness. Whereas the loving and saving God would like to save humankind from the bondage of sin, the holy and righteous God cannot condone or forgive the sin of humankind without the sacrificial death of his only-begotten Son, God the Son. Thus, the event of the cross where the painful death of God himself takes place can meet the demands of both God's love and his righteousness at one and the same time, so that it may become the sole, appropriate, and perfect way of accomplishing the redemption of humanity.

Fujii Takeshi, one of Uchimura's reliable followers, published an essay entitled "Tanjun naru fukuin" ("The Simple Gospel") in the March 1916 issue of the monthly biblical journal *Seisho no Kenkyū (The Biblical Study)*, a journal Uchimura had initiated and of which he had been in charge. Fujii argued that the view of God as the God of righteousness was derived from the Old Testament and that this old faith should be replaced by faith in the loving God and his gospel. Recognizing the problem of Fujii's argument only after it was published, Uchimura made a critical response to it in the essay "Kami no funnu to shokuzai" ("God's Wrath and the Atonement") in the same journal published in the following month.

Uchimura's essay expressed several points against Fujii's arguments. First, it is not necessarily correct to say that there exists no wrath on the part of God. According to Uchimura, God is the God of passion who so deeply loves humanity that he can show holy anger for humanity. Uchimura insisted that righteous wrath and holy anger belong to divine virtue.

---

13. Cf. Jürgen Moltmann, *Der gekreuzigte Gott* (Munich: Chr. Kaiser Verlag, 1972), 184-267.

Second, without God's righteous wrath against the sins of humankind, the cross of Christ is unthinkable. For the cross of Christ is the manifestation of the substitutive punishment and atonement at one and the same time; it is the only comprehensible solution on the part of God's attitude toward the sins of humankind. Third, the righteous God can now save the sinner through righteousness, so that the grace of forgiveness may now infinitely abound to the sinner through his or her repentance.

Fourth, Uchimura argued that strict love alone deserves the name of true love. According to him, love that does not undergo righteous penalty cannot be trusted. He claimed that truth often takes the shape of an ellipse, so that it has two centers as cardinal virtues, that is, love and righteousness. Lastly, Uchimura maintained that, as Fujii claimed, the gospel of the cross is simple and yet simplicity takes various forms. In the cross of Christ is contained everything such as God's love, righteousness, wrath, and forgiveness (22:237-45). To sum up, Uchimura's understanding of the atonement in the light of the tension and yet continuity notwithstanding between God's love and his righteousness within the triune God can be understood as basically consonant with the views held in the mainstream Protestant theological traditions that go back to Luther and Calvin.

(4) **Eschatological Life and Spirituality**   The fourth component of Uchimura's understanding of eschatological atonement is an important one, although it is often neglected and paid little attention. This is the theme I like to call eschatological life and spirituality. In June of 1920, during the last phase of the second-coming movement, Uchimura published an important and interesting article entitled "Sairin shinkō no ni hōmen" ("Two Directions of the Faith of the Second Coming"). In this article he clearly wrote about the implications of eschatological faith for daily Christian life and spirituality, although he did not use the term "spirituality" as we frequently use it today (25:491-95).

First, Uchimura maintained that there are two directions or aspects in the second coming of Christ, outward and inward. The former, that is, Christ's outward second coming, is, for instance, described in the book of Revelation and is fraught with eschatological images such as great catastrophes, the last judgment, the establishment of a new heaven and earth, and so on. The second aspect, that is, Christ's inward second coming, is attested by the spiritual workings in the heart of each believer who awaits with longing the return of Christ. The second inward dimension of the second coming is, Uchimura insisted, spiritually experienced on a daily-life basis by each believer. In her or his heart, the clear hope of the second coming abides as assurance. Thus, this experience — Uchimura preferred to call it "spiritual experiment" — of the "inward second coming" can become the believer's strong personal ground for living the eschatological life of faith, love, and hope (25:492).

This eschatological life is different from mere optimism. That is a kind of hope-ism, so to speak. According to this hope-ism of the believer, salvation was already achieved in the events of the cross, the resurrection, and the bestowment of the Holy Spirit; victory was already won and it became a certainty. Thus, the believer's vocation is to advance further this reality of salvation and victory that the kingdom of God has inaugurated on earth in action and in power. It means to engage in daily mundane life of labor, work, and action with a forward-looking and forward-moving spiritual vista of eschatological hope. Such daily life is penetrated moment by moment under the power of the Holy Spirit by the spiritual climate of freedom, love, and justice, by gratitude and joy, and above all by hope. I believe this is Uchimura's message of eschatological life and spirituality. That is a lifestyle daily lived out with "the gospel in the midst of the secular" *(sezoku no nakano fukuin)*, as Sekine Masao, a follower of Uchimura and an Old Testament scholar, later expressed it.[14]

Furthermore, Uchimura explained the importance of an "inward second coming" by showing that the second coming as outward phenomenon is such a gigantic event beyond the limit of human reasoning that it may easily lead the believer astray from the path of a solid and stable Christian life. Therefore, the believer needs to keep himself and his faith healthy and well balanced by internalizing the event of Christ's second coming. Thus, Uchimura insisted, "Sound faith in the Second Coming has to be the one where the external Second Coming and the internal Second Coming have to be combined with each other" (25:493).

(5) The Redemption of Nature and the Completion of the Universe

The final distinctive aspect of Uchimura's atonement eschatology is that Christ's redemption not only reaches humankind but also incorporates and covers the whole universe and the nature that God created. It is "a cos-

14. Sekine Masao, *Sezoku no nakano fukuin (The Gospel in the Midst of the Secular)* (Tokyo: Kirisutokyō Yakan Kōza Publishers, 1967), 135. Cf. Shin Chiba, "Christianity on the Eve of Postmodernity: Karl Barth and Dietrich Bonhoeffer," in *Christian Ethics in Ecumenical Context: Theology, Culture, and Politics in Dialogue,* ed. Shin Chiba, George R. Hunsberger, and Lester Edwin J. Ruiz (Grand Rapids: Eerdmans, 1995), 203-4.

mic affair," as Uchimura usually expressed it. As was already indicated, one of his astounding discoveries about eschatological redemption was that its effect would reach not merely the whole of humankind but also the entire cosmos. Nature, now under the bondage of decay, would then find its own redemption. When he was on his deathbed in March 1930, Uchimura was reported to have prayed not merely for the "prosperity of Japan" and the "salvation of humankind" but also for the "completion of the universe." This message of the redemption of the whole universe and nature came to be articulated in his *Romasho no Kenkyū (The Study on Paul's Epistle to the Romans)*, published in its entirety in 1924.

In Romans 8:18-25 Paul wrote that the whole of nature groaned for its own redemption from futility and bondage to decay. And Paul continued to argue that with the liberation of humankind from its bondage to sin, nature itself would become free from its subjection to futility and be finally saved. Commenting on these verses, Uchimura proclaimed that the entire cosmos, namely, all the created things and the whole world, would be finally redeemed and that there would be no greater hope than that! He thought that only with the redemption of the whole universe would the salvation of humankind become really perfect (26:307-13).

Uchimura saw a strange thread of solidarity that united humankind with the whole of nature (26:310). A human being has his own nature within himself — that is, the body — so that he knows what its subjection to futility and decay is like. Therefore, each and every human being often groans together with nature. Uchimura wrote the following:

> Thus, human beings and nature will be saved together, so that all things may be completed and become perfect; thus, peace and joy may come to be filled in the whole heaven and on the whole earth.
>
> Without this great hope, the Gospel cannot be the Gospel. Without this great realization of redemption, God cannot be God. If the Gospel is less than this, the Gospel cannot be the Gospel. Human beings and nature will be saved together; this is indeed nothing but the evangelical salvation. Here the hope of humankind is at stake. (26:312-13)

*   *   *

To summarize this section, one can say that the five aspects discussed above can be considered the distinctive, cardinal features and components that make up the content of Uchimura's atonement eschatology.

Uchimura's idea of eschatological life and spirituality — namely, his emphasis on the internal aspect of the second coming of Christ — has sounded an echo in later twentieth-century discussions of eschatological inwardness, existentialism, and spirituality. Here I have in mind diverse theological lineages of the late nineteenth century and twentieth century developed in various parts of the world such as S. Kierkegaard and R. Bultmann and their discussion of eschatological existence of Christian faith and decision, or such as father and son Blumhardt and K. Barth and their theology of reconciliation and redemption, or such as variant types of theology of the kingdom of God and of hope elaborated by Leo Tolstoy, Kagawa Toyohiko, J. Moltmann, and others.

Uchimura's emphasis on the internal dimension of eschatology can be understood as an antecedent — or an expected parallel from the Orient — of the theology of eschatological existence. It is also interesting to compare the cosmic dimension of Uchimura's atonement eschatology to the reemergence of apocalyptic themes and motifs observable in such diverse types of twentieth-century theologians from various parts of the world as Teilhard de Chardin, Karl Rahner, Suh Nam-Dong, Wolfhart Pannenberg, Jürgen Moltmann, Gustavo Gutiérrez, and José Miguez Bonino. Moltmann, for instance, developed an ecological "theology of nature" from his cosmic and eschatological perspectives.[15]

Moreover, Uchimura's atonement eschatology that developed from 1918 to 1920 was astoundingly similar to what Karl Barth later elaborated on reconciliation and the eschatological alteration of the human situation in the history of salvation ("history of covenant" in Barth's case). These eschatological notions were elaborated not in the well-known *Die Römerbrief* (1919 and 1921) written by the early Barth, but rather in the later Barth's *Die kirchliche Dogmatik* IV/3.1-2 (1959). The later Barth wrote about eschatological redemption in terms of the "alteration of human situation" enacted by one single event of God's presence (παρουσία) that took place in different times and in different forms, such as Christ's resurrection, the bestowment of the Holy Spirit, and Christ's second coming.[16]

---

15. E.g., Jürgen Moltmann, *Gott in der Schöpfung: Ökologische Schöpfungslehre* (Munich: Chr. Kaiser Verlag, 1985). See the following works on Uchimura's ideas of nature and ecology: Miura Nagamitsu, *Gendai ni ikiru Uchimura Kanzō* (Tokyo: Ochanomizu Shobō Publishers, 2011); Chiba Shin, "Uchimura Kanzō no shizenkan to ekoroji" ("Uchimura Kanzō and His View of Nature and Ecology"), *Uchimura Kanzō Kenkyū* (*Uchimura Kanzō Studies*), no. 30 (October 1994): 72-98.

16. E.g., Karl Barth, *Die kirchliche Dogmatik* IV/3.1 (Zollikon-Zürich: Evangelischer

Similarly, Uchimura understood the events of salvation — such as Christ's resurrection, ascension, second coming — as "God's comings" in his own words, that is, a series of salvific occasions of God's presence or arrival (παρουσία).[17] There is a fascinating congruence or similarity between these two thinkers. They had in common a large-scaled perspective of the history of salvation.

Uchimura expresses eschatological spirituality in terms of walking on the path of life with faith, hope, and love. The daily walk of life is sustained and invigorated by the inward second coming of Christ.[18] It is a life and spirituality filled and guided by the power of the Holy Spirit. He once used the expression "a believing automation" to express his own understanding of christocentric eschatological life: "The Lord Jesus Christ is my wisdom from God, and righteousness and sanctification and redemption. He is my all. Indeed, for me to live is Christ. I by my faith let Him live and work in me, and myself become a believing automation, a fit instrument of righteousness in His hand. All is so simple and so good. 1 Cor. 1:30" (24:516E).

III. Atonement Eschatology and the
Possibility of Universal Salvation

1. The Hazardous Nature of the Idea of Universal Salvation

Uchimura alluded to the possibility of universal salvation at the end of an article already taken up, "Sairin shinkō no ni hōmen" ("Two Directions of the Faith of Second Coming"). Needless to say, the theme of universal salvation is a sensitive and even dangerous one in many ways. Its hazards can be stated in various ways. The idea of universal salvation, for instance,

---

Verlag A. G., 1959), 338-43; *Die kirchliche Dogmatik* IV/3.2 (Zollikon-Zürich: Evangelischer Verlag A. G., 1959), 1044-45.

17. "Sairai no igi" ("The Meaning of the Revisit"), March 1918, 24:77; "Matai den dai 26 shō 64 setsu nitsuite" ("On Matthew 26:64"), August 1918, 24:276-77.

18. Uchimura did not use the expression of eschatological spirituality, because in his days the term "spirituality" was not in common usage. Cf. Mutōh Yōichi, "Uchimura Kanzō to reisei" ("Uchimura Kanzō and Spirituality"), *Uchimura Kanzō Kenkyū (Uchimura Kanzō Studies)*, no. 31 (November 1995): 11-32; Shibuya Hiroshi, *Kindai shisōshi niokeru Uchimura Kanzō (Uchimura Kanzō in the History of Modern Thought)* (Tokyo: Shinchi Shobō Publishers, 1988), 268-89; Hakari Yoshiharu, *Mukyōkai no tenkai (A Development of Mykyōkai)* (Tokyo: Shinchi Shobō Publishers, 1989), 27-36; Tomioka, *Uchimura Kanzō*, 195-212; Jinpo Yuji, *Uchimura Kanzō* (Tokyo: Kōsōsha Publishers, 1990), 143-218.

might deprive the believer not merely of the will to make a sincere effort for salvation but also of the aspiration to share the gospel with the non-believing world; it gives an absolute, privileged, and even imperialistic status to the Christian idea of salvation; it might deprive human beings of the hellish fear of Gehenna; and so forth. Thus, the theme of universal salvation has been treated with caution as a perilous one in the mainstream theological tradition of Christianity.

To be sure, Uchimura well understood the hazardous nature of the theme. From time to time he nevertheless alluded positively to the possibility of universal salvation. He was certainly aware of its possible distortion and abuse, and he avoided dogmatizing this idea, thinking that the whole issue was beyond human comprehension, reasoning, and competence. For he thought that the theme of universal salvation did not belong to the category of human jurisdiction but to the category of God's freedom and sovereignty over the whole of the created world. Uchimura nowhere reflected on the pros and cons of universal salvation; it looks as if he even refused giving systematic thought to the problem. There remains the fact, however, that he now and then did allude to the possibility of universal salvation. What does this mean?

2. *True and Genuine Salvation?*

Whenever he wrote about the possibility of the salvation of every human being, Uchimura did so with an attitude of profound fear and trembling. According to Uchimura, while the negative aspect of the second coming clearly consists in the last judgment of humankind, its positive aspect is that the last judgment of humankind is not the final aim of the second coming. Rather, Uchimura maintained that the positive aim of the second coming consists in the salvation of each and every repentant sinner who is justified by faith in Christ. He continued to argue that the final aim of the second coming of Christ is to save everyone. But what explains the logical — and soteriological — connection between the justification by faith alone and the salvation of everyone? How can Christ save everyone? And finally, what is genuine salvation like?

Uchimura gave an interesting response to these questions. He said Christ will save all men and women by meeting those who have not yet encountered him. But Uchimura was not reintroducing the idea of purgatory as medieval scholasticism had proposed it. Rather, his suggestion was that

Christ will encounter in heaven itself those who had not met him yet. Furthermore, the second coming of Christ will not merely save all humankind but also will usher in the glorification of humankind, the advent of a new heaven and earth, and the construction of new Jerusalem. Uchimura summed up this argument as follows:

> A human being is not worthy even if he or she alone is saved. Salvation becomes genuine and true salvation, only when I am saved together with all my brothers and sisters. God will create an entirely sacred society with sanctified souls. In doing so, God will visit and provide both individuals and humankind with the greatest and ultimate grace. This is nothing else than genuine salvation. Apart from this there is no salvation of individuals. The time of the second coming of Christ is the time of the completion of all created things. This is nothing but a matter to rejoice at, a matter to praise, and a matter to thank for. (25:496)

It seems that during and after his participation in the second-coming movement from 1918 through 1919, Uchimura began to speak more concretely than ever of the content of universal salvation. He explained that Christ will come again in order to encounter everyone dead and alive and will bestow saving grace on every human being. Grace comes first, and then follow repentance, justification, and sanctification; and finally comes glorification. Uchimura further maintained that everybody is blessed with the same abundance of God's grace and goodness. But among those who receive the blessing, the way of being blessed is different from individual to individual. "Each in his order," wrote Uchimura. For example, Christians shall be blessed with a new resurrection life, and they shall serve the whole of the universe together with Christ. Jews shall be bestowed with messianic blessings and serve the world and universe. And the Gentiles shall be blessed as those who shall receive the brightness of God's glory and shall return the glory of all things to God and praise him all in all.[19]

It is clear that Uchimura severed the very theological connection be-

---

19. "The Aim of the Second Coming," 24:451-52E. "Banmin nikakawaru dainaru fukuin" ("The Great Gospel for All People"), February 1919, 24:458, 461. Cf. Harashima, "'Kyusaishi' to 'sekaishi' no setten," 60-70; Miyata Mitsuo, "Yotei setsu to bannin kyūsai setsu: shūkyō kaikakusha, Uchimura Kanzō, Karl Barth" ("The Doctrine of Predestination and the Doctrine of Universal Salvation: The Reformers, Uchimura Kanzō, Karl Barth"), *Shisō (Thought)*, no. 782 (August 1989): 5-30; Tanaka Osamu, *Uchimura Kanzō to keishōsha (Uchimura Kanzō and His Successors)* (Nagoya: Aichi Shobō Publishers, 1995), 15-29.

tween the doctrine of predestination and justification by faith alone, that is, both moments that Luther and Calvin wanted to organically connect. But Uchimura neither showed well the reasons for this severance nor explained persuasively enough the aporia necessarily derived from the idea of universal salvation, that is, the compatibility between his emphasis on the justification by faith alone and his reference to universal salvation.

Here I see again the theological affinity between Uchimura, on the one hand, and Karl Barth and Emil Brunner, on the other. Three thinkers engaged in an epoch-making theological endeavor that suggested the possibility of a christocentric bestowal of universal grace upon the whole of humankind. In so doing they tried to underscore an open possibility of universal reconciliation and salvation under a merciful God. But these three thinkers also shared some logical incompleteness in their insistence.

These three thinkers never took universal salvation for granted. Despite Brunner's constant charge against Barth that the latter held the doctrine of universal salvation in a principled and a priori manner, this criticism was not correct. For Barth the salvation of everyone totally depended on the fact that it might become the event of God's free grace. Neither Uchimura nor Barth and Brunner ever insisted on universal salvation either as a dogma or as a doctrine or as a "logical rational solution" (Brunner). Perhaps this is the main reason that there remained some logical incompleteness in their discussions. Free saving grace of God and his bestowal of it upon humanity and the whole cosmos are always beyond human comprehension and remain a great mystery. So any discussion of the possibility of universal salvation is bound to remain logically imperfect or unfinished. But these three thinkers have all alluded to the possibility that under divine mercy and free grace, as implied in the *kerygma* of Christ, such a mysterious, salvific event could actually take place.[20]

Epilogue

When Uchimura was a student at Sapporo Agricultural College, he asked himself: "What kind of Christianity can afford to save humankind?"

20. E.g., Emil Brunner, *Die christliche Lehre von Gott,* vol. 1 (Zurich und Stuttgart: Zwingli Verlag, 1946), 310-20; *Die christliche Lehre von der Kirche vom Glauben und von der Vollendung: Dogmatik,* vol. 3 (Zurich und Stuttgart: Zwingli Verlag, 1960), 474; *Eternal Hope,* trans. Harold Knight (London: Lutterworth, 1954), 184; Karl Barth, *Die kirchliche Dogmatik* II/2 (Zollikon: Verlag der Evangelischen Buchhandlung, 1942), 127-83, 355-60.

Looking back over his whole life, I now think that one answer to this question was what I called in this chapter atonement eschatology, that is, "Crucifixianity," to use his own expression. As was indicated earlier, Uchimura claimed to be neither a theologian nor a scholar of *Dogmatik* in the strict sense of the term. He called himself a student of the Bible and a preacher of the old and ancient gospel. His language was plain and readable, confessional and experimental, passionate and practical. Furthermore, he hated the type of "theology" that had the tendency to contract gigantic theological themes to fit a small human logic.[21]

But as was indicated throughout this chapter, Uchimura proved to be a stimulating theological thinker especially in his later period, when he wrote about the needs for a "second Reformation," as well as the importance of atonement eschatology. One could observe in his writings the presence of tenacious questionings and responses with regard to complicated and tough issues of God and humanity, the universe and nature, the destiny of the world and history, and salvation. His inquiries and responses were also based on his dispassionate and astute reasoning, although they were predicated upon his own passionate faith. Perhaps Mitani Takamasa was right, when he wrote that Uchimura could be regarded as the greatest theologian that Meiji Japan had ever produced.

---

21. Uchimura once wrote in his diary during his study sojourn in America as follows: "Theology is too big a theme to be comprehended by small men. When small minds find themselves too small for such a gigantic theme, they construct their own theologies fitting their own smallness, and throw anathemas at those who comprehend it better than they. O my soul, do not contract theology to fit thy smallness, but expand thyself to fit its largeness." From *How I Became a Christian*, in *Zenshū*, 3:135E.

Contributors

Andrew E. Barshay

Professor of History, Department of History, University of California, Berkeley, USA. Author of *State and Intellectual in Imperial Japan: The Public Man in Crisis* (University of California Press, 1988); *The Social Sciences in Japan: The Marxian and Modernist Traditions* (University of California Press, 2004); *The Gods Left First: The Captivity and Repatriation of Japanese POWs in Northeast Asia, 1945-1956* (University of California Press, 2013).

Chiba Kei

Professor of Philosophy, Faculty of Letters, Hokkaido University, Sapporo, Japan. Author of *Arisutoteresu no Keijijyōgaku no Kanōsei (Aristotle on the Possibility of Metaphysics)* (Keisō Shobō Publishers, 2002); "Aristotle on Essence and Defining-Phrase in His Dialectic," in *Definition in Greek Philosophy,* ed. David Charles (Oxford University Press, 2010); "Aristotle on Heuristic Enquiry and Demonstration of What It Is," in *The Oxford Handbook of Aristotle,* ed. Christopher Shields (Oxford University Press, 2012).

Chiba Shin (coeditor)

Professor of Political Thought, Department of Politics and International Studies, International Christian University, Tokyo, Japan. Coeditor of *Christian Ethics in Ecumenical Context* (Eerdmans, 1995); *Peace Movements and Pacifism after September 11* (Edward Elgar, 2008); *Building New Pathways to Peace* (University of Washington Press, 2011).

Lee Kyoungae

Former Associate Professor of Christian Studies, Orio Aishin College, Kitakyūshū, Japan. Author of *Uchimura Kanzō no Kirisutokyō Shisō (The Christian Thought of Uchimura Kanzō)* (Kyūshū University Press, 2003); "Meiji Jidai ni okeru Shinkaron no Ichi Danmen: Uchimura Kanzō no Yūshinron teki Shinkaron" ("A Cross Section of the Theory of Evolution in the Meiji Era: Uchimura Kanzō's Theistic Evolutionism"), *Orio Aishin Tanki Daigaku Ronshū (Journal of Orio Aishin Junior College)* 44 (December 2011).

Miura Hiroshi

Lecturer, Department of International Studies, Shikoku University, Tokushima, Japan. Author of *The Life and Thought of Kanzo Uchimura, 1861-1930* (Eerdmans, 1996).

Ohyama Tsunao

Former President and Professor Emeritus of History, Keisen Women's College, Tokyo, Japan. Author of *Sapporo Nōgakkō to Kirisutokyō (Sapporo Agricultural College and Christianity)* (EDITEX, 2012); coauthor of "Uchimura Kanzō at Amherst," in *Culture and Religion in Japanese-American Relations: Essays on Uchimura Kanzō,* ed. Ray A. Moore (University of Michigan, Center of Japanese Studies, 1981); *Hokkaido to America (Hokkaido and America)* (Sapporo Gakuin University Press, 1993).

Shibuya Hiroshi (coeditor)

Professor Emeritus of History of Western Political Thought, Faculty of Law, Meiji Gakuin University, Tokyo, Japan. Author of *Pyūritanizumu no Kakumei Shisō (The Revolutionary Thought of Puritanism)* (Ochanomizu Shobō Publishers, 1978); *Kindai Shisōshi niokeru Uchimura Kanzō (Uchimura Kanzō in the History of Modern Thought* (Shinchi Shobō Publishers, 1988); *Omoiyari no Shu Iesu to tomoni (A Life with Jesus, the Lord of Sympathy* (Seigakuin University Press, 2001).

Shogimen Takashi

Associate Professor of History and Associate Dean (Research), Division of Humanities, University of Otago, Dunedin, New Zealand. Author of *Ockham and Political Discourse in the Late Middle Ages* (Cambridge University Press, 2007; paperback, 2010); "'Another' Patriotism in Early Showa Japan (1930-1945)," *Journal of the History of Ideas* 71, no. 1 (2010); "Censorship, Academic Factionalism and University Autonomy in Wartime Japan: The Yanaihara Incident Reconsidered," *Journal of Japanese Studies* (forthcoming).

Takahashi Yasuhiro

Associate Professor of Western Political Thought and American History, Faculty of Humanities, Niigata University, Niigata, Japan. Author of "Martin Luther Bokushi no Heiwa Shisō" ("The Peace Thought of Pastor Martin Luther"), in *Heiwa no Seiji Shisōshi (The History of Political Ideas on Peace)*, ed. Chiba Shin (Oufū Publishers, 2009); "Contemporary Christian Pacifism in the United States: Political Activism of Jim Wallis," in *Glauben und Wissen in der Geistesgeschichte*, Niigata University Scholars Series, vol. 12 (Niigata University, Graduate School of Modern Society and Culture, 2011).

Yagyu Kunichika

Professor Emeritus of History of Western Political Thought, Faculty of Law, Tōhoku University, Sendai, Japan. Author of *Seiji to Shūkyō: Weber Kenkyūsha no Shiza kara (Politics and Religion: From the Perspective of a Scholar on Weber)* (Sōbunsha Publishers, 2010); "Max Weber und Ernst Troeltsch in Japan: Die Rezeption ihrer Werke bei Maruyama Masao," in *Max Weber und das Moderne Japan*, ed. Wolfgang Mommsen and Wolfgang Schwentker (Vandenhoeck & Ruprecht, 1999); "Der Yasukuni-Shrein im Japan der Nachkriegszeit: Zu den Nachwirkung des Staatsshinto," in *Erinnerungskulturen: Deutschland, Italien, und Japan seit 1945,* ed. Christoph Cornelissen, Lutz Klinkhammer, and Wolfgang Schwentker (Fischer, 2003).